PASSING THE TORCH

PASSING THE TORCH

DOES HIGHER EDUCATION FOR THE DISADVANTAGED PAY OFF ACROSS THE GENERATIONS?

PAUL ATTEWELL AND DAVID E. LAVIN

IN COLLABORATION WITH
THURSTON DOMINA AND TANIA LEVEY

A Volume in the American Sociological Association's
Rose Series in Sociology

Russell Sage Foundation · New York

Library of Congress Cataloging-in-Publication Data

Attewell, Paul A., 1949-
  Passing the torch : does higher education for the disadvantaged pay off across
the generations? / Paul Attewell and David Lavin ; in collaboration with
Thurston Domina and Tania Levey.
        p. cm. — (American Sociological Association's Rose series in sociology)
  Includes bibliographical references.
  ISBN 978-0-87154-037-9 (cloth)   ISBN 0-87154-038-6 (paperback)
  1. Youth with social disabilities—Education (Higher)—United States.
2. Educational equalization—United States. 3. College graduates—
United States—Economic conditions. 4. Social mobility—United States.
I. Lavin, David E. II. Title.

    LC4069.6.A87 2007
    378.1'98269420973—dc22

                                                                2006033291

The paper used in this publication meets the minimum requirements of American
National Standard for Information Sciences—Permanence of Paper for Printed Library
Materials.   ANSI Z39.48-1992.

Text design by Suzanne Nichols.

RUSSELL SAGE FOUNDATION
112 East 64th Street, New York, New York 10021
10 9 8 7 6 5 4 3 2

Previous Volumes in the Series

Forthcoming Titles

The Rose Series in Sociology

The American Sociological Association's Rose Series in Sociology publishes books that integrate knowledge and address controversies from a sociological perspective. Books in the Rose Series are at the forefront of sociological knowledge. They are lively and often involve timely and fundamental issues on significant social concerns. The series is intended for broad dissemination throughout sociology, across social science and other professional communities, and to policy audiences. The series was established in 1967 by a bequest to ASA from Arnold and Caroline Rose to support innovations in scholarly publishing.

Douglas L. Anderton
Dan Clawson
Naomi Gerstel
Joya Misra
Randall G. Stokes
Robert Zussman

Editors

For the next generation:
Steven and David
Nina, Jennifer and Taylor, and Samantha and Mark

Contents

About the Authors

Paul Attewell is professor of sociology at Graduate Center of the City University of New York.

David E. Lavin is professor of sociology at Graduate Center of the City University of New York.

Thurston Domina is postdoctoral research associate in the Office of Population Research at Princeton University.

Tania Levey is assistant professor of sociology at York College of the City University of New York.

Acknowledgments

Participation in American higher education has grown with especial rapidity during the last thirty-five years. One of the key events in this growth was the program of open admissions initiated in 1970 at the large multicampus system of the City University of New York. Although the CUNY experiment has sometimes been viewed as a unique event in American higher education, this book shows that by 1980, open access to college was the rule in the United States, rather than the exception.

The great expansion in college going has been accompanied by controversy. Some have argued that too many students cannot profit from college, that efforts to accommodate them have led to a decline in academic standards, and that the value of college degrees has declined. As a result, college graduates have been getting less payoff from their questionable credentials.

This book takes a detailed look at two major aspects of college going. First, over the long term—that is, over a thirty-year period—how well have students done in terms of graduation and in terms of the returns to college degrees in the labor market. Second, what has been the influence of educational attainment on the educational chances of the second generation—that is, on the educational careers of the children of those who started college decades earlier?

Analysis of these topics yields little to support the criticisms aimed at colleges and their students. Over a thirty-year period, graduation rates are considerably higher than shown for periods of four to six years and payoffs to degrees are quite robust. Moreover, college completion by parents has many positive effects on the educational careers of their children.

Various sources of support have enabled us to complete this work. The Andrew W. Mellon Foundation, The Ford Foundation, and the Spencer Foundation provided generous funding so that we could collect new data, conduct analyses and complete the drafting of this book. Harriet Zuckerman at Mellon provided not only substantial funding but gave a number of strategic suggestions that helped us to successfully complete a large new data collection. Alison Bernstein at Ford originally helped us with funding for a pilot study that allowed us to assess whether we could locate and interview former students, thirty years after beginning college. Ford later made a substantial grant that helped us to make great progress in data analyses. Spencer support allowed us to complete these analyses and to make major progress in completing the write up of results.

A number of graduate students made important contributions. Aviva Zubida did much of the initial work in setting up our historical data sets and in generating a method that allowed us to sample former CUNY students to interview. David Adox conducted a number of special, in depth interviews. Amy Adamczyk also helped with interviews. Roderick Graham provided assistance in compiling bibliography, and Josh Howard did a great deal of work in editing the bibliography and checking page proofs.

The editorial board of the American Sociological Association's Rose Monograph Series gave us much thoughtful feedback that improved the quality of the manuscript. We especially want to thank Robert Zussman for all his help.

The staff at Shulman, Ronca, and Bucevalas ran a highly professional and effective case finding survey operation so that we were able to attain a high response rate for our interviews.

Our two main research assistants Thurston Domina and Tania Levey conducted often complex data analyses with a high degree of initiative, and provided excellent editorial assistance that clearly improved the quality of our written work. Consequently, we have included them as junior authors of the book.

Finally, we want to thank our almost 2000 respondents who were so generous in giving their time to be interviewed.

Chapter 1

Passing the Torch:
An Overview

A central theme in our culture is that "getting an education" is the key to upward mobility. Americans hold dear the belief that young people can escape from poverty or disadvantage if they persevere in school and work their way up to a college degree. We also expect that once the first generation in a family has struggled to complete a college education, succeeding generations will sustain this advantage.

Through most of the twentieth century, these popular beliefs coincided with increased access to higher education for an ever-broader swath of Americans, including racial minorities and the poor.[1] In recent decades, however, dissident voices have been raised, arguing that public universities are admitting people who are unqualified and ill suited for higher education. Colleges have been criticized for dumbing down curricula while tolerating grade inflation, which protects the academically incompetent. Access to higher education has gone too far, according to these critics, and public colleges are conferring devalued degrees upon unworthy students.

Important changes in public policy have accompanied this shift in perception. The first thing to go was a long-standing tradition of free tuition at some public colleges. This was followed by decades of reductions in state funding for public higher education, forcing state universities to hike tuition, to the detriment of students from less affluent families. Opportunity programs such as affirmative action and "second chance" policies such as remedial education and open admissions were attacked as unfair or as a waste of resources, reflecting the belief that underprepared students would not succeed in college.

The political backlash against mass higher education has undercut or eliminated many policies aimed at helping underprivileged students: affirmative action has come under a judicial cloud; in several states, women on welfare may no longer attend college while receiving public support; restrictions have been placed on remedial education; needs-based financial aid has lost ground to merit-based scholarships; and so on.

This sea change regarding educational opportunity policies reflects larger disputes over the validity of government intervention, especially the extent to which public education should attempt to ameliorate class and racial inequalities in society. These disagreements over social values and political philosophies are deep-seated and not easily resolved. At the same time, the criticisms of mass higher education are built upon allegedly factual claims—that affirmative action does not help minorities and makes them feel inferior, that degrees have become cheapened, and that university graduates lack basic work skills, among others. Researchers are well placed to adjudicate these factual matters, by investigating the outcomes of opportunity policies in the recent past.

To date, the best-known scholarship looking into these controversies has focused on affirmative action policies. For example, William Bowen and Derek Bok, in *The Shape of the River*, convincingly documented the achievements of students admitted through affirmative action, after surveying graduates from the nation's most prestigious private and public universities. The authors found that affirmative-action students in highly selective institutions were very successful in terms of degrees, earnings, and professional accomplishments.[2]

Selective colleges and universities are gateways to the most highly rewarded positions in the occupational world, so it is understandable that affirmative-action policies have received the scrutiny they have. Still, affirmative action in highly selective colleges is just the tip of the iceberg of educational access in America.[3] The overwhelming share of the burgeoning enrollment of poorer and minority Americans has occurred in less selective institutions,[4] places—mainly in the state colleges and universities—where the tide turned several decades ago in the direction of mass higher education. In this sector of the higher education enterprise "nontraditional students" are found in greatest numbers.

The research in this book centers on these public institutions. Our principal concern is with the many thousands of poorly prepared high school students from economically disadvantaged families who enter college and try to make their way into the American middle class. We focus on two critical issues: First, are young people from underprivileged backgrounds able to benefit from higher education, given their poor preparation in high school? Questions here concern the proportions of students who ultimately obtain a degree, and whether those credentials really pay off in terms of earnings and mobility.

Second, what is the impact of higher education upon the next generation? Do the benefits of college opportunity produce an intergenerational momentum that carries over to children in the next generation? That is, when disadvantaged young people do get into college and obtain a credential, are they able to transmit this advantage to their own offspring? Do their children fare better in school, or do they still resemble the children of poor and working-class families? How many of the children in this second generation ultimately equal or exceed their parents' educational success, and how many fall backward into lower-class patterns of educational and occupational achievement?

We suggest that the appropriate measure of success for mass higher education should not just be the earnings and occupational attainment of those who get into college—though obviously those are important— but also whether, by going to college, students from underprivileged backgrounds break the cycle of disadvantage and lift their children into the middle class. To the extent that this transpires, a national investment in greater access to college has a higher and more permanent payoff.

[margin note: Measure of Success]

Contrast this multigenerational focus with debates that took place over the last decade or so, as legislators undertook welfare reform. Initially much was said about the cycle of poverty, of welfare mothers raising daughters who themselves ended up on welfare. Unfortunately, policy alternatives soon became constricted to a choice between moving women off welfare directly into work, and providing them with training in basic work-life skills prior to job placement. Higher education, which was once an alternative for many welfare and poor mothers, largely disappeared from the policy agenda. By focusing on the short term, rather than on the intergenerational consequences of various policies, welfare reformers overlooked an important option for breaking the cycle of disadvantage.

To examine these issues, we investigate the extent to which children of college-educated parents who come from underprivileged backgrounds gain an advantage over their counterparts by dint of their parents' education. How much of a difference does a parental degree make? Does even a partial exposure to higher education (short of graduation) confer advantage to their children? These are questions that we pose in this book.

If the second generation does fare better in terms of its own education and occupational trajectory, then what are the mechanisms that produce this effect? Do college-educated parents from underprivileged backgrounds become more involved in their children's education? Or do they guide their children into better schools? Do they raise their children with higher expectations, or pass on some of the knowledge and cultural capital they learned in college? How much help are the greater economic resources typically associated with parents' college completion for the children? On the downside, do other aspects of people's lives such as marital disruptions undercut or vitiate the benefits that parental college education can confer on children?

[margin note: Questions]

Our point of departure in this study is an important experiment in opening the doors to college that took place in New York City in the early 1970s, when the eighteen-campus (with 250,000 students) City University of New York (CUNY) guaranteed all graduates of the city's high schools admission into the university. David E. Lavin and his colleagues began tracking the fate of this generation immediately (see Lavin, Alba, and Silberstein 1981; Lavin and Hyllegard 1996). Many of the CUNY students in this cohort came from poor and near-poor families, but working- and middle-class students were also well represented.

Nearly thirty years later we launched a new follow-up study of those ex-students. With financial support from the Andrew Mellon, Ford, and Spencer foundations, we traced and interviewed a representative sample of almost two thousand women drawn from the original cohort in order to assess their current social and economic well-being and document the occupational and educational achievements of their children. The response rate for this survey was 71 percent, and the sample of women we studied in the year 2000 closely mirrored the larger cohort who entered CUNY in the 1970s.[5]

We chose to collect data from women for this thirty-year follow-up study because of our focus on how their children were doing. After marital disruptions, mothers are far more likely than fathers to have custody of their children, and therefore women tend to have more reliable information about offspring. The same is true for those women who had children outside of marriage. The data we collected on mothers and their children in the year 2000 were then merged with the historical data gathered about these same women in the 1970s.

To further validate and extend our findings, we undertook additional analyses using a different government-sponsored longitudinal survey known as the National Longitudinal Survey of Youth, or NLSY. That study was begun in 1979, when several thousand young women were selected to participate. It inquired about occupation and earnings, education and marital status, both for the women and for their children. This information was updated every year or two after 1979, up to the year 2000. The NLSY allows us to determine whether various findings about the CUNY women also hold for a wider national population. In addition, it enables us to supplement certain analyses by including measures not available in the CUNY data. For example, the NLSY contains measures of women's IQ that enable us to separate the effects of having a mother who went to college from simply having a mother of high intelligence. Finally, we occasionally employ two other national sources of information as benchmarks, the Current Population Survey, produced by the U.S. Census Bureau, and the U.S. Department of Education's National Educational Longitudinal Study.

The findings that emerged from our analyses are startling and unprecedented. Other research stops short of the truly long-term picture needed to evaluate the payoff of opening the doors to college. Our long-range perspective shows that disadvantaged women ultimately complete college degrees in far greater numbers than scholars realize. Fully 71 percent of the CUNY cohort earned a degree, and over three-fourths of these completed a bachelor's degree. Twenty-six percent completed a master's or higher degree.

These accomplishments can take a long time: 29 percent of women completed their degrees over ten years after they first entered college, and 10 percent completed them twenty or more years after entry. The nationwide NLSY survey shows a similar pattern. The low graduation rates that scandalize critics of public higher education are typically measured only four or six years after entry to college. When one takes a longer view, a much more positive picture emerges.

Community colleges or junior colleges have drawn the ire of commentators who claim that very few students who enter associate of arts (A.A.) degree programs ever make it through to bachelor's degrees. Others say that associate's degrees are worth little in terms of earnings. While it is true that community college entrants are less likely to earn B.A. degrees than comparable students who start at four-year colleges, our long-term study reveals that 31 percent of women who entered a junior college in the CUNY system ultimately completed a bachelor's degree, a much larger proportion than previously noted. Moreover, in some applied fields, the A.A. degree paid off better in the long term than some B.A. majors. Thus, community colleges provided genuine benefits to many students, both in the New York and nationwide surveys.

Mass education has not made a college degree worth less. At both the A.A. and B.A. level, the educational credentials gained by women from poor backgrounds were not devalued in earning power. Women who started at CUNY earn as much as other women of the same age and degree level in national data sets. On a national scale, greater access to higher education has been accompanied by growth in the earnings premium for a college degree, rather than a collapse in the value of this credential.

Higher education has a financial payoff even for those who begin but do not complete a degree. Women who completed some college short of a degree enjoyed an earnings premium over otherwise equivalent persons who were only high school graduates, as shown by national NLSY data.

For women who complete a given level of education, family background ceases to matter in predicting earnings and occupational prestige. In this restricted sense, higher education compensates for childhood disadvantage. However, women from the most severely disadvantaged backgrounds are less likely to complete their studies and obtain a credential than women from more affluent families.

Racial differences in earnings are small, once education is taken into account. Black women had personal earnings roughly equal to those of white women with equivalent education. However, race continues to make a big difference in household income. Educated black women have lower household incomes, have less wealth, and are less likely than whites to be homeowners, principally because of African Americans' lower rates of marriage and greater marital instability.

White and Hispanic women who come from modest backgrounds and enter college are usually able to attain upward mobility in two ways: directly, through their own credentials and earning power, and indirectly, by marrying educated men who become occupationally successful. Black women of similar background and education are often limited to the first path, because they are far less likely to marry. Furthermore, college-educated black women who do marry are less likely to have a spouse with high occupational prestige. Thus, the formation of dual-earner professional families becomes a critical point in the translation of higher education into upward mobility.

College-educated mothers pass important educational advantages on to their children. We find that a mother's level of educational attainment has a positive effect on her offspring's likelihood of educational success, net of race, mother's family or class background, her IQ, and other factors.

Although these benefits of maternal education are clearly visible among all groups, race continues to impact children's outcomes, even when mothers have "made it." College-educated black women are less likely to have academically successful children and are more likely to have downwardly mobile children than either white or Hispanic women with similar credentials. This is particularly true for young black men, who are less likely to equal their mother's achievements than young black women. Among African American mothers, 49 percent of sons and 35 percent of daughters did not attain their mother's degree level.

College enrollment changes the way women raise their children. From increased educational expectations to greater involvement in schooling to the presence of books and computers in the home—college-educated mothers from poor backgrounds invest more time and resources in the next generation. These parenting practices are in turn associated with significantly better educational outcomes for their children, from elementary school on. This effect of parenting practices on children's outcomes is separate from benefits accruing from the higher incomes of college-educated mothers.

Where does this leave us? For many Americans, college conjures up memories of young people fresh out of high school, living on campus, immersed in a liberal arts curriculum focused on great thinkers from Plato through Freud. For social commentators such as William Bennett, today's universities have forsaken that traditional model and instead offer a degraded version of a college education.[6] While we share a respect for a classical liberal arts education, it was only accessible to a minority of Americans. Over the last half century, American universities have broadened their scope to accommodate many new students who cannot afford to attend college full-time or to live on campus, as well as students who have an interest in more applied subjects. Today only 27 percent of undergraduates nationwide match the traditional undergraduate profile.[7] We argue that one should not underestimate the success of today's mass higher education simply because it is different from its older and socially more restrictive counterpart.

A tiny proportion of our nation's minority and economically disadvantaged college students are enrolled in America's most selective universities; public universities and the community college system serve most of these kinds of students. A broad population of students, including those with poor high school preparation, enters the doors of public colleges. In response, these institutions have extended remedial courses—which were always offered to wealthy students in Ivy League colleges—to any students who need them. Is that remediation a bad investment? Contrary to critics' contentions, our analyses suggest that remedial courses do not depress graduation rates for most students, and that remediation may reduce college dropout rates in the short term.

Taken as a whole, the evidence presented in this book indicates that the democratization of public higher education has not generated hordes of unemployable graduates or worthless degrees. Those who graduate with a college degree from public universities earn significantly more than high school graduates, net of background characteristics. For hundreds of thousands of underprivileged students, a college education is the first step up the ladder of social mobility, and their college attendance generates an upward momentum for most of their children. Yet higher education cannot rest on these laurels—the effects of poverty and race still reach across the generations. Access to four years of higher education does not eradicate those disadvantages, but it substantially reduces their influence and facilitates upward mobility for many in the second generation. That is no small accomplishment.

The majority of the evidence in this book comes from sample surveys involving thousands of respondents, so our analyses are predominantly statistical. That makes sense, because we want to make well-grounded generalizations about the outcomes of increased access to higher education for large parts of our population. Nevertheless, we do not forget that our numbers are distilled from the lives of thousands of people, and that our statistics represent in barest outline the complex struggles of many individuals, each with their own particularities. In pursuing hard numbers we risk losing the human drama and fascinating details of individual cases, which some find the most compelling of evidence. In partial remedy, we devote the remainder of this chapter to the stories of two women who entered college at CUNY in the early 1970s. Their accounts illustrate many of the themes that will reappear in the later analytical chapters of this book. (The names of these women and a few personal details have been changed to protect their privacy.)

Ramona Rodriguez

If you phone Ramona Rodriguez nowadays, her assistant intercepts the call and informs you that you have reached the offices of Counselor Rodriguez. With a law degree and a six-figure salary in a prestigious law firm, Ramona has come a very long way from her hardscrabble childhood in New York City. The oldest of four girls, she was raised almost completely by her mother, an immigrant from the Dominican Republic. Her father had left the family several times while she was very young, abandoning the family for good when she was eight.

Watching her mother come home exhausted from a day of doing piecework in the garment district is a childhood memory that still resonates with Ramona. Life was a constant struggle for her mother, with five mouths to feed, and Ramona, as the oldest child, shouldered part of the burden, beginning a part-time job at age twelve to help support the family.

Ramona's mother's schooling ended at the third grade and she could read and write only a little in Spanish and not at all in English. So she rarely discussed school matters and never helped her daughter with her homework. "But we were all expected to do our work," says Ramona. "Even though she didn't help us, I think she taught us to be more independent and make sure we got our work done."

Schoolwork proved difficult for Ramona. "I really had a problem with education. I was able to get away with certain tricks. I was able to fool my teachers for many years. It wasn't until I was in seventh grade that my teachers realized I couldn't read," she recalls. "I was what you might call now learning disabled." After this discovery, Ramona was put in an intensive after-school reading program. It worked: by the time she got to high school, she was reading above grade level.

After graduating from high school in 1970, Ramona enrolled at one of the four-year colleges of the City University of New York. "With open enrollment they couldn't turn me down, so once I got the application, I was in college, as far as I was concerned. . . . I was encouraged to apply to other colleges, but to me there was no real alternative. I lived in the neighborhood. I could walk to school. I didn't have to worry about carfare. It was very convenient."

Though she was still living at home, college expanded her world far beyond the five-block radius that had constituted her world for the first eighteen years of her life. "My exposure to different people, different cultures and goals—it broadened me." Because she still found reading arduous, Ramona became attracted to mathematics and subjects that involved numbers and logic. A first-semester economics course drove her career aspirations sharply upward: "I thought I was going to be the economics adviser to the President of the United States. I was going to go to Washington and solve all our national problems," she reminisces.

All that changed during her junior year of college, when at age twenty she became pregnant. Once it became apparent that Ramona was not going to marry the child's father, her mother decided that she was a bad influence on her younger sisters, and asked her to leave home. "I felt like I lost my mobility, so I had to change my goals." Ramona began considering stereotypically female careers such as social work, and she took on a work-study job in New York's family court system. After taking one semester off when her daughter was born, she returned to college and graduated a year or so later with a B.A. degree in mathematics and economics.

Working in the courts had made a strong impression on Ramona, and she started thinking about becoming a lawyer, but her family was far from encouraging. "What do you want to do that for?" her mother asked. "My sisters told me I was going to fail: 'You? A lawyer?' " Looking back, Ramona explains: "I can see my mother was trying to insulate me from disappointment—the disappointment that *she* had felt, trying to get ahead. She didn't think that her daughter, you know, would be able to go to law school, be an attorney. So that was her way. But that motivated me more."

As a single mother on public assistance with a two-year-old daughter in tow, Ramona dove into the first-year grind at law school. "It was rough. Looking back at that now, I don't know if I could ever do that again," she says. "I only had two things, my daughter and my school; there wasn't room for much of anything else." But she persisted. Twenty-some years later, Ramona has had six children, two marriages, and a successful career as an attorney.

Contrasting her own upbringing with the ways she raised her children, Ramona emphasizes that the main thing she wanted to do differently from her mother was "to encourage [my children] to be all they can be and let them know that they have options, and that through hard work and sacrifice, anything is possible." She deliberately "exposed them to a lot more, culturally. As they were growing up, I took them to museums, the zoo, and the aquarium. On weekends we would go out and explore things. The Bronx Zoo was a big thing for us, the botanical gardens. When they were little I took them to real plays where they could see actors. Those were things I was never exposed to."

When it came to getting directly involved in her children's schoolwork, though, matters proved complicated. "I left that to them because I always had a big problem reading. To this day, because my frustration level and the pain I went through in the past, I cannot help my children with their homework without feeling all those old feelings all over again. . . . My oldest [adult] daughter talks about that today, how I never helped her with her homework."

Although Ramona didn't help with her children's studying, she did become heavily involved with their schools. "I am one of those parents who's there all the time. If necessary, I am there every day. They all know me at the school as a concerned parent. I get involved with the PTA. . . . One of my sons, he's always getting into problems at school. I'm always having to go to school to smooth things over for him. In some aspects, I may have become an enabler, if you know what I mean. I try not to do that, but I stick up for them."

In other areas, Ramona has taken a more hands-off approach, allowing her children to make their own decisions. They chose their own courses, for example: "It's up to them; it's up to their interests. . . . With their peers and friends, I try to give them advice without getting too much involved . . . [but] one of my big sons does. He decided that some of my younger son's friends are not acceptable in the apartment. I guess because he's young and he sees the interaction between them, whereas I'm so busy that I don't notice it. It's good I have someone looking over my shoulder and helping me with that."

Ramona has very consciously taught her kids about the process of getting ahead: "That's a process that's foreign to a lot of the people who grow up in the ghetto. I know, a lot of my peers, when I graduated high school—they thought you go to college just by showing up, just like you go to grammar school or junior high. I was familiar with the application process. I was able to help my children with that. I showed them how to write a résumé, how to look for a job. I had these how-to's, and I was able to pass on some strategies, basically."

Raising her kids in the same city neighborhood where she grew up meant that violence and crime were among Ramona's greatest fears. "I live in a very drug-infested neighborhood. The drugs, the crime— they call out to our children." It would have been costly to send her six children to private school, but in any event she rejected that idea on principle: "I insist that my children stay in public school because the problem with our community is the brain drain. All our talent moves away. It's important for us to remain here to make sure not only our kids get a good education, but the community kids, too."

That strong commitment to the local community has its limits. "I remember there being a drive-by shooting in my neighborhood and an innocent child being shot in the leg." That same year, Ramona sent her older sons to the South to live with their father during junior high and high school, while keeping her oldest daughter and two youngest children in the city. "Especially young black men are hard to discipline. I just thought that they would have a much better foundation if they grew up in the South, in a suburban, slower environment. That decision has haunted me for years because the flip side is that they weren't with me."

Ramona's parental efforts and involvement seem to have paid off, though not in every respect. Her two oldest children have graduated from college and are well on their way to professional jobs. One other son won a scholarship to an out-of-state college, but dropped out after his freshman year and has come back to live at home. She has three children still in school; two of them are doing well academically, but her youngest boy has been held back to repeat a grade.

Ramona Rodriguez's story is one of great personal success, and she has raised several very accomplished children as a single parent. But despite her extraordinary endeavors, it has not been straightforward to pass her advantages on to her offspring. The children clearly benefited from their mother's school involvement, her career advice, and her efforts at cultural enrichment, but they also had to grow up with a busy professional single mother, and negotiate their way in a dangerous neighborhood. In a pattern that seems especially common among the minority families in our surveys, Ramona's children went in educationally divergent directions, some able to use their parent's success as a springboard for upward mobility, while others struggled unsuccessfully to equal her level of education.

Janet Swallow

Janet Swallow, an African American woman in her forties, provides a contrasting story of marriage and deferred career. Like Ramona, Janet's parents, who both moved to New York City from the South, had received little formal education. Her dad had a fourth-grade education and was, according to his daughter, "a functional illiterate." Janet's mother had left school after eighth grade. Nevertheless, Janet grew up in a church-going family where education was valued and parental expectations were very high. Her parents wouldn't accept an average grade from Janet or her five siblings; they insisted on superior grades. They wouldn't tolerate idle time at home, either. Janet and her brother and sisters had to find something to read, or to work on a project, once homework was finished

Even though her parents weren't able to help her with schoolwork themselves, it was understood that homework was done first, before everything else. Fortunately, Janet as the youngest child could turn for help to her older sisters, one of whom was "quite the student." Not only was academic success a priority in her family, but Janet's mother had strong views about what kind of schooling Janet should get: "My mother wouldn't let me be on the general track, or commercial track.

My mother wouldn't even let me take a typing class. She said you'll either be a teacher or a nurse—a professional. That's what you'll be."

Janet was the kind of child who loved school, enjoyed studying, and devoured books. She is still nostalgic about her high school: "I cried my way through graduation because I loved it so much," she told us. "High school was the best time of my life. . . . I met a lot of teachers whom I admired so much because they pushed me. They saw things in me that I didn't see in myself and they pushed me to be better than I was. They pushed me to desire, to want more, to go for it."

After her tearful graduation, Janet dreamed of leaving New York and going away to college: "I wanted to go elsewhere and see the world. But it wasn't feasible, financially." Once again, it was her mother who decided what Janet would do, and that fall, Janet enrolled in the local community college, a branch of CUNY. To her surprise, the academic work proved quite difficult at first. In her first semester, Janet recalled, "I had an English professor who was really tough, and I got my first D. I was devastated." It took time to adapt to the greater challenge of college, but she persevered and steadily improved her grade point average.

Two years later Janet graduated with an associate's degree and transferred immediately to the nearest public four-year college to work toward a B.A. in English. Finally completing that bachelor's degree gave Janet an enormous sense of accomplishment: "I had gotten myself through four years of college, and everything else that went with it—the papers, the projects. I felt empowered, not only as a woman but as an educated woman. I realized that I didn't just have to settle for a place for me that was decided by someone else. I could make changes and move on to areas that people didn't expect me to. I knew that anything I really wanted to do, I could do."

Those feminist sentiments notwithstanding, Janet decided to start a family with the man she had married in the spring of her senior year in college. She had three children over the course of the next seven years. "I stayed home for twelve years raising kids because I didn't want anyone else raising them," she explained. "I knew that I could help my children, that I could be actively involved in their education. I knew if there was a conflict that I could go and reason with the teacher. My parents never went to [my] school. I always felt I was out there by myself. I wanted [my children] to know that I would go to bat for them for whatever reason, and they did know that." When one of Janet's oldest child's teachers humiliated him in front of the class, Janet immediately went to school and talked both with the teacher and with the school principal.

She adopted a very different stance from that of her parents toward education: "The main objective of my parents was to put food on the table and a roof over our heads. I wanted to raise little individuals who had personalities and could develop into responsible adults. . . . I wanted to instill in them a love for learning about the simplest things. I wanted them to be inquisitive. I made trips to the library, to museums, all the things that I knew would make them question the world around them." Janet helped her children with schoolwork, running all over town to get materials for projects.

"I was really concerned about public schools because I had heard all the press about them: how dangerous, inadequate, that private schools were much better. I bought into it." . . . "The two oldest kids went to parochial schools . . . and I was very involved because I wasn't working. The PTA, chaperone, reading partner—I did all that."

Despite her extensive involvement in her children's education, Janet tried to respect her children's autonomy and avoid the authoritarian approach of her own parents. "I don't do advice," she explained. "I listen, I might throw out a question, but advice, no. I was not given advice as a child. I was told what to do and when to do it. I didn't want to do that [to my kids]. I wanted them to think for themselves. . . . I really didn't have any influence [over their choice of friends]. They made good choices, no problem with the wrong crowd. There were bad characters, but [my kids] somehow just internalized my value system."

Two things marred what otherwise appears to be a strikingly successful example of a mother putting her own career on hold in order to invest in the next generation. First, Janet's husband was far less of a partner in these efforts than she had hoped. "He was there physically, but anything that had to do with kids was my responsibility. I hope that my boys looked at him and saw an example of what they shouldn't be like, and I know my daughter will be very careful when she chooses a mate. . . . Giving [my kids] a normal home life because there were issues with their dad, that was very hard. I wanted them to have a sense of a normal family in spite of all the controversies in the home." Janet and her husband split up when the youngest child was a teenager.

A second disappointment was the racial composition of the schools. "The problem was that we were in a predominantly Caucasian area and my kids were the only African Americans in the school. I wasn't happy about that, having them so isolated. . . . There wasn't a choice at first. We had to go where we could afford to. I didn't purchase a house till ten years ago. Then it mattered . . . in a place where the kids could be with their own."

Janet's decisions paid off for the children, and ultimately for her. "After twelve years of being at home with *Mr. Rogers* and *Sesame Street*," when her children were grown, Janet returned to college, earned a master's degree, and now works as an educator. Two of her three children have graduated from college and begun professional careers. However, "the youngest child is not a scholar, which was a bitter pill to swallow. He wasn't interested in reading or studying." Yet this son proved to be an enormous emotional support to Janet during her divorce, and has begun training in a technical field.

Janet celebrates her choices and her children. "I am proud of all three of them. They have grown into very sensitive and caring young people. They are focused, know what they want, and how to achieve it. . . . We all have a destiny to fulfill, and this was mine. I often wonder what the future of my family will be like. Will my children instill this in their children? I look at my children as better versions of myself, and hope this continues through the generations."

Ramona Rodriguez and Janet Swallow exemplify several issues that are important for this book. Ramona had children before her educational career was completed, a common pattern among college women from less affluent backgrounds. Being a mother and a student typically affects the time it takes to attain a degree and the final amount of education that a woman completes, important issues that we examine in the following chapter, using survey data. Whether a woman finds a husband or partner while in college, and whether that person sticks by her, was a pivotal issue for both women. In chapter 6, we discuss how much the presence of a father affects the educational prospects of his children. Finally, both women expressed strong views about parenting and the kinds of cultural stimulation that mothers should provide to their children. This belief proves to be an important reason why maternal education pays off for the next generation.

In the following chapters we will examine each of these issues, drawing on our survey data, generated from following the lives of several thousands of women from youth to middle age. Although certain technical aspects of these analyses become fairly complicated, we have aimed our discussion at the general reader, and have tried to minimize technical discussions in the text. Instead, we have provided a methodological appendix at the end of this book (appendix A), where we provide details on the statistical methods we used in our study and the samples and expand on issues of response rates. Our social scientist colleagues will no doubt scrutinize that appendix, but other readers who do not care about technical aspects can ignore it. Similarly, our chapters are sprinkled with tables that display the statistical evidence for our conclusions, but we have been careful to provide a thorough discussion of each finding in the text of each chapter, so readers will not lose the thread of our argument nor miss the evidence behind our claims if they choose to skip over the tables.

⸻ Chapter 2 ⸻

Thirty Years Later:
Educational Attainments

C ollege going in the United States has expanded rapidly throughout the last half century, growing from about 2.3 million undergraduates in 1950 to nearly 15 million by 2001 (National Center
for Education Statistics 2003b, 2005a). This huge growth in enrollment
was partly driven by population growth and demographics: the giant
baby boom cohort entered college in the 1960s and 1970s, and their children, another huge cohort, poured into higher education from the 1990s
until the present. However, population growth is only part of the story.
Beginning in the early 1970s, universities began opening their doors to
groups who previously had little representation in higher education:
racial minorities, and Americans from poorer or less-educated families
(Karen and Dougherty 2005). Community colleges and many public universities began accepting high school graduates with very diverse skills,
including many who had earned weak grades in high school.

The Development of Open Access

Among the first institutions to implement a policy of open access was
the City University of New York (CUNY), a university system at that
time consisting of seventeen campuses: nine four-year colleges and
eight community colleges. After CUNY initiated its open-admissions
policy in 1970, freshmen enrollments across the sprawling system doubled in the ensuing few years, and total enrollments grew to 250,000
students by 1975.
CUNY's new program was one important expression of a growing
national concern with racial and ethnic inequality that had emerged
during the 1950s and '60s. In that period, new migrants to New York
City—at the time predominantly African Americans from the American
South and Puerto Ricans—were highly disadvantaged in the increasingly stiff academic competition for seats in the university.[1] Their weak
position stemmed largely from their typically inadequate academic
preparation in the ghetto high schools of New York. Although minority

students were a growing presence in New York's public schools, they were starkly underrepresented in CUNY's colleges.

The growing mobilization of minorities across the nation, especially among African Americans, over issues of inequality, combined with the liberal establishment's efforts to advance equity, were reflected in New York City around a number of issues, not the least of which was access to higher education. Conflict over this issue escalated, leading to militant action on the part of students, most notably at the system's flagship school, the City College of New York (CCNY), located in Harlem. Student demonstrations, combined with support from both the CUNY chancellor and the administration of the liberal Republican mayor, John Lindsay, led CUNY in 1970 to initiate a second-chance program often referred to as "open admissions." Under this program, every high school graduate in the city was guaranteed a seat somewhere in the system.

This policy represented a sharp break from the highly selective CUNY admissions system previously in effect. Although open admissions provided a seat in the university for all high school graduates, it did not guarantee a place in baccalaureate programs. To qualify for a spot in a four-year college, graduates had to have either an average of at least an 80 in their college-preparatory courses in high school or a ranking in the top 50 percent of their high school graduating classes. Students who did not meet either of these standards could enroll in one of the system's community colleges.

On its face, this new admissions procedure was racially and ethnically neutral. In practice, however, it was pathbreaking because it functioned especially to broaden access to B.A. programs for minority students, who typically attended ghetto high schools where grades tended to be low. College admissions policies that emphasized GPA consequently worked against minority access. Where neighborhood schools are highly segregated by race, however, admitting on the basis of a student's rank in the high school graduating class served as a color-blind mechanism that benefited minority applicants. In CUNY's case, allowing graduates in the top half of these segregated high schools entry to B.A. programs proved crucial in opening the doors to previously excluded students.[2] In 1969, the last year before open admissions, blacks and Hispanics made up 4 percent of senior college enrollment. In 1970 they jumped to 16 percent.

The CUNY approach to access was pathbreaking in other ways, too. The university attempted to embrace a concept of opportunity that included not only access but also outcome. Presaging what would become a national trend, programs of skills testing, remediation, and other support services were put in place, aiming to enhance students' chances for achieving academic success.[3] Finally, CUNY had in place an ideal financial aid model: its century-old tradition of free tuition. Taken together, these features formed an open-admissions blueprint. The CUNY program was more baccalaureate-oriented in its focus than other higher education systems such as California's.[4]

Despite a widespread perception of City University's access policy as unique and unprecedented,[5] by the late 1970s and early 1980s, much of the rest of American public higher education had come to look more like CUNY. The academic, economic, and ethnic profile of CUNY's early 1970s "open-admissions" cohorts was in many ways similar to the nationwide profile of college-goers a decade later. In effect, the CUNY initiative was a harbinger of national currents that were gaining momentum and visibility. By the end of the 1970s, broader access was a widespread feature of the public higher education systems across the country.

Of course, the national trend toward wider access to college was not an expression of a singular, clearly articulated policy initiative, as it was at CUNY. Rather, it evolved from various demographic and institutional influences. Among these were the growing rewards of college credentials in the labor market, which created ever-widening incentives to attend college, even for academically weaker students and for those who were older than the traditional age for entry into college. These developments spurred the rate at which new institutions (four-year, two-year, and proprietary vocational) were founded. Growth in the number of new colleges created the necessity of filling student seats, which in turn reinforced the broadening of access.

Issues and Questions About Open Access

A number of important questions arise about the educational outcomes of open-access policies. How well were students who came to college with academic and economic handicaps able to capitalize on educational opportunity? What proportion of these students received undergraduate degrees, and what factors influenced the chances of degree completion? Did the collegiate tier in which students were initially placed—that is, in associate's degree programs in community college or in B.A. programs— affect the chances of earning a baccalaureate degree? What proportions of bachelor's degree recipients went on to complete postgraduate studies? How long did it take to climb the various rungs of the educational ladder? And how long did degree completion take for minority students compared with whites? These are the major questions we address in this chapter.

The data sets we have deployed at both CUNY and nationally are strategic for addressing these issues.[6] Never before have these questions been examined over a span of three decades, as we have done for CUNY. The national survey's twenty-year time span is also unusually long. A different picture emerges than that usually seen over shorter, more conventional time periods for following student progress. For example, when graduation rates are measured after four or six years, large differences are seen between ethnic groups—indeed, they are still apparent even after a decade (Lavin and Hyllegard 1996). However, after thirty years, do such differences narrow, and if so, by how much? If narrowing occurs, to what is this due?

Overall, we will argue, the broadening of American higher education has been a success in terms of students' postsecondary attainments. As this chapter will demonstrate, by the year 2000, more than 70 percent of the women who entered CUNY in the early 1970s had earned a degree of some kind. More than three-fourths of these women earned a B.A. degree or higher. National graduation rates are similarly impressive. Alongside this success is the fact that substantial ethnic inequalities in education persisted: African American and Hispanic students remain less likely to go to college, and once they do, they are more likely than whites to be placed in two-year community colleges and less likely to graduate. Nonetheless, we will demonstrate that the expansion of opportunities for college has helped to narrow ethnic disparities.

Who Entered College Under Open Access?

Large proportions of those who entered college after the admissions gates opened wider would not by any conventional yardstick have been viewed as "college material." Many of the new enrollees came from modest, often impoverished, economic backgrounds. At CUNY, more than 80 percent of black and Hispanic women—more than twice the percentage of whites—came from families with incomes of less than $10,000 (in 1970 dollars).

As table 2.1 makes clear, most CUNY minority women entered with educational disadvantages, too. Heavy majorities of these women were the first generation in their families to attend college, so they could be thought of as strangers entering a strange land. Their high school grades were decidedly average or below average: over 80 percent of African Americans and almost two-thirds of Hispanics had C averages or lower, whereas the majority of whites had A and B averages. Minority women were a half year or more behind whites in their college-preparatory course work.[7]

Nonacademic factors may also have affected educational attainments. Blacks and Hispanics were more likely than whites to be twenty or older when they entered college. This could affect the likelihood of attaining postgraduate degrees, since older students might be less likely to contemplate going on to postgraduate studies after completing undergraduate work. Whether women had children is another consideration. Those who became mothers[8] while in college might have found it more difficult to continue in school or might have been delayed in graduating as a consequence of having child-care responsibilities. Women of color were far more likely than whites to become parents before or during the initial years of college.

As we suggested earlier, women in the national NLSY sample were not so different from those at CUNY. Although on average the national students entered college with somewhat stronger high school grades (they were more likely to have A or B averages), more than 40 percent of them entered college with averages of C or lower. Among minority students, the figure was 60 to 65 percent. Minority women in the national sample, like their CUNY counterparts, were less likely to have parents with college experience, were more likely to come from impoverished families, and were much more likely to have children. Thus, by the 1980s, broad access to college—in terms not only of academics but also of socioeconomic characteristics—was a reality both at CUNY and nationwide.

Getting Started: Students' College Placement and Early Experiences

The level at which students begin college typically has a major impact on eventual educational attainments—not only in terms of how far students go, but also how long it takes. There is a consensus among researchers that starting in a community college lowers the odds of completing a bachelor's degree (Alba and Lavin 1981; Breneman and Nelson 1981; Brint and Karabel 1989; Dougherty 1994, 2002; Karabel 1972; Lavin and Hyllegard 1996; Monk-Turner 1990). This reduces the chances of earning postgraduate credentials and diminishes economic payoffs.

After the open-admissions policy was initiated at CUNY, minority women were more likely to start college at the B.A. level than they had been before the program started. Nonetheless, the majority of them were still found in community colleges. Around 60 percent started in these two-year schools, whereas whites typically were placed in four-year institutions (see table 2.1).[8] Although differences in white-minority levels of entry (at a four-year versus at a community college) were not as unequal nationally as in New York, nationally, whites were still more likely than minorities to start in a B.A.-granting institution.

Table 2.1 Socioeconomic and Academic Characteristics of CUNY and National Women (Percentages Except as Noted)

	CUNY Women				National Women College Entrants			
	White	Black	Hispanic	All	White	Black	Hispanic	All
Ethnicity	70.7%	18.1%	11.2%	100%	79.0%	14.7%	6.3%	100%
Father's education								
Has some college or more	33.3	16.1	12.9	28.5	42.7	20.6	18.8	38.5
Received degree	17.2	3.5	4.6	13.7	29.1	10.1	11.9	25.7
Mother's education								
Has some college or more	23.1	17.0	6.7	20.3	33.0	20.2	11.9	29.9
Received degree	8.4	6.2	2.4	7.3	17.0	7.2	3.9	14.8
Neither parent attended college[a]	58.5	72.0	83.7	63.2	47.6	65.3	71.2	51.3
Family income at entry under $10,000[b]	38.7	81.5	84.2	51.8	20.6	67.2	63.3	30.1
Family income at entry under $4,000	3.0	17.9	24.5	8.2	4.4	21.7	18.2	7.9
Degree aspirations[c]								
None	0.9	2.3	3.2	1.4	11.2	11.1	20.3	11.7
A.A.	14.7	24.2	21.2	17.0	15.2	12.4	15.6	14.9
B.A.	27.2	32.4	35.3	28.9	44.4	41.2	35.9	43.6
Higher than B.A.	57.3	41.0	40.4	52.7	29.1	35.3	28.1	29.9
High school average								
A	10.0	1.2	1.5	7.6	17.7	3.8	6.1	15.2
B	46.6	14.2	33.2	39.6	44.8	31.2	36.5	42.5
C	37.0	48.6	52.7	40.7	31.6	48.3	41.7	34.4
Lower than C	6.3	35.9	12.7	12.1	6.0	16.8	15.7	7.9

Mean high school average	81.2	72.9	77.4	79.4	84.0	77.3	78.6	82.9
Mean rank in high school	63.9	50.4	62.8	62.0		—e		
Ranked below top half of class	28.0	50.0	28.8	31.0		—e		
Mean number of college-preparatory credits	13.5	10.6	11.0	12.7	16.3	15.6	16.3	16.3
Mean age at college entry	17.6	19.9	18.9	18.1	20.1	20.2	20.9	20.2
Age twenty or older at entry	2.2	23.4	15.3	7.5				5.1[d]
Entered four-year college	63.1	36.1	40.5	55.7	54.7	51.1	45.0	53.6
Entered community college	36.9	63.9	59.5	44.3	45.3	48.9	55.0	46.4
Open admissions students								
In four-year college	24.6	74.8	48.3	32.1		—e		
In community college	44.1	73.4	50.4	52.3				
GPA in first year	2.62	2.06	2.22	2.48		—e		
Took remedial courses	32.2	66.2	58.2	41.3		—e		
Mean number of remedial courses taken[f]	1.6	2.9	3.1	2.2				
Employed full-time as undergraduates		—e			11.8	9.7	13.0	11.5
Had first child before entry	0.8	15.7	6.4	4.1	13.6	30.0	23.9	16.7
Had first child within five years of entry	6.9	23.0	20.5	11.3	29.3	55.0	47.5	34.2

Sources: CUNY Women File and NLSY79–Adults.

[a] Students who entered college neither of whose parents attended may be designated as "first-generation college attenders."

[b] 1970 dollars for CUNY women and 1979 dollars for NLSY women; 1979 dollars were converted to 1970 dollars.

[c] Degree aspirations for the NLSY women were measured closest to the age of eighteen and include only women who entered college by the age of eighteen.

[d] Figure taken from Alexander W. Astin et al. (1987) for the years 1970 to 1972.

[e] Data unavailable

[f] Calculated only for those who took remedial courses

In a program such as CUNY's, which aimed to increase minority opportunity for higher education, level of entry needs to be scrutinized because it is in itself an important dimension of opportunity. A multivariate analysis helps to clarify the reasons for unequal placement. In our analysis we predicted level of entry, using a number of variables we expected might influence the placement process.

A clear set of findings emerges from the analyses (table B.1 in appendix B). By far the most important influence on college entry level at CUNY was high school academic background.[9] Students with stronger records—higher GPAs, more college preparatory course work, and higher rankings in their graduating class—were much more likely to enroll in four-year colleges.[10] The CUNY admissions process stipulated that placement should be determined by high school record, and our analysis shows that this is in fact the primary determinant of level of placement. Minorities' disadvantage in access to four-year colleges was a direct consequence of their weaker high school preparation.

CUNY's use of rank in high school graduating class did, however, enable more minority students to enter these schools than would otherwise have been the case. Among students who had comparable high school records, black women were more likely than whites to enroll in four-year schools, and Hispanics were equally likely. The policy of making all those in the top half of the high school graduating class eligible for four-year schools in fact paved the way for many students to enter those institutions, even those with low high school averages.

The national data tell a similar story. As at CUNY, high school record was the most important influence on level of placement.[11] However, there was clearly an attempt to redress racial inequality in high school preparation: with controls for high school preparation, black women emerge as significantly more likely than whites to enter four-year colleges, and there is no significant difference between Hispanics and whites.

Both at CUNY and nationwide, widening the access gates partly compensated for educational and economic disadvantages that previously would have made entry to four-year colleges—or, for that matter, community colleges—impossible. That ethnic disparities continue to be seen in level of placement is mainly a function of the stark inequalities in high school performance that remain between white and minority high school graduates.

Thirty Years Later: A Scorecard on Educational Attainment

As we noted earlier, thirty years after entry more than 70 percent of former CUNY entrants had earned a degree of some kind (table 2.2). At the same time there were clear ethnic inequalities in degree outcomes.

Table 2.2 Educational Attainment of CUNY Women After Thirty Years, by Level of Entry and Ethnicity (Percentages)

	Four-Year College				Community College				All CUNY			
	White	Black	Hispanic	All	White	Black	Hispanic	All	White	Black	Hispanic	All
Early dropout[a]	4.7	12.4	15.7	6.4	15.0	22.4	19.1	17.5	8.4	18.5	17.7	11.3
Some college[b]	12.9	19.4	22.5	14.5	21.9	22.4	22.1	22.0	16.3	21.3	22.3	17.9
Associate's degree	3.0	11.6	6.7	4.2	31.8	24.1	31.3	29.8	13.6	19.6	21.4	15.5
Bachelor's degree	38.0	30.2	30.3	36.6	21.4	21.5	16.8	20.7	32.0	24.6	22.3	29.6
Master's degree	36.1	22.5	23.6	33.5	8.7	8.3	9.9	8.8	26.0	13.4	15.5	22.5
Advanced degree[c]	5.3	3.9	1.1	4.8	1.2	1.3	0.8	1.1	3.7	2.5	0.9	3.2
N of cases[d]	357	304	335	996	345	330	300	975	702	634	635	1,971

Source: CUNY Women File.
[a]Earned less than one semester's worth of credits.
[b]Earned more than a semester's worth of credits, but no degree.
[c]Includes Ph.D. and professional degrees such as M.D. and L.L.M.
[d]Unweighted number of cases.

Only about 25 percent of white women failed to complete any college degree, compared with about 40 percent of minority women. More than 60 percent of whites earned a B.A. or higher, whereas among blacks and Hispanics the figure was closer to 40 percent.

How do the graduation results for the CUNY women stack up against national ones? As of the year 2000, most of the CUNY women were forty-five to forty-nine years old. We compared their thirty-year record with a national one compiled by the Current Population Survey (CPS) for women in this age group. Results after thirty years seem quite comparable (table 2.3). The 70 percent of CUNY women who completed some kind of degree is almost matched by the national rate of 68 percent.[12] Minority women at CUNY were as likely as minority women nationally to earn a bachelor's degree, and they outdid their national counterparts in completion of master's degrees. Though the difference between the national and the CUNY groups in the percentage of women who got M.A.s is most substantial for whites, CUNY minority women also outdid their national counterparts (table 2.3). The CUNY group is more urban than is the national sample, and the labor-market demand for teachers and social service workers with master's degrees may be greater as a consequence.

One aspect of the debate surrounding the issue of academic standards concerns the institutions where degrees were completed. Notwithstanding criticisms of open admissions as leading to the admission of unqualified entrants who were not college material (and who, therefore, earned "bogus" degrees), many CUNY graduates who continued into postgraduate programs were admitted to institutions outside the walls of CUNY and successfully met their standards. About three-fourths of associate's and bachelor's degrees were earned at CUNY, but at the master's level, the figure falls to 35 percent. Almost 90 percent of advanced degrees were earned elsewhere.

All in all, the data indicate that the long-term academic success of CUNY women compares favorably with the national record. In both samples, minority women did rather well, but not as well as whites.

Predictors of B.A. Attainment

To examine the processes that affect the attainment of a B.A. degree, we predicted from a number of variables,[13] including ethnicity, parents' education and income, high school record, age at entry to college, degree aspirations, level of entry to college (bachelor's or associate's program), whether students worked full-time as undergraduates, the number of remedial courses taken, GPA in the first year of college, and whether a woman had a child during the first five years of college (table B.2).

Table 2.3 Educational Attainment, by Ethnicity, of CUNY and National Women (Percentages)

	CUNY Women				National Women[a]			
	White	Black	Hispanic	All	White	Black	Hispanic	All
Some College[b]	24.7	39.8	40.0	29.2	30.4	40.7	42.1	32.0
Associate's degree	13.6	19.6	21.4	15.5	17.7	17.9	14.9	17.6
Bachelor's degree	32.0	24.6	22.3	29.6	33.3	29.1	28.9	32.7
Master's degree	26.0	13.4	15.5	22.5	15.1	10.1	12.0	14.4
Advanced degree[c]	3.7	2.5	0.9	3.2	3.4	2.2	2.1	3.2
N of cases[d]	702	634	635	1,971	4,737	604	242	5,583

Sources: CUNY Women File and Current Population Survey, March 2000.
[a]National data for women aged forty-five to forty-nine who entered college.
[b]For CUNY women, "Some college" includes the category "Early dropouts" from table 2.2.
[c]Includes Ph.D. and professional degrees such as M.D. and L.L.M.
[d]Unweighted number of cases.

To begin we remind the reader that overall at CUNY, over 60 percent of whites earned a B.A., compared with about 40 percent of African Americans and Hispanics. These are the white-minority gaps we examined. To assess the sources of these differences, we first examined the extent to which they are determined by characteristics that students brought with them to college, such as their family background and their high school grades, academic courses taken, and rank in their high school graduating classes.

For the CUNY students, parental educational attainment and parental income were not associated with the chances of graduating with a B.A. Perhaps this is because a free tuition policy was in effect during the initial five years of open admissions and helped to minimize the effects of low income on economic ability to stay the academic course.

High school grades and exposure to an academic curriculum in high school were especially crucial in augmenting graduation chances. When we control for these school background factors, ethnic differences in graduation are erased. The more academic courses students took in high school, the better were their B.A. chances. In addition, high school grades influence graduation indirectly through their effects on grades in the first year of college. First-year college grades seem to forecast quite well the eventual chances of B.A. completion. For example, a student who earned a B average as a college freshman had a 40.7 percent chance of getting a B.A., whereas a student comparable in other ways who earned a C average had a 27 percent chance.

The level at which students enter college is another important consideration. We wanted to find out whether, measured over a period of three decades, the negative community college effect (meaning that those who attend community college seem less likely to attain B.A.s) might wane—if, for example, those who completed A.A.s decided to return to college for further study much later on. Our analysis suggests that the effect does not disappear. Even thirty years after students started college, community college entry retains a strong negative influence on B.A. attainment. With other factors held constant, a student who started in community college had only a 35 percent chance of earning a B.A., compared to 61 percent for a similar student whose initial matriculation was in a four-year college.

Another influence on B.A. attainment is the choice of curriculum while in college. Many students in community colleges concentrated in vocational or technical studies. However, those who majored in liberal arts, the conventional transfer track, were more likely to complete a B.A. degree. Students' degree aspirations strongly affected the chances of B.A. attainment over and above their high school academic background.

Some students had to work while undergraduates. Full-time employment (measured in the NLSY) lowered the chances of getting a B.A., partly because it had a negative influence on the grades students earned. CUNY's minority women were more likely than whites to hold such jobs.[14] The ethnic gap in graduation rates is partly a result of this.

We had anticipated that factors such as becoming a parent within the first five years after college entry and being older when one started college would affect B.A. chances. Although the coefficients for each were in the expected direction—for example, women who had a child before or in the first five years of college appeared as less likely to complete a B.A.—none were statistically significant.

Taking remedial courses did not predict B.A. attainment at CUNY. Students who took remedial courses were not less likely to graduate. (We will consider issues and controversies surrounding college remediation in detail in chapter 7.)

These multivariate analyses highlight the causes behind ethnic differences in graduation rates. Minority women took fewer academic courses in high school, were more likely to start college in a two-year school, had weaker averages in their freshman year, were less likely to aspire to a postgraduate degree, and more often held full-time jobs. If minorities were comparable to whites on these factors, black women would actually be more likely to complete a bachelor's degree than whites, and Hispanic B.A. completion would be no different from whites' (table B.2).

In a few important respects, the national NLSY data are not consistent with the CUNY findings. Nationally, socioeconomic origins—including both low parental income and parents' education—continued to matter in predicting B.A. graduation, even controlling for college variables, age, and full-time work. The role of low income seems to loom larger in the national picture, perhaps because there was no policy of free tuition nationally, as there was at CUNY in the initial years of its open-admissions program. Also, having a child within five years of entering college significantly lowered B.A. graduation chances in the national sample but not at CUNY. Again, the absence of free tuition may have made it more difficult for women with children to continue in college.

These analyses teach us a great deal about the sources of ethnic disparities in B.A. attainment. They suggest that even with open access, high school preparation and college performance as indicated by grades remained important, as one would expect if academic standards were in place. At the same time they indicate the importance of open access in narrowing ethnic inequalities. Without the expansion of college enrollment created by a broad access policy, ethnic gaps in degree attainment would have been far greater.

The Timing of Degree Attainment

Whether students capitalize on educational opportunity by completing a degree is obviously one crucial piece of the story of broader access to higher education. In addition, how long it takes matters a great deal. Traditionally, graduation with a bachelor's degree has taken four years and with an associate's degree has taken two years. But as the college-going population has become more diverse, many students have needed more than the conventional period to complete their studies.

For example, the process of degree attainment may become more extended among students with weaker academic preparation for college, among older students, among those with heavy employment responsibilities, and among students who are parents and not infrequently single mothers. Low income or parental responsibilities may oblige some students to attend college part-time; others must interrupt their attendance entirely for a period; and remedial or compensatory course work may not carry graduation credits, perhaps slowing progress toward a degree among students who take such courses. It is increasingly understood that six years and even longer is necessary for degree completion if one is to count substantial portions of students who eventually graduate.[15] Time intervals that are too short often lead researchers to misclassify eventual graduates as dropouts, thus understating graduation rates over the longer term. Even in the case of studies such as those conducted by the U.S. Department of Education's National Center for Education Statistics (NCES), where students are followed for as long as twelve years (see Adelman 2004), study periods may not be sufficiently long to catch all who graduate.

Although degree attainment typically enhances occupational status and earning power, extended time to attain a degree may partly undercut these benefits. First, delayed graduation means that degree recipients will spend less time in the labor market with their educational credentials working for them. Second, it is increasingly the case that the better-rewarded jobs in the U.S. economy require postgraduate credentials, and so a drawn-out undergraduate career may ultimately diminish the chances that a graduate will continue to climb the educational ladder. For example, it makes a difference whether one completes a B.A. at age twenty-two or age thirty. Older graduates are more likely to face life-course events that create conflicts between school, family, and work responsibilities.

Our thirty-year time perspective for assessing graduation completion leads to a number of interesting and surprising results. Both at CUNY and nationally, many students required far longer than the traditional length of time needed to complete degrees at various levels. In the nominally two-year associate degree programs, CUNY students

Table 2.4   CUNY and National Women's Mean Number of Years to Highest Degree, by Ethnicity and Level of Entry[a]

	CUNY Women							
	Four-Year College				Community College			
	White	Black	Hispanic	All	White	Black	Hispanic	All
Associate's degree	10.3	9.7	15.0	10.7	4.3	6.7	6.3	5.1
Bachelor's degree	6.4	8.1	7.9	6.7	10.2	11.5	14.9	11.1
Master's degree	10.7	15.1	12.4	11.2	14.9	16.7	16.3	15.6
Advanced degree	15.4	19.1	13.7	15.7	16.4	14.1	18.9	15.8

	All CUNY Women				National Women			
	White	Black	Hispanic	All	White	Black	Hispanic	All
Associate's degree	5.1	7.3	7.4	5.9	5.3	6.6	5.9	5.5
Bachelor's degree	7.3	10.0	11.0	8.0	5.8	7.1	8.3	6.0
Master's degree	11.3	15.7	13.9	11.9	11.4	13.9	11.9	11.5
Advanced degree	15.5	17.2	15.8	15.7	8.9	12.8	9.5	9.3

Sources: CUNY Women File and NLSY79–Adults.
[a]Women in the CUNY sample are followed up to thirty years after entering college. Women in the NLSY79 sample are followed on average for twenty years.

on average took almost six years to finish the A.A., while nationally five and a half years were needed.[16] CUNY women took an average of eight years to finish supposedly four-year B.A. programs, and nationally the figure was six years. The CUNY data also show that B.A. recipients who started in community colleges needed almost four and a half years more than B.A. recipients who began college in a senior college (table 2.4).

Ethnic differences in time to complete a B.A. degree are quite visible. Minority women at CUNY received B.A.s three to four years later than whites.[17] Thus, African Americans on average needed ten years to finish B.A.s and Hispanics eleven years. Since the mean age at entry to CUNY was almost twenty for blacks and nineteen for Hispanics, women of color were typically about thirty when they graduated (among whites the average graduation age was about twenty-five).[18]

As one would expect, those who went beyond the B.A. to attain postgraduate degrees took many years to complete their education. M.A. recipients earned this credential an average of twelve years after they began college. Again, minority women generally took much longer than whites. Those attaining advanced degrees (Ph.D.s and professional degrees) took close to sixteen years in the CUNY sample. Overall, minority women were not far behind whites at this level.[19]

Although it is clear that many women took more than the normative period of time to complete degrees, the chronology of the degree attainment process is surprising. What stands out is the substantial proportion of degree recipients who, by conventional standards, took extremely long to graduate. For example, 16 percent of CUNY B.A. recipients and 8 percent of national B.A. recipients took fifteen or more years to complete their degrees (note that the CUNY and national results are not entirely comparable because the CUNY sample was followed longer). Substantial numbers of women of color took a very long time to graduate: more than a fifth of black CUNY B.A. graduates needed fifteen or more years, and 30 percent of Hispanic B.A. holders took at least fifteen years (table B.3).

To give a further sense of how important an extended time perspective is for getting a complete picture of degree attainment and for making ethnic comparisons, if B.A. rates at CUNY were counted after just six years, one would erroneously classify as dropouts 25 percent of the white women who in fact eventually graduated; 56 percent of black B.A.s and 53 percent of Hispanic ones would erroneously be classified as having fallen by the wayside. Similarly misleading impressions are evident in the national data.

Many policy documents and government statistics report B.A. graduation rates measured after relatively short intervals such as four, six, or eight years after college entry. Such figures seriously overstate ethnic inequalities in attainment, so that minority success rates seem much worse than white rates. Because minority women take longer to graduate, rates measured after long time periods show much narrower ethnic gaps in educational success. Thus, shorter tracking periods can have the effect of reinforcing stereotypes of minorities as "high-risk" students with only modest chances of success, whereas longer-term follow-up studies portray them as more similar to whites. Thus, choice of time interval for measuring graduation is no mere methodological issue, but can have important political implications.

What explains the ethnic gaps in the amount of time required for degree completion? To examine this question we carried out regression analyses. All B.A. recipients are counted in these analyses, including those who later went on to complete postgraduate degrees. For the total group of bachelor's recipients in the CUNY sample, white B.A.s finished an average of 2.7 years faster than blacks, and 2.9 years earlier than Hispanics (table B.4). When social origin and high school record variables are controlled, these large ethnic time-to-B.A. disparities are no longer statistically significant. The number of college-preparatory courses taken in high school is the most important factor explaining them. High school record exerts its influence through its effects on level of college entry and grades in the first year of college. A student who completed the freshman year with a B average graduated a year and one quarter ahead of one who was comparable in other respects but had a C average. Starting in a community college added more than two and a half years for B.A. completion compared with students who were similar in other ways but who started in four-year colleges.[20]

We reported earlier that among CUNY women, having a child in the early part of one's college career did not diminish the chances of earning a B.A. However, parental status clearly put women on a much slower track for getting a degree. Graduation was delayed by three years for B.A. recipients who had a child before or during the first five years of college. Having to work full-time in college also delays progress to the B.A., and is especially common among minority women.[21]

The joint influence of these variables is very substantial. A mother who had a child before or within five years of college entry, who started in a community college, worked full-time, and had a C average rather than a B would have needed about nine years more than an otherwise comparable woman who had no children, started in a four-year college, had a B average, and did not work full-time. A comparable analysis of the national sample yields similar results.[22]

Who Gets Postgraduate Degrees?

One reason for the importance of the bachelor's degree is that it makes one eligible to apply for graduate study and, hence, access to better-rewarded jobs. Just as the proportion of the population earning bachelor's degrees has been growing—from 11 percent in 1970 to 26 percent in 2000 (National Center for Education Statistics 2003b)—so, too, has there been an upswing in the proportions having master's degrees and advanced degrees (table 249). Women have clearly participated in this upswing, as their growing share of degree holders in the high professions attests (table 249).

A large proportion of the CUNY women earned graduate degrees; more than 25 percent of all CUNY entrants and 46 percent of B.A. recipients completed some kind of graduate study at either the M.A. or advanced degree level (table 2.5). Ethnic differences are visible—minority

Table 2.5   Percentage Completing Postgraduate Degrees, by Level of Entry and Ethnicity (CUNY and National Results)[a]

| | CUNY | | | | | | | |
| | Four-Year College | | | | Community College | | | |
	White	Black	Hispanic	All	White	Black	Hispanic	All
All entrants	41.4	26.4	24.7	38.3	9.9	9.6	10.7	9.9
B.A. recipients	52.1	46.6	44.9	51.1	31.6	30.9	38.9	32.4
	All CUNY				National			
	White	Black	Hispanic	All	White	Black	Hispanic	All
All entrants	29.7	15.9	16.4	25.7	18.5	12.3	14.1	17.6
B.A. recipients	48.1	39.2	42.3	46.5	35.7	29.7	32.8	35.0

Sources: CUNY Women File and Current Population Survey, March 2000.
[a]Postgraduate degrees include master's, professional, and doctoral degrees.
National figures calculated for women aged forty-five to forty-nine who entered college.

women's rates of postgraduate attainment are below those of whites, but the gaps are considerably smaller than they are for B.A. attainment: 62 percent of whites got B.A.s, compared with 41 percent of blacks and 39 percent of Hispanics (see table 2.2)—around a 20-percentage point white-minority gap—differences in postgraduate attainment among B.A. holders narrow to 9 percentage points between CUNY whites and blacks and 6 percentage points between CUNY whites and Hispanics. It appears that much of the winnowing—the creation of the white-minority gap—occurs during the process of reaching the B.A. Once that threshold is crossed, minority chances for going further become similar to those of whites.

Nationally women's postgraduate attainment rates are lower than CUNY women's, but they are still substantial: 35 percent of women B.A. holders nationwide earned a postgraduate degree. The same pattern of ethnic differences was observable in the national data, but the white-minority gaps were narrower than for CUNY.

Conclusion

Widening the gates of academe for nontraditional students provided educational opportunities for many at CUNY and nationally who otherwise would have had no chance for college. In spite of the disadvantages that they brought to college with them, a substantial number were able to translate educational opportunity into results. Our long-term follow-up reveals that graduation rates were fairly high, around 70 percent; on this the CUNY and national samples were very similar.

Broad access especially augmented the proportions of minority women who completed degrees. Calculations we made for CUNY show that its open-admissions policy more than *doubled* the number of black women who completed B.A.s. Among Hispanics, the number of B.A.s almost doubled, and even among whites, the number of B.A. recipients increased 1.3 times (in chapter 8 we shall examine in more detail a variety of benefits produced by open access).

In effect, open access performed a compensatory function, both adding to the number who entered the university and boosting the number of degree recipients. Still, this significant achievement must be tempered by the recognition that even though open admissions made a substantial dent in the ethnic disparities in educational attainment, it was not able to erase inequalities entirely. Students, especially minority women, came to college with disadvantages that subsequently generated yet additional disadvantages. Such students were more likely to be placed in community colleges. They more often had to take full-time jobs. Weaker academic skills and full-time work added to the chances that they would start off with poorer grades in the freshman year. These factors contributed to lower rates of baccalaureate attainment. Among B.A. recipients, rates of progress were often significantly slowed for women who became mothers before or during the initial years of college, and working full-time was also an important delaying factor. Starting in a community college not only lowered the odds of graduation, it also added significantly to the time it took to finish. Extended time to B.A. in turn lowered the odds of earning postgraduate degrees. Minority women were the ones most affected.

Although broad college access helped to increase the number of minority graduates, the use of conventional time spans for tracking graduation can produce a severe understatement of the numbers of students who receive bachelor's degrees, especially minority B.A. graduates, because surprising proportions graduated after six, ten, and even fifteen years.

Notwithstanding the greater difficulties minority women faced in completing undergraduate work, surprising numbers did earn postgraduate degrees. In this connection, it is worth noting—especially because of the furor about academic standards under open access—that 90 percent of these degrees were earned at institutions outside the walls of CUNY. Other institutions clearly accepted CUNY graduates into postgraduate degree programs, an indication they viewed CUNY degrees as valuable.

As we noted in chapter 1, it has sometimes been asserted that the admission of students with weak academic backgrounds is a cruel hoax. It has been said that first their appetites for higher education are whetted; then, because of weak academic skills, their aspirations meet with failure. The consequence is that students end up with little or nothing to show for their efforts, and there are needless institutional costs, as large amounts of public funds are wasted. The evidence of this chapter flies in the face of such a conclusion.

Ultimately, a fundamental test of educational attainment is its contribution to material well-being. How achievements in higher education translated into economic payoffs is the question to which we now turn.

Chapter 3

How Families Fared:
The College Payoff

Despite the fears of some critics that CUNY's open-admissions policy would prove a failure as thousands of weak students foundered on the harsh realities of academic requirements, we saw in chapter 2 that substantial proportions graduated, often despite serious disadvantages in their academic and socioeconomic backgrounds. However, not all critics of open admissions expected that students' academic weakness would lead to massive rates of failure. Some predicted that political pressures for academic success would instead produce passing grades for students, even if their performance was subpar—an example of "social promotion" making its presence felt in higher education. Ultimately, students' degrees would be merely a patina of learning overlaying superficial academic achievement. According to this prediction, CUNY credentials would have limited value in the labor market.

In this chapter we will examine the economic payoffs to educational attainments both for the CUNY and national NLSY populations. Decades later, as CUNY women neared age fifty and as the national sample of women neared forty, how well off were they in terms of material resources? How were they doing in terms of their personal earnings? More broadly, what were the economic resources of their households, as indicated by household income and important aspects of economic well-being, such as home ownership, savings, equities, and retirement plans?

We distinguish between two dimensions of material well-being. The first is women's individual outcomes in employment, especially their earnings. The second concerns the women's household and family contexts and their household material resources. Taken together, these two dimensions offer a more complete picture of economic well-being, and a fuller understanding of the resources available to children.

Our aim is not only to provide a picture of economic well-being, two decades (NLSY) and three decades (CUNY) after these women started in higher education but also to give a sense of the processes through which educational attainments, work, family, and children have influenced these material results. Ethnic differences are a major theme. Because

35

educational opportunity policies such as open admissions aimed to erase or at least narrow differences in life chances between white and minority students, it is of fundamental importance to consider how the economic payoffs to minority women's education compare with those of whites.

Does Broad College Access Payoff? 1. Personal Earnings

Personal earnings are crucial for evaluating the success of open access policies for women who came from families with modest economic resources.[1] Median personal earnings in the year 2000 for women in the CUNY sample were $38,968 for all workers and $43,000 for full-time workers (table 3.1). The issue of full-time versus part-time employment is of importance with regard to ethnic differences in earnings. Minority women are more likely to hold full-time jobs than whites. For example, in the CUNY sample, eight in ten black and Hispanic women were working full-time, compared with about six in ten whites. We focus our discussion on those who are employed full-time.

As we noted, some critics, believing that academic standards would unravel under open access, expected that the economic value of credentials would plummet. Two aspects of the earnings data in table 3.1 indicate that this devaluation did not happen. First, comparison of CUNY results with earnings for same-age women in the Current Population Survey (U.S. Census Bureau 2000) shows that the earnings of CUNY women exceed those of women at the same educational level in the national sample, in almost every case. We considered whether this occurred because many CUNY women lived in the New York metropolitan area. However, comparisons with national women of comparable education who live in urban areas (also reported in table 3.1) reveal that the two groups have very similar earnings.

A second aspect of the data supports the idea that degrees remained valuable: the progression of earnings payoffs as one moves up the credentials ladder. As a regression analysis (table 3.2) shows, payoffs are substantial for each incremental level of educational attainment. For example, CUNY women who completed credits short of a degree earned 14 percent more than early dropouts, a finding consistent with the work of others (Kane and Rouse 1995a) who have found benefits conferred by the accumulation of credits. Associate's degree completers earned 22 percent more than early dropouts; B.A. recipients earned 33 percent more, while those who completed graduate degrees earned 63 percent more. These comparisons do not support the idea that CUNY credentials "fell from grace" under its open admissions policy.

Payoffs to college attendance will be overestimated if they are intertwined with prior socioeconomic advantages or high school experiences.

Table 3.1   Median Personal Earnings of CUNY and National Women,[a] by Educational Attainment, Ethnicity, and Employment Status

	All Workers		Full-Time Workers		
	CUNY	National	CUNY	National	National Urban[b]
All races					
High school[c]	26,000	21,000	30,000	23,211	25,100
Some college	31,000	26,000	35,000	28,884	32,565
Associate's degree	35,000	27,500	40,783	30,100	34,000
Bachelor's degree	36,351	36,050	42,063	40,000	46,000
Postgraduate degree	50,000	47,766	54,545	50,000	55,900
Total	38,968	28,000	43,000	30,600	36,000
White					
High school	22,000	21,095	34,040	24,000	27,982
Some college	31,134	25,450	34,326	28,847	33,210
Associate's degree	33,000	27,500	44,239	31,017	36,138
Bachelor's degree	35,000	35,969	40,030	40,035	46,000
Postgraduate degree	50,000	48,335	54,238	50,446	58,330
Total	38,000	28,292	45,000	31,762	38,576

(Table continues on p. 38.)

Table 3.1 *Continued*

| | All Workers | | Full-Time Workers | | |
	CUNY	National	CUNY	National	National Urban[b]
Black					
High school	26,000	20,321	26,028	21,514	23,400
Some college	31,414	28,000	35,165	29,536	30,337
Associate's degree	40,000	26,948	40,936	28,421	33,000
Bachelor's degree	45,000	38,042	47,689	39,000	46,000
Postgraduate degree	55,026	41,616	55,924	41,616	42,048
Total	40,000	26,200	40,639	28,000	30,000
Hispanic					
High school	31,362	18,000	33,000	20,000	22,000
Some college	30,358	25,000	34,232	27,040	35,000
Associate's degree	35,000	28,000	38,401	30,000	30,000
Bachelor's degree	40,000	37,000	40,000	40,000	45,032
Postgraduate degree	50,000	45,000	51,326	45,400	41,151
Total	36,000	24,030	39,000	28,080	30,084

Sources: CUNY Women File and Current Population Survey 1998 to 2002.

[a]National data include black, white, and Hispanic women aged forty-five to forty-nine.

[b]A city of 5 million or more, as determined by the CPS.

[c]"High school" in the CUNY sample refers to early dropouts—women with less than sixteen college credits.

To account for this possibility, we added measures of social and educational background to regression models (table 3.2).[2] When we did this, **Variables** payoffs to degrees in the CUNY sample, though slightly reduced, remain robust (for those who had completed "some" credits, the payoff was marginally significant). Between the two factors, it is high school record rather than social origins that is significantly associated with greater earnings. We replicated these analyses using propensity score modeling **Methodology** (discussed in appendix A), and the substantive results are entirely consistent with the original findings. The evidence is clear: access to higher education significantly improves women's earnings.

As for ethnic differences, there are no statistically significant earnings differences between African American and white women in the CUNY sample (model 2 of table 3.2). However, Hispanics lag behind, earning about 13 percent less than whites. These findings change when educational attainment, high school background, and social origins are controlled statistically. Then, black women's earnings actually *exceed* those of equivalent whites, and Hispanic women's earnings do not differ from whites' (model 3). This is to say, a black woman who is comparable to whites in educational attainment, family background, and high school record would earn significantly more than whites, and the earnings of Hispanics would be the equal of whites.

Another way of conceptualizing this issue is to consider the size of the boost in earnings that a woman obtains from getting a degree compared to not completing. Does this boost to earnings vary according to ethnicity? To assess this question we added interaction terms to our CUNY regression model (see column 5 of table 3.2). Our analyses show that African Americans receive a significantly larger earnings boost than do whites, of about 30 percent at the B.A. level and about 26 percent at the advanced degree level (the latter is marginally significant). The payoffs that Hispanics received were not significantly different from those received by whites. In sum, in the CUNY data, earning an academic credential pays off even more strongly for African American women than for others.[3]

In the main, national data are consistent with the CUNY findings. What differences there are seem to be matters of magnitude rather than kind. There are strong payoffs to all levels of educational attainment. With controls for social background and high school preparation, these payoffs are reduced but remain robust. Initial earnings disparities distinguishing whites from minorities are larger in national data: blacks and Hispanics both earn less than whites, on average. When we control for high school record and family background, these earnings disparities in favor of whites disappear, and minority women emerge as earning significantly more than equivalent whites (the black coefficient is marginally significant). This is to say that initial ethnic disparities are

Table 3.2 Logged Full-Time Earnings of CUNY and National Women (Unstandardized OLS Coefficients)

	Model 1	Model 2	Model 3	Model 4	Model 5
CUNY women					
Constant	10.289***	10.642***	9.5337***	9.5656***	9.5789***
Some college[a]	.13879*		.10372	.10685	.03139
Associate's degree	.21931***		.19158**	.18383**	.12079
Bachelor's degree	.32884***		.2268***	.22081***	.12039
Advanced degree	.62921***		.51065***	.50066***	.41865***
Black[b]		-.05886	.14721**	.14289**	-.05894
Hispanic		-.13161**	.03658	.03739	-.01874
Age			-9.6e-05	.00025	8.5e-05
Low income of family of origin[c]			-.04938	-.05051	-.04585
Parents' highest grade completed			-.015	-.0146	-.01395
Grades in high school academic courses			.0067*	.00663*	.00712**
Units of high school academic courses			.02718***	.02591***	.02655***
Married or partnered				-.0635	
Any children				-.14631***	
Ever a single mother				.05997	
Spouse's prestige				.00241	
Black—some college					.18192
Black—associate's degree					.18048
Black—bachelor's degree					.30048*
Black—advanced degree					.25894
Hispanic—some college					.01711
Hispanic—associate's degree					.02241
Hispanic—bachelor's degree					.09988
Hispanic—advanced degree					.05753
Adjusted R-square	.1119	.0041	.1335	.1457	.1326

National women

Constant	9.8659***	10.215***	9.6677***	9.6545***	9.7356***
Some college	.15258***		.07805*	.0662*	-.05391
Associate's degree	.30118***		.17378***	.16001***	.08265
Bachelor's degree	.66337***		.39359***	.34507***	.36179***
Advanced degree	.85809***		.52996***	.46663***	.42643***
Black		-.21406***	.0672	.078*	-.05313
Hispanic		-.07579*	.16275***	.15419***	.04853
Age			-.00486	-.00299	-.00492
Low income family of origin			-.05188	-.04476	-.05198
Parents' highest grade completed			.00795	.00566	.00758
Grades in high school academic courses			.05114*	.04717*	.05014*
AFQT80			.00624***	.0059***	.00632***
Married or partnered				.02938	
Any children				-.13732***	
Ever a single mother				.00811	
Spouse's prestige				.00239**	
Black—some college					.22968***
Black—associate's degree					.19531*
Black—bachelor's degree					.03314
Black—advanced degree					.24107
Hispanic—some college					.21958**
Hispanic—associate's degree					.11969
Hispanic—bachelor's degree					.08045
Hispanic—advanced degree					.21653
Adjusted R-square	.1648	.0193	.2237	.2343	.2265

Sources: CUNY Women File and NLSY79–Adults.

[a]Reference category is an early dropout in the CUNY sample, defined as having less than sixteen college credits; in the NLSY sample, a high school graduate.

[b]White is the reference category. Women of "other" ethnic groups are not included in the CUNY or NLSY samples.

[c]Defined as less than $10,000 in 1970 dollars.

*p < .05; **p < .01; ***p < .001

largely explained by prior ethnic inequalities in high school educational experience. In some respects (interaction terms are significant for some college and for A.A. but not for B.A.), African Americans in the national data receive a larger earnings boost from their higher education than whites (table 3.2, model 5).

Personal Earnings and the College Dropout

The emphasis in the preceding discussion has been on the earnings payoffs for those who completed A.A., B.A., and advanced degrees. However, as we saw in chapter 2, about 30 percent of entrants, both at CUNY and nationally did not complete any degree, even decades after entering college. Among minority students, the figure was about 40 percent. These percentages are not trivial and they raise the question: Are there economic payoffs of college attendance even to college dropouts? Did they experience economic benefits in terms of personal earnings? Did they do better than they would have if they had not entered college at all? These questions are best examined using the national sample, because it can use high school graduates as the basis of comparison with college students who earned credits but never graduated.[4]

Nationally, there is a 7 percent earnings boost to those who earned credits short of a degree, and minorities who earn some credits receive a significantly bigger earnings increment than whites (table 3.2, NLSY models 4 and 5). This earnings advantage exists after controls for family background, high school preparation, and IQ. A trend in the same direction occurs in the CUNY data, but it does not reach statistical significance, undoubtedly because of the reference category. The national results were confirmed when we used propensity modeling. Clearly, then, those who had some college experience received significant personal-earnings payoffs, especially minority individuals.

Personal Earnings and College Major

The payoffs of educational credentials vary according to the field of study (Bauman and Ryan 2001; Jacobs 1986, 1995), both at CUNY and nationally. At CUNY, average A.A.-level earnings vary from a low of $30,734 for an education major to a high of $48,948 for health and social services majors. At the B.A. level there is a range of almost $14,000 with education being the least lucrative major and business the most lucrative (table 3.3).

Because of the effects of major or field of study, some A.A. majors produce higher average earnings than some B.A. majors. In fact, CUNY women A.A. graduates who majored in health or social services earned significantly more than B.A.s who were education majors, and no less than any of the other B.A. majors (table 3.3).[5] Indeed, with other variables

Table 3.3   The Influence of College Major on Logged Full-Time
Personal Earnings[a]

	CUNY Women		National Women	
	Mean Earnings	Adjusted OLS Coefficients[b]	Mean Earnings	Adjusted OLS Coefficients
Associate's degrees				
Arts, humanities, social sciences	$37,947	−.3261**	$31,912	−.07089
Business	46,289	−.1122	40,244	.03695
Education	30,734	−.5059**	22,586	−.28213*
Health, social services	48,948		31,295	
Math, natural sciences, computers	39,859	−.17866	32,028	−.03702
Secretarial, legal, vocational	36,830	−.31847 **	24,015	−.24969*
Bachelor's degrees				
Arts, humanities, social sciences	50,698	−.11731	49,395	.11431
Business	53,206	−.03031	54,430	.30515***
Education	39,235	−.29989***	34,933	.01947
Health, social services	50,557	−.02415	49,484	.36281***
Math, natural sciences, computers	48,931	−.09679	56,611	.25329**
Other	40,000	−.00748	44,041	−.13923
Postgraduate degrees				
Arts, humanities, social sciences	60,083	−.00528	38,519	.14709
Business	73,678	.39025***	70,671	.4556***
Education, library science	50,175	.03783	44,512	.25598**
Health and social services	61,928	.21944*	55,381	.35583**
Math, natural sciences, computers	84,793	.47844***	56,308	.30384
Medicine and law	104,572	.63765***	91,312	.77939***
Adjusted R^2		.1656		.2267

Sources: CUNY Women File and NLSY79–Adults.

[a]The reference category is the associate's degree in health and social services.

[b]Coefficients are adjusted for ethnicity, age, parents' education and income, grades in high school academic courses, and units of academic courses in high school in the CUNY sample and AFQT scores in the NLSY sample.

*p < .05; **p < .01; ***p < .001

controlled, A.A. degrees in health and social services produced earnings as high as those with postgraduate degrees in education and in arts and humanities. So although it is true in the aggregate that credential level is linearly associated with earnings, when credentials are disaggregated by major, a more nuanced picture is revealed. These effects of major were not as strong in the national NLSY data, but here, too, some A.A. fields yielded payoffs equal to the earnings of some B.A. majors.

Within specific fields of study—for example, arts and humanities and social sciences or business—it is invariably the case that earnings are higher as one moves up the ladder from the A.A. level to the B.A. to postgraduate. For example, among CUNY women who majored in business, A.A. recipients earned an average of almost $38,000, B.A. holders were over $53,000, and those who completed postgraduate business degrees were earning over $73,000.

Ethnicity is also an issue in relation to college major. African American and Hispanic women were significantly more likely to be found in the high-earning majors than whites. That is one reason why minority women do rather well in earnings relative to whites.

Personal Earnings: Conclusion

Our analyses of earnings data fly in the face of criticisms that expanding access would produce at best puny economic benefits. Going to college paid off for all, and the earnings boost was sometimes greater for minority students. These findings are consistent with a long-standing status-attainment approach in documenting that educational attainment has a powerful influence on earnings (Blau and Duncan 1967; Hauser and Featherman 1977; Sewell and Hauser 1975; Warren, Hauser, and Sheridan 2002). They show that opening the gates to academe to minorities and the less affluent has not undermined the earnings-boosting power of academic degrees.

Does Broad College Access Payoff?
2: Household Income and Assets

Personal earnings are only one part of economic well-being. Several decades after they had started college, most women were living in households with children and were or had been married to partners or spouses who contributed economically. To understand this, we switch our focus to college attendance and wider economic resources, including not only household income but also home ownership and the value of homes. We shall also consider financial assets that help to provide security such as equities, retirement plans, and savings.

Household Income

As one might expect, women's household incomes substantially exceed their personal earnings: among all workers in the CUNY sample, median personal earnings are almost $39,000, but their median household incomes are $70,000 (table 3.4). In the national sample, the analogous figures are $28,000 and $72,500. Overall, women's personal earnings make up 56 percent of total household income in the CUNY sample and 42 percent nationally. In both samples, educational attainment is positively associated with household income.[6] For example, among CUNY women the median household income for B.A. recipients is $15,000 higher than for those with A.A.s and $25,000 higher than that of early dropouts. The national picture is very much the same. Regression analysis confirms the influence of educational attainment on household income (table 3.5, model 1), except that these payoffs are somewhat diminished when social origins and high school record are controlled.

The most striking aspects of the household income data are the dramatic ethnic gaps. In contrast to personal earnings, where the story was basically one of ethnic equality among women, the picture revealed by household income is one of stark inequality: the household incomes of minority women lag far behind those of whites (table 3.4). Among CUNY women, a gap of $30,000 separates white and black household incomes, and a gap of $25,000 separates white and Hispanic household incomes. Similar ethnic disparities are apparent in the national data.

Very large racial and ethnic differences in household income are apparent even for women with equal amounts of education. Among women holding bachelor's degrees, for example, CUNY whites' household incomes exceed blacks' by more than $20,000. Even the smallest gap shown by our data—$11,000 in the national results separating the household incomes of white B.A.s from their Hispanic counterparts'—is large.

The magnitude of these inequalities is further brought home when one realizes that on average a black woman with an advanced degree has the same household income as a white woman who left college with less than a semester's worth of credits. In the national data there are similar household inequalities, although they are not as wide as in the CUNY sample.

These inequalities cannot be attributed simply to ethnic differences in personal earnings, since we saw in our earlier assessment that earnings differences among ethnic groups were quite narrow. The source of ethnic disparities in household income must therefore be found elsewhere— as we shall see, in family of origin, and in family-context variables, including, most prominently, ethnic differences in rates of marriage and marital interruption, and in the earning power of spouses.

We assessed these influences through regression analyses (table 3.5) and confirmed the wide initial ethnic gaps in household income noted

Table 3.4   Comparison of Median Household Income of CUNY and National Women, by Educational Attainment and Ethnicity

	CUNY				National[a]		
	White	Black	Hispanic	All	White	Black	Hispanic	All
High school[b]	$70,000	$40,000	$50,000	$50,000	$56,786	$32,009	$43,643	$52,000
Some college	75,000	45,000	49,734	59,074	63,150	41,000	56,223	59,537
A.A.	70,000	51,132	49,020	60,000	66,200	47,466	57,577	62,660
B.A.	79,303	57,210	65,000	75,000	85,180	60,000	74,232	81,153
Advanced degree	100,000	69,937	85,060	100,000	99,923	65,231	109,032	97,584
Total	80,000	50,000	55,000	70,000	76,400	49,546	66,307	72,500

Sources: CUNY Women File and Current Population Survey (1998 to 2002).

[a]Calculated for black, white, and Hispanic women aged forty-five to forty-nine with high school diplomas or higher.
[b]High school refers to a college entrant with less than sixteen college credits in the CUNY sample, and a high school graduate in the CPS sample.

Table 3.5 Logged Household Income of CUNY and National Women (Unstandardized OLS Coefficients)

	Model 1	Model 2	Model 3	Model 4	Model 5
CUNY women					
Constant	10.802***	11.205***	11.264***	10.598***	11.347***
Some college[a]	.11126*		.03606	.04193	-.04146
Associate's degree	.10366		.0619	.08069	-.0587
Bachelor's degree	.33872***		.19264***	.14649**	.08191
Advanced degree	.59499***		.40241***	.32836***	.28474***
Black[b]		-.40967***	-.15942***	.0278	-.42496***
Hispanic		-.34947***	-.11419*	-.03143	-.22438
Age			-.01721***	-.01407**	-.01741***
Low income of family of origin[c]			-.1346***	-.09056**	-.13561***
Parents' highest grade completed			.02899*	.02375	.0307*
Grades in high school academic courses			.0033	.00064	.00376
Units of high school academic courses			.01644*	.01856**	.01511*
Married or partnered				.43173***	
Any children				.02592	
Ever a single mother				-.06731	
Spouse's prestige				.00858***	
Black—some college					.17824
Black—associate's degree					.40839**
Black—bachelor's degree					.30917*
Black—advanced degree					.37711**
Hispanic—some college					.09267
Hispanic—associate's degree					.03991

(Table continues on p. 48.)

Table 3.5 *Continued*

	Model 1	Model 2	Model 3	Model 4	Model 5
Hispanic—bachelor's degree					.17252
Hispanic—advanced degree					.18952
Adjusted R-square	.0959	.0662	.1602	.3377	.1633
National women					
Constant	9.8612***	10.619***	9.8495***	9.3058***	10.064***
Some college	.30905***		.21494**	.22057**	.0717
Associate's degree	.61972***		.41144***	.33232***	.12549
Bachelor's degree	1.0808***		.59621***	.47376***	.35195**
Advanced degree	1.3054***		.70119***	.57505***	.49044**
Black		-.77523***	-.33343***	-.01747	-.49792***
Hispanic		-.42669***	-.07804	.00095	-.49294***
Age			-.00837	-.01252	-.01087
Low income of family of origin			-.09875	-.06858	-.09765
Parents' highest grade completed			-.00103	-.00317	.00038
Grades in high school academic courses			.15367*	.09536	.15023*

AFQT score			.0082***	.00786***	.00848***
Married or partnered				1.0147***	
Any children				-.069	
Ever a single mother				.08241	
Spouse's prestige				.00523**	
Black—some college					.1295
Black—associate's degree					.34917
Black—bachelor's degree					.45825*
Black—advanced degree					.26854
Hispanic—some college					.49974**
Hispanic—associate's degree					.82889**
Hispanic—bachelor's degree					.68401*
Hispanic—advanced degree					.71468
Adjusted R-square	.0507	.0334	.0900	.1539	.0923

Sources: CUNY Women File and NLSY79–Adults.

[a]Reference category is an early dropout in the CUNY sample, defined as less than sixteen college credits, and a high school graduate in the NLSY.

[b]White is the reference category. Women of "other" ethnic groups are not included in the CUNY or NLSY samples.

[c]Defined as less than $10,000 in 1970 dollars.

*p < .05; **p < .01; ***p < .001

above. Family structure proved to be the largest determinant of racial gaps in household income (table 3.5, model 4). On average, CUNY women with husbands or partners had household incomes 43 percent greater than otherwise comparable women who were single. When we interviewed them in 2000, only a little more than 40 percent of black women were married, compared with 75 percent of whites, and 59 percent of Hispanic women. The obvious explanation for this association between ethnicity and household income is that minority households more often miss the economic contribution made by a spouse or partner.[7] As we shall see in chapter 6, and as the literature notes, women with more educational attainment are significantly more likely to marry (Sweeney 2002). Over and above this, however, is the fact that at any level of education, black women have much lower marriage or partnering rates than whites (Attewell et al. 2004).

A related domestic factor that helps to account for household income disparities is the job status of the husband or partner. Spouses with higher job prestige typically earn more, thus contributing more to household income.[8] We found that college-educated minority women tended to marry men with lower job prestige than comparable white women. Moreover, this white-black discrepancy in spouse's prestige was widest at the top level of women's educational attainment.

What contributes to these ethnic discrepancies in spouse prestige is not entirely clear. They are consistent with previous studies showing that black women outdistance black men in educational attainment, so that in terms of the principle of educational homogamy in mate selection, there is a thinner pool of higher-attaining black men available to comparably educated black women (Attewell et al. 2004; *Journal of Blacks in Higher Education* 1997; Slater 1994). One consequence is that black women—if they marry—are more likely to marry black men with lower levels of education and thus lower earnings. Job discrimination against black males may also contribute to ethnic inequality in household income.

The NLSY survey confirms the CUNY results (table 3.5, NLSY panel). In the national survey, having a spouse or partner is the most critical factor in accounting for disparities between white and minority household income. The job status of husband or partner has an additional influence. The national data show that blacks and Hispanics get a larger household income boost from a B.A. than whites, but these increments do not fully compensate for racial differences in the frequency of marriage and in marital disruption.

In sum, these analyses suggest that when we broaden the idea of economic well-being to include household income, educational attainment continues to make a positive contribution, but ethnic differences in marriage rates undercut education's benefits by reducing household income. Also, among minority women with a spouse or partner, the occupational prestige and earnings of that partner are likely to be lower than for comparably educated whites.

Real Property

Home ownership is an especially significant asset—typically, the single most important source of wealth among Americans. As researchers have pointed out, owning a home can make a fundamental contribution to the ability of families to maintain their standard of living. Assets can be important even in the case of low-income families (Spilerman 2000, 500):

> Even modest financial assets, which normally provide only a small addition to total income, can cushion a family from the economic shock of illness or job loss, enabling . . . bills to be paid for a number of months and thereby preventing a temporary loss of employment from snowballing into a wider crisis for the family. Households with few financial assets, especially African-American families . . . are particularly vulnerable to such financial dislocations.

Even where job loss or illness is not an issue, an asset such as a house can often ease the strain of expenses such as college costs for children because it makes possible the refinancing of mortgages and other maneuvers to gain extra cash. The literature suggests that for both historical and contemporary reasons, there are very large ethnic differences in home ownership rates (Conley 1999; Flippen 2001; Oliver and Shapiro 1995; Rosenbaum 1996).

Both the CUNY and national samples contain home ownership data, and the NLSY survey provides additional information on the value of homes. For these two measures we see a similar pattern: higher educational attainment is positively associated with likelihood of home ownership and with the value of homes.

Regression analyses further specify the influence of college attainments on these housing measures (tables B.6 and B.7). Among CUNY women, the completion of B.A. and advanced degrees increases the odds of home ownership. Nationally, all credentials are associated with increased odds of owning a home and a higher value home. When family origins and high school record are controlled, educational attainment continues to influence the ownership and value of homes (model 3 in the regressions). In the CUNY sample, the benefits for home ownership are seen only for those who were at the upper end of the education ladder, (among advanced degree holders). In the national sample, however, these benefits are more widespread (apparent as well among both A.A. and B.A. recipients). Moreover, among home owners, each step up the credential ladder is associated with increased value of the home.

Again there are generally sharp ethnic inequalities favoring whites on both outcomes: whites are more likely to own a home, and whites' homes are much more valuable than blacks' and, to a smaller extent, Hispanics' (table 3.6). With controls for social origins (parental education, income in family of origin), high school record, and educational attainment in college, ethnic gaps, while narrowed, still remain substantial (tables B.6 and B.7, model 3).[9]

Family structure clearly has a large effect in determining home ownership and home value. In both the CUNY and national samples, being married, having children, and having a spouse with relatively high job prestige greatly improve the odds of home ownership (and in the latter survey, the value of the home).[10] Ever having been a single mother diminishes them.

Why do home ownership gaps in favor of whites remain, even after accounting for these marital factors? We think the key for African Americans lies in their historical situation, especially their difficulties in acquiring property, even after the Civil War (Conley 1999; Gutman 1976; Oliver and Shapiro 1995). More recently, in the massive migration out of cities and into suburbs that occurred after World War II, blacks were largely excluded from this migration, both because many were poor and had relatively little education, and because redlining often prevented them from acquiring mortgages. Many of those who did attempt to move to suburbs faced intense racism (Massey and Denton 1993).

To summarize, educational attainment clearly improved the chances of acquiring real property with higher valuation. Without access to college, minority individuals would have been even further behind whites in acquisition of these resources. Nevertheless, ethnic disparities clearly persist. These seem due to a combination of historic inequalities that have limited the chances of minorities, especially blacks, to acquire wealth in the form of housing, and to the greater difficulties that minority women face in establishing and maintaining two-wage-earner households.

Other Financial Assets

In addition to real property, other material resources such as savings, certificates of deposit, stocks, other investments, retirement plans, and inheritances affect financial well-being. Increasing educational attainment is strongly associated with possession of more such assets (table 3.7). Among high school graduates, the average value of these assets was about $38,000, while for those who completed a postgraduate degree, it was over $127,000—more than three times greater. Even college dropouts had 37 percent more financial assets than high school graduates, and B.A. recipients were almost 200 percent ahead of high school graduates. With controls for social and high school background, these

Table 3.6 Home Ownership Rates of CUNY and National Women and Value of Home, by Educational Attainment and Ethnicity

	Own a Home (Percentage)				Median Value of Home			
	White	Black	Hispanic	All	White	Black	Hispanic	All
CUNY women								
High school[a]	80.5	39.4	53.8	63.7		N/A		
Some college	73.6	46.7	51.0	64.7				
A.A. degree	78.1	57.1	65.2	71.3				
B.A. degree	84.7	64.4	69.4	80.3				
Postgraduate degree	88.8	67.3	74.3	85.5				
Total	82.8	55.0	62.4	75.5				
National women								
High school	74.7	38.0	45.3	66.8	$100,000	$60,000	$94,793	$95,000
Some college	74.6	39.4	56.5	65.8	125,000	80,000	115,765	120,000
A.A. degree	78.6	53.7	67.6	73.7	125,000	79,289	121,624	120,000
B.A. degree	86.3	56.3	79.3	83.2	178,000	100,000	160,468	170,000
Postgraduate degree	85.1	77.3	71.4	84.1	180,000	118,741	160,000	175,000
Total	78.6	43.9	57.4	71.8	135,000	80,000	120,000	130,000

Sources: CUNY Women File and NLSY79–Adults.
[a]High school refers to a college entrant with less than sixteen college credits in the CUNY sample, and a high school graduate in the NLSY sample.

Table 3.7   **Mean Value of National Women's Other Financial Assets,
by Educational Attainment and Ethnicity[a]**

	White	Black	Hispanic	All
High School	$42,314	$13,026	$20,885	$37,908
Some college	63,618	24,618	42,223	55,205
Associate's degree	74,068	15,965	54,426	64,742
Bachelor's degree	118,595	44,537	90,972	111,185
Postgraduate degree	134,230	67,598	68,742	127,440
Total	77,724	25,517	44,863	69,360
Number of cases	3,246	487	237	3,970

Sources: NLSY79–Adults: white, black, and Hispanic women with high school diplomas
or higher, in 1996, 1998, and 2000 waves.
[a]Assets consist of the total dollar value of savings, CDs, stocks, other investments,
retirement plans, and estates. Top-coded at $350,000.

educational effects are somewhat diminished but remain statistically
significant (table B.8).

Ethnic inequalities are also dramatic (table 3.7). Total mean asset value
for whites is $77,724, more than triple the average value for African
Americans and more than one and a half times the value for Hispanics.
A regression analysis provides insight into the sources of these large
ethnic differences (see table B.8). Social background is one. Women with
better-educated parents had more valuable assets. White women's parents were the ones who went further in education. Parental income also
made a difference: growing up in a lower-income family was associated
with lower asset value in the next generation. Minority women more
often came from less affluent families. Doing well in high school had
continuing positive effects on asset value. College educational attainment made an important contribution. Even women who had some college experience short of a degree had assets that were worth 25 percent
more than those of otherwise comparable women who did not attend
college. B.A. recipients' assets were over twice as great, net of other factors. When all of these factors are taken into consideration, they explain
virtually the total difference between whites and Hispanics and account
for half of the disparity between whites and blacks.[11]

Household factors have an additional influence. Married women's
assets were 86 percent greater than those of otherwise comparable single
women. Having a spouse with relatively high job status also increased
the value of assets. Whites were more likely to be married and have husbands with more job prestige. When these factors are taken into account,
the white-black gap is again halved,[12] and Hispanic-white differences
are no longer significant. Although whites retain a 34 percent advantage
over blacks in asset value, this disparity is much narrowed from the
original gap, where whites' assets were triple those of blacks.

Conclusion: The Potential and Limitations of Educational Opportunity Policies

In this chapter we examined the economic payoffs to education decades after college entry, asking whether attainments made possible by broad access helped to erase or narrow ethnic inequalities in material well-being. The data we have reviewed teach us quite a lot about education's influence over this lengthy time period. Consistent with a long line of research flowing from the work of Peter M. Blau and Otis Dudley Duncan (1967; see also, for example, Jencks et al. 1972; Jencks et al. 1979; Sewell, Hauser, and Wolf 1980; Sewell and Hauser 1975), educational attainment was found to have a potent influence on how well individuals do in the labor market. Those who go further in higher education are more likely to hold jobs that are more rewarded in terms of earnings and other material benefits. Overall, educational attainment is among the most important influences on personal earnings.

Minority women had personal earnings comparable to those of whites. Educational opportunity created by broad access to college was especially critical for minority women. Because of the weakness of their educational backgrounds and their typically modest or even impoverished economic status, many undoubtedly would not have attended any college without open access. Opportunity translated into substantial educational achievement, and this in turn helped to produce economic leverage in the labor market. These findings provide no support for those who believed that broader access to college would undercut the value of college credentials in the labor market.

When the spotlight switches from personal earnings to household economic resources, the story takes a different turn. Even though educational attainment has a large positive influence on household income, home ownership, and possession of other financial assets, the role of marriage and household factors also looms large. Family variables—marital status, single motherhood, and the job status of spouses and partners—strongly affect the material well-being of households. Minority women are often less well off economically because they are far more likely to be single or divorced. Women's educational attainments are positively associated with the job prestige and earnings of spouses, but such marital payoffs from higher education are weaker for minority women than for whites. In addition, minorities are more likely to have been single mothers. These family context variables largely explain the extreme ethnic inequalities in household income and in measures of wealth such as home ownership and other material assets, and they seem to stand largely outside the field of educational effects.

White women who come from modest backgrounds and enter college are usually able to attain upward mobility in two ways: directly, through their own credentials and earning power, and indirectly, by marrying college-educated men who gain access to highly rewarded jobs. Thus, the formation of dual-earner professional families becomes a critical point in the translation of higher education into upward mobility. Fewer college-educated minority women are able to benefit from the indirect path.

Extreme ethnic inequalities in some outcomes, such as home ownership and financial assets, are not fully explainable through the variables we have deployed for analyses. White-minority differences, especially in ownership of real property, have historical roots that continue to result in diminished wealth accumulation among minority families. Their historical origins mean that these conditions are less amenable to influence by educational opportunity. Although educational opportunity has narrowed differences in personal earnings, wealth gaps remain extreme.

This discussion has left open the status of women of Hispanic origin. Hispanic women in our sample generally accumulated more wealth and assets than African American women, despite the fact that typically they had parents who were impoverished when they immigrated to the United States. The sources of Hispanics' economic disadvantage are not so rooted in historical issues of race, and this seems to be a decisive factor in their wealth accumulation.

These analyses of educational opportunity and the economic well-being of individuals and families have not so far explicitly touched upon implications for the second generation—the children of the women whose situations we have been assessing. Since a major focus of our work is the association of educational attainment in one generation with outcomes in the next, the complexities of education and family contexts that we have considered in this chapter might be expected to pose problems for the analysis of children's outcomes in the chapters to follow. But here we must remind the reader that the implications of educational attainment go beyond economic well-being. Those who have gone further in education may as a consequence have different ways of thinking about many issues, including child rearing, and their parenting behavior may be quite different from that of parents who did not go as far in higher education. We now turn to the analyses of children's outcomes.

= Chapter 4 =

Breaking the Cycle of Disadvantage: Maternal Education and Children's Success

In previous chapters we examined how going to college affects the lives of women, particularly their subsequent earnings, household income, and home ownership. Our concern in this chapter is whether higher education for women also translates into benefits for the next generation. If a mother's college education spills over to improve her children's chances of success, then increasing maternal access to college may reduce the transmission of disadvantage down the generations, and serve as a positive force for social mobility.

Considering families across several generations reframes social inequality as a dynamic process. Some families rise out of poverty into affluence, from grandparents who were high school dropouts to grandchildren with advanced degrees. Others slide downward in the course of two or three generations. So rather than think of a family as located in one class or social position, we will stress its trajectory from one generation to the next and then look at the role of education in this process.

An emphasis on intergenerational mobility and family trajectories also draws us away from the world of Horatio Alger, where each person forges a destiny through personal talent and effort. Instead, we allow that a person's success depends in part on parents and other family members. This viewpoint conceives of families as accumulating (or sometimes losing) educational, occupational, and financial resources over several generations. Thus, the success of one generation generates resources or advantages that may (or may not) be handed down or transferred to the younger generation.

Sometimes a resource consists of specific skills or aptitudes: a mother passes on her mathematical skills to her child, or a father his love of reading. In other instances, the transfer is more a matter of expectations: some parents communicate that going to college is expected of their children and thereby motivate the children to strive in high school. Psychological orientations can also be passed down the generations: some families inculcate their children with a belief that you are the master of your own destiny; others instill a more fatalistic or pessimistic creed. Each of these elements, inherited from the family, can enhance a child's likelihood of success during school and beyond.

The notion of intergenerational accumulation and transfer might seem to suggest a high degree of social inertia, because families that have lots of skills and resources to begin with can pass them on, whereas families that lack them cannot. This would imply that the rich get richer across the generations, while the poor get poorer. Our view is not that pessimistic, however. Sometimes important resources are available from outside the family. Success in school, attending college, and marrying are paramount examples of external influences that can change an individual's and a family's mobility trajectory. Moreover, transferring skills, expectations, and psychological orientations from one generation to the next doesn't always work. Some children rebel against family influence, and others lack their parents' talent or drive, despite parental encouragement. The transmission of privilege and disadvantage is therefore a probabilistic process, a matter of inheriting better or worse resources for success, but there are always some people who beat the odds and others who lose despite initial advantages.

If maternal higher education does play a significant role in enhancing children's success, we then need to identify the mechanisms through which this process works. Is it the higher income of a college-educated mother that matters? Or her ability to find a more educated husband or partner? Or the impact of her occupation and career? Or does she raise her children differently, by dint of her own educational experiences? In chapters 5 and 6 we will examine each of these mechanisms, but the present chapter focuses on the logically prior question: How much of a difference does maternal education make for children?

The Children's Data

As in previous chapters, we analyzed data drawn from two longitudinal studies. The CUNY (City University of New York) study assembled baseline information on a cohort of women college entrants in the early 1970s, and collected new information about the women and about the educational and occupational status of their 2,632 children in the year 2000.

Our other main source of data is a nationwide survey of mothers and children, called the NLSY (National Longitudinal Survey of Youth) Mother-Child Sample. The NLSY population is broader than the CUNY study in two important ways. First, the NLSY study includes women from all educational levels, including high school dropouts, high school graduates, and those who went to college. By contrast, the CUNY study only includes women who attended college. Second, the NLSY drew its sample from all over the United States, whereas the CUNY women all attended college in New York City in the early 1970s, although many have since moved to different regions of the country.

The mothers of the NLSY sample were first interviewed in 1979, when they were between fourteen and twenty-one years old, and have been re-interviewed every year or two since then. Whenever a woman had a child, that girl or boy also became a member of the NLSY sample and was followed over time thereafter. By 2000, there were 11,211 children in the study. Information was collected about these children that included standardized tests of vocabulary and reading and numerical ability. Parents were asked about the ways they raised and interacted with a child. Researchers visited the families at home to observe and measure parent-child interactions. As the children aged, information was also collected about school activities and parental involvement, and later about the child's college attendance and work experiences. (Additional details about these surveys can be found in the appendix A.)

Who Are the Children?

In the year 2000, about a third of the NLSY children were eighteen or older: roughly college age or beyond. The rest of the NLSY children were still of school age: 57 percent were between six and seventeen years old, and at the youngest end, 9 percent were under six. Girls and boys were represented in close to equal numbers. The NLSY deliberately oversampled minority women; as a result under half of the children are non-Hispanic whites (47 percent), about one quarter are African Americans (28 percent), a fifth are Hispanic, and the remaining children are Asian, Native American, or other ethnicities.

The mothers in the CUNY sample are somewhat older than the NLSY mothers, and consequently their children are also a little older on average than the NLSY children. Almost half of the children in the CUNY sample are eighteen or older, and most of the rest are aged six through seventeen. There are almost equal numbers of boys and girls. In the CUNY study, 71 percent of the children are non-Hispanic whites, 18 percent are African Americans and 11 percent Hispanics.

In both surveys, African American children are on average older than their white and Hispanic counterparts, reflecting the fact that black mothers tended to bear children at an earlier age. So in the NLSY, the average age for black children is fifteen years old, compared to fourteen for non-Hispanic whites, while in the CUNY sample, the average black child is twenty-two years old, compared to nearly seventeen years for whites.

We employed several indicators of the financial status of the families in which the children grew up, including their family's household income at various points in the child's life,[1] as well as whether a family income was below the federally defined poverty level. The United States is an affluent country, but in the NLSY 47 percent of children lived in families whose incomes fell below the poverty level at some point in the child's first five years, and 56 percent of children were in poverty families at some point between the ages of six and ten. The picture changes when we look at persistent poverty, rather than occasional poverty. A smaller but still large proportion—27 percent of the NLSY children—lived in families whose average income was below the poverty line during the first five years of the child's life, and 21 percent of the children had average incomes below the poverty line between the ages of six and ten. In short, a large proportion, but by no means all, of the children in these national samples grew up in families struggling with poverty.

The distribution of childhood poverty varies by race and ethnicity. About two-thirds of black children in the NLSY experienced poverty at some point before age six, compared to about one-third of white children. Looking at persistent poverty between the ages of six and ten, in the national NLSY sample, 36 percent of African American children lived in poverty, compared to 26 percent of Hispanic children and 11 percent of white children. When later we notice large discrepancies in educational outcomes between white and black children in our surveys, we should recall these huge ethnic differences in childhood poverty.[2]

Not all minority children in our analyses were raised in low-income families, however. Substantial numbers of African American and Hispanic children in both the NLSY and CUNY surveys grew up in middle- or high-income families. In the NLSY, 16 percent of black children were in the top income quartile (the top quarter of the whole sample in terms of income) and 18 percent in the next-to-highest income quartile. For Hispanic families, 23 percent of children were in the highest income quartile. So although there is a clear association between minority race or ethnicity and growing up in a low-income family, the surveys include substantial numbers of minority children who grew up in relative affluence. This will allow us to untangle the effects of race and ethnicity from those of family income or poverty in the statistical models that follow.

Because household incomes often fluctuate dramatically from year to year, some researchers choose to characterize families according to parental occupation, which is more stable, rather than household income. Moreover, scholars have linked occupational prestige and complexity to different styles of child-rearing, an occupational effect that operates even after controlling for income (Kohn 1969; Parcel and Menaghan 1994). When we categorize the NLSY children according to their parents' occupational standing (known as their "socioeconomic index" or Duncan SEI score) when the child was aged six to ten, we observe racial and ethnic inequalities, though not as extreme as for income. In the NLSY, 19 percent of white children were raised in families in the lowest quarter or quartile of occupational standing, compared to 30 percent of black children and 25 percent of Hispanic children. And in the highest occupational quartile, we find 32 percent of the white children, 19 percent of black children, and 23 percent of Hispanic children. In short, there are clear inequalities between racial and ethnic groups in terms of the occupational standing of children's parents, but there are nevertheless also lots of high-status minority families in these surveys.

The CUNY children are similarly diverse in terms of family income and occupational prestige. For household income, 31 percent of whites were in the top income quartile, compared to 9 percent of African Americans and 11 percent of Hispanics. At the bottom income quartile, we find 15 percent of whites, 43 percent of blacks and 39 percent of Hispanics. Even though these are all children of women that attended college, the racial and ethnic disparities in income remain quite large.[3]

Media commentators often assert that children from two-parent families have better life chances than children who grow up in single-parent households. Scholars are more divided on this issue, and there have been heated debates about the effects of being a child of a single or a divorced mother.[4] Some researchers assert that providing a child with a stable family environment and the kind of dependable routines and support that a two-parent family can provide matters more than the family's material or educational advantages. Other scholars dispute this, decrying the view that a two-parent family is superior, suggesting that this is a disguised form of class or race prejudice. Yet other researchers suggest that the contrast between single-parent and two-parent families is misplaced. What matters, they argue, is whether a family remains stable over time—irrespective of its configuration. A stable family life is a prerequisite for children to flourish. This shifts the emphasis to family breakup or re-formation as potentially harmful events for children.

In our analyses, we used multiple indicators of family structure that are oriented toward these debates: whether children lived with only one parent during their early years; whether they experienced a family transition—such as a divorce, separation, or gaining a stepfather—before their thirteenth birthdays; and whether children were living in two-parent households at the time when the educational skill tests were administered. Although these variables diverge in some analyses, they provide a consistent picture when it comes to race and ethnic differences: as table 4.1 reports, African American children in both the national NLSY and CUNY samples were far less likely to be reared in two-parent families than white children were. Hispanic family patterns fall somewhere between those of whites and blacks, but are closer to the white pattern.

Table 4.1   Family Structure and Race or Ethnicity (Percentage)

	Raised Mainly With Single Mother[a]	Experienced Family Transition[b]	Has Husband or Partner[c]
NLSY sample			
White	3	33	84
Black	34	48	44
Hispanic	9	40	75
CUNY sample			
White	7	25	87
Black	36	70	47
Hispanic	25	52	66

Sources: NLSY Child File; CUNY Child File.
[a]Defined as between birth and age ten for the NLSY sample; for most of the child's life for the CUNY sample.
[b]A transition is defined as divorce, separation, or remarriage for both samples.
[c]Measured when the child took major test battery around age seven, for NLSY children, and measured in 2000 for the CUNY sample.

These racial and ethnic differences in family structure are so marked that one might well expect family structure to be an important factor in explaining inequalities in the life chances of the children. We will analyze this issue in depth in chapter 6.

Family size is another dimension that researchers have previously linked to children's outcomes. On average, children who grow up with many siblings tend to be somewhat less successful in their educational careers than children with fewer brothers and sisters. The disadvantage of being raised with many siblings persists even after controlling for family income, parental education, and other factors (Downey 1995; Parcel and Menaghan 1994, 159; see also the debate among Guang 1999, Downey et al. 1999, and Phillips 1999). Scholars hypothesize that the amount of individual attention that each child receives from a parent is less in large families, a phenomenon known as dilution, and that this produces the differences observed in educational outcomes.

In the NLSY—which includes a full spectrum of educational backgrounds, from mothers who were high school dropouts through women with advanced degrees—we observe in table 4.2 that white children are slightly less likely than black children to grow up as an only child, and that white children are considerably less likely than minority children to grow up with three or more siblings. By contrast, in the CUNY sample— women who all went to college—the racial patterns in family size are different. Black and Hispanic children were slightly more likely than whites to be the only child in their family. In our later analyses about the importance of maternal education, we will control for number of siblings.

Table 4.2   **Numbers of Siblings, by Race or Ethnicity (Percentage)**

	Only Child	Three or More Siblings
NLSY		
White	7	18
Black	9	32
Hispanic	7	34
CUNY		
White	13	8
Black	19	11
Hispanic	17	7

Sources: NLSY Child File; CUNY Child File.

Measuring a Child's Educational Success

Both surveys assessed each child's educational standing or skills relative to other children at several points during the child's life. The earliest NLSY assessment measured the vocabulary and verbal ability of children before or immediately after they began school (ages three to five). Known as the Peabody Picture Vocabulary Test (or PPVT-R), this widely used and well-regarded assessment presents a child with several pictures at a time. The tester reads out a word to the child and the child is asked to point to the one image that corresponds to the word's meaning. There are 175 vocabulary items of increasing difficulty, keyed to children of different ages. The number of correct answers is translated into a score that represents each child's verbal ability relative to national norms for children of that age.

Even at this young age, children exhibit large differences in vocabulary that are clearly associated with family income, social class, race and ethnicity, and parents' education and IQ. Researchers have shown that early vocabulary differences among children do not decline or become irrelevant after children enter school; on the contrary, they persist and have serious consequences. A child's preschool vocabulary score is a strong predictor of how well the child will subsequently learn to read, which in turn predicts school grades and achievement up to the teenage years.[5]

Social scientists who hold that inequalities in school skills reflect early linguistic and cognitive skill differences are not arguing for genetic determinism. Vocabulary and linguistic skills are learned. The most crucial learning period, however, occurs between birth and age three, leading several leading researchers in this area to advocate early intervention activities aimed at enriching learning environments for babies and toddlers.

The second occasion we chose for assessing children's educational standing in the NLSY came when the child was under seven years old. The Peabody Individual Achievement Test (PIAT) measures skills in mathematics, reading recognition, and reading comprehension. The math scale starts with the simplest school math skills, such as understanding numerals, and progresses to topics of greater difficulty. A child begins the test with relatively easy items appropriate to her or his age and answers multiple-choice questions of increasing difficulty. The reading recognition and reading comprehension tests have a similar structure. The PIAT assessment is widely used and has high test-retest validity. It yields separate age-adjusted scores for mathematics and for reading. In our analyses, however, we constructed a combined math-reading score because the math and reading scores were quite highly correlated.

The NLSY re-administered the PIAT test battery on several occasions. We chose as a later educational milestone the retest that occurred when the children were between thirteen and sixteen years old.

The Behavior Problems Index (known as the BPI), an assessment widely used in child development studies that the NLSY undertook for children age four and above, is based on a questionnaire filled out by a parent (usually the mother). It consists of twenty-eight items compiled from several psychological instruments that measure the "frequency, range and type of children's behavior problems" on multiple dimensions: antisocial behavior, anxiety or depression, headstrongness, hyperactivity, immaturity, dependency, and peer conflict or social withdrawal. The questions refer to the child's behavior in the prior three months. The NLSY repeated the assessment on several occasions from age four on. For our analyses we focused on each child's mean BPI overall score between ages six and ten.

Another indicator of school success is the track in high school a student is placed in. For many decades, high schools in America assigned students into separate tracks, such as college-academic, general, vocational, or remedial–special education, on the basis of grades, test scores, or teacher recommendations. Once in a track, students used to take most courses in that single track. Each track had its own curriculum, which differed from other tracks in its difficulty and scope. The result was a kind of educational segregation or caste system in schools. It was difficult, if not impossible, for a child to move up from one track to a more challenging one, so the system made little allowance for the possibility that a child might be strong in certain subject areas and weaker in others. During the 1980s, academic critics mounted a successful campaign against tracking in U.S. high schools (Oakes 1985). The result is that many high schools have abandoned the old system. Many schools still distinguish individual classes according to level of difficulty (for example, honors, regular, remedial), but nowadays most students take courses at different levels, combining, say, honors English with remedial math, honors French with non-honors science, and so on (Lucas 1999). According to researchers, however, students still classify themselves as being predominantly in a certain track. The variable that we use is a dichotomy that contrasts a college-preparatory track with all other tracks.

The NLSY also provided information on whether a child had been held back a grade between kindergarten and twelfth grade. Having to repeat a year can be an early sign of serious learning problems. Most scholars find that being kept back undercuts students' educational progress thereafter: students who repeat a year become bored or frustrated, and their school performance grows even worse.[6] We created a variable that indicated whether at any point between kindergarten and twelfth grade the student had been retained in grade.

The final outcome measure we derive from the NLSY is whether a child who had graduated from high school went to college. Unfortunately, we were unable to analyze later milestones—the occupations and incomes of grown children—because there were not enough children of this age group in the NLSY to ensure statistically valid comparisons.

Unlike the NLSY, the measures developed for the CUNY survey do not include test scores. They are based instead on mother's reports of the children's school standing at various stages of their educational careers. The first measure pertains to the child during elementary school, and is a composite of a child's grades and of the degree to which the student got on well with teachers. A second composite measure focuses on middle and high school and combines questions about grades, attendance, and finishing homework on time. A third combines questions about missing school, tardiness, getting into trouble at school, and earning low grades. We also created a fourth variable that indicated whether a student was in the college-prep track during high school. For children old enough to have finished high school, we created an outcome measure that indicates whether or not they attended a college (two- or four-year), and a separate variable, limited to children over twenty-one years old, for the kind of degree the student earned.

To summarize, we have multiple assessments of each child's academic standing relative to other children, measured at different points in the child's life. We will analyze each indicator separately, to determine the effect of maternal education on that particular child outcome. What we find, in most cases, is a great deal of consistency across outcome indicators. The variables that are associated with a child's educational success at age three in many cases are still important when we look at determinants of high school status or college going. We will report the results for individual child outcome measures in tables, and discuss the overall pattern in the text, noting any exceptions to the general pattern.

Table 4.3   Educational Upward Mobility: Percentage of Grandchildren of High School Dropouts Who Enroll in College

	CUNY	NLSY
All grandchildren	84.0	32.5
Female		
Black	75.0	38.2
White	100.0	40.0
Hispanic	90.3	45.4
Male		
Black	71.1	22.5
White	92.1	37.3
Hispanic	80.0	25.2

Sources: NLSY Child File; CUNY Child File.
Note: "High school dropout" means that neither maternal grandparent had a high school diploma.

Patterns of Intergenerational Mobility

The last thirty years have seen a rapid expansion in secondary schooling and in college attendance in America. In 1970, about 57 percent of whites but only a third of black students had four years of high school. By the year 2003, most non-Hispanic whites (89 percent) and most African Americans (80 percent) were high school graduates. In 1970, only a small percentage of whites (12 percent) and even fewer blacks (5 percent) had four years of college. By 2003, those numbers had risen to 30 percent and 17 percent, respectively.[7]

Viewed in terms of multigenerational trajectories, this means that many American families have jumped in two generations from having less than a high school education to college attendance. As shown in table 4.3, in the national NLSY, about one-third of the grandchildren of people who never completed high school are now college goers. About 45 percent of the grandchildren of grandparents who were high school graduates have gone to college. The prevalence of upward mobility into college differs by race and gender, with whites and Hispanic families outpacing African Americans, and females outpacing males, for reasons we shall discuss in due course.

Upward mobility is even more prevalent in the CUNY sample than in the national data. In the former, 84 percent of the grandchildren of high school dropouts enrolled in college, and 88 percent of the grandchildren of high school graduates went to college. These figures are much higher than the national norm because the CUNY sample was deliberately constituted of families where the second generation (of women in our case) was able to get to college. In the large majority of

Table 4.4   **Educational Downward Mobility: Percentage of Offspring of B.A. Recipients Who Failed to Enter College**

	CUNY Sample	National GSS	National PSID	NLSY
All offspring	7.8	14.1	15.1	19.0
Females				
Black	7.5	20.8	31.1	25.0
White	0	13.5	15.1	28.6
Hispanic	5.9	25.9	8.3	25.0
Males				
Black	22.5	24.3	26.1	18.8
White	5.6	13.8	13.6	16.7
Hispanic	21.1	14.7	1.5	12.5

Sources: See General Social Survey 1972 to 2000, and Panel Study of Income Dynamics 2006.
Note: In the CUNY, General Social Survey (GSS), and Panel Study of Income Dynamics (PSID) surveys, the sample includes only offspring who are twenty-one years old or older. For the NLSY survey, the figure includes offspring twenty or over.

these families, which have risen from modest backgrounds, the grand-children are college goers.

However, the picture is not all rosy. It is not always the case that after a parent attains a B.A., their children are able to equal that level of education. On the contrary, American society resembles a game of educational chutes and ladders. To estimate the amount of intergenerational downward mobility, we analyzed several national surveys, each of which covers somewhat different age groups. The results are summarized in table 4.4. Nationwide, we find that somewhere between one in seven and one in five children of B.A. parents fail to begin college, let alone graduate with a degree. The amount of downward mobility among the CUNY families was under half of these national figures—about 8 percent of children, which is still substantial.

Social Background and the Probability of Educational Success

To what extent do social privilege and social disadvantage reach across the generations and affect the life prospects of grandchildren? Table 4.5 answers such questions for the CUNY sample, reporting the results of logistic regression models that use family background characteristics, measured before a child was born, to predict a child's educational outcomes.[8] Later analyses will include a host of additional influences—from mother's and father's income and education to their marital history to family size to the kind of neighborhood where the family lives—and assess their effects on children's outcomes. However, we think of these

Table 4.5   **Effect of Maternal Family Background on Children's Chances
of Educational Success for CUNY Sample (Percentages)**

	Percentage Strong in High School		Percentage Enrolled in College	
	Unadjusted	Adjusted	Unadjusted	Adjusted
Grandparents' income				
Bottom quartile	21.48	22.48	80.71	85.69
Top quartile	48.79	36.85	95.77	91.95
Grandparents' education				
Less than high school	31.91	30.41	84.16	87.14
College graduate	46.71	33.17	94.65	91.24
Mother's College Admissions Average				
Bottom quartile	24.11	23.68	81.79	84.08
Top quartile	50.53	41.57	96.32	93.87
Race				
Black	23.25	26.83	81.14	85.99
White	43.80	37.37	95.47	93.83
Hispanic	26.27	27.26	85.17	88.54

Source: CUNY Women File.
Note: The "Adjusted" columns control statistically for race, maternal grandparents' income, and highest degree, and for mother's high school GPA in academic courses. All reported differences are statistically significant at $p < .05$.

latter variables as proximal, or immediate, influences on children's outcomes: they stand between family background and children's outcomes, and are to some degree influenced by the background variables. For now, in table 4.5, we look solely at earlier influences: the social origins of the mother, before she finished her education or got married.

First consider the social-class origins of the family, represented in table 4.5 by two variables, the maternal grandparents' income and their education. In the "Unadjusted" column of the table, we see that in the CUNY sample the grandchild of someone in the bottom income quartile has a 21 percent probability of doing well in high school, compared to a 49 percent probability of doing well for grandchildren from the top income quartile. A child with low-income grandparents has an 81 percent chance of going to college, compared to a 96 percent probability for a child with high-income grandparents. A similar pattern is found for grandparents' education. When grandparents' education and income are taken together, it is clear that the social-class origins of a family are strongly associated, two generations later, with a child's chances of educational success.

Shifting to the mother's characteristics measured during her youth, there are again clear influences on child outcomes. About 50 percent of the children of mothers who were in the top quartile in high school performance do well in high school and 96 percent go on to college. The equivalent probabilities for children with mothers with weak high school performance are substantially lower: 24 percent and 82 percent.

Race has an effect too: minority children are considerably less likely than white children to do well in high school and are also less likely to go on to college, but the racial gap in college going is smaller than that in high school performance.

These probabilities in the "Unadjusted" columns report relationships between one family background factor and one child outcome at a time (so-called bivariate effects). However, the four indicators of family background—grandparents' income, grandparents' highest academic degree, mother's high school preparation, and race—overlap to a considerable extent. Minority grandparents are more likely to have low incomes and less education, for example. So what appears to be, say, an income effect may partly reflect or incorporate the effects of race. To remedy this, the figures reported in table 4.5 in the columns titled "Adjusted" separate out the effects of each variable by controlling statistically for all the others (race, grandparents' income and education, and mother's high school preparation). In the "Adjusted" columns, we note, for example, that a child whose grandparents were at the bottom income quartile has a 22 percent chance of doing well in high school, compared to a 37 percent chance for a child of high-income grandparents, when their values on all other background characteristics were identical.

These adjusted estimates are smaller than the unadjusted or bivariate effects, but they are still statistically significant and substantial in size. All four of the background characteristics are independently associated with child outcomes in the CUNY sample. We also note that family background appears to affect how well children do in high school more than their college attendance.

These analyses of the CUNY sample document the enduring intergenerational effects of family background, even for children whose mothers all got as far as college. One might imagine that once a mother gets to college, her family background would not matter for the way her children turn out, but these analyses prove that family background does remain influential.

When analyzing the NLSY sample, in table 4.6, we consider a broader population, including many mothers who did not go to college. As a result, we might expect even stronger intergenerational effects than we found for the CUNY women, since one way that differences in class and educational background express themselves is through differences in maternal access to college. In other respects, this analysis is similar to the one for the CUNY women, except that it adds two new background variables: the mother's cognitive skills, or IQ, measured by her score on the Armed Forces Qualification Test (AFQT); and a psychological measure called the Pearlin Mastery Scale, which measures the extent to which mothers perceive themselves as being in control of forces that impact their lives.

Table 4.6   Effect of Maternal Family Background on Children's Chances of Educational Success for NLSY79 Children Sample (Percentages)

	Percentage Strong on High School Tests		Percentage Enrolled in College	
	Unadjusted	Adjusted	Unadjusted	Adjusted
Grandparents' income				
Bottom quartile	21.47	28.92	42.90	48.25
Top quartile	55.65	32.26	65.75	57.11
Grandparents' education				
Less than high school	23.38	27.67	45.39	49.00
College graduate	64.29	40.95	67.25	59.73
Mom's College Admissions Average				
Bottom quartile	18.07	24.72	39.48	44.83
Top quartile	56.27	37.01	64.89	56.62
Mom's AFQT				
Bottom quartile	12.63	16.79	38.59	43.22
Top quartile	64.38	50.15	71.32	65.16
Mom's Pearlin Mastery				
Bottom quartile	25.22	28.54	35.46	38.95
Top quartile	40.92	31.96	58.55	55.36
Race				
Black	17.13	20.91	45.44	50.76[†]
White	51.10	37.40	56.05	48.44
Hispanic	29.39	34.18	51.11	54.77
Other	37.88	28.15	42.86	36.16

Source: NLSY79 analyses.
Note: The dependent variable reports whether a child scored in the top third in high school tests of math and English (the PIAT) between ages thirteen and seventeen. Unadjusted or raw percentage versus estimated percentages after controlling for race, grandparents' income, grandparents' highest degree, grandparents' SEI, mother's high school GPA, mother's AFQT score, and mother's Pearlin Mastery score. All reported differences except the one marked [†] are statistically significant at p < .05

The two child outcomes that we focus upon are high scores on the PIAT reading-math score, assessed between ages thirteen and seventeen (children who scored in the top third were counted as high scorers), and a variable that indicates whether or not the child enrolled in college.

In the adjusted columns in table 4.6, we see that five aspects of family background significantly affect both children's outcomes. One outcome, the probability of going to college, does not differ between white, black, and Hispanic students, after grandparents' income and education and mother's IQ and high school preparation are taken into account. Race, however, is significantly associated with having a high PIAT score: a black student has an adjusted 21 percent probability of scoring high, compared to an otherwise similar white student's 37 percent and a Hispanic student's 34 percent, after controlling for other factors.

In sum, grandparents' social class, as represented by their income and education, is associated with grandchildren's outcomes. Several maternal characteristics also affect children's educational outcomes. Mother's IQ, as measured by the AFQT test, strongly influences child outcomes. Children of mothers in the bottom AFQT quartile have a 17 percent probability of scoring high on the PIAT tests, compared to 50 percent for children of high-AFQT mothers, holding other background characteristics constant. Similarly, 43 percent of children of low-AFQT mothers go to college, compared to 65 percent of children of high-AFQT mothers, controlling for the other background characteristics. Mother's high school preparation has a similar effect: substantial but not nearly as large as that of AFQT.

Mastery—a sense that one controls one's own fate—is a psychological trait that has been shown to correlate with academic and occupational success. In our data, children of women with high mastery are considerably more likely to go to college than those with mothers who are low on mastery, even when the other background variables are made equal. Mastery, in other words, reaches across generations. This is partly because this psychological orientation is itself passed on from mother to child, so that high-mastery women bring up high-mastery children.

In conclusion, we find that the probability of a child's educational success is substantially related to the resources of the maternal grandparents and mother, measured in most cases before the child was born. Several aspects of maternal family background reach across the generations: the family's class origins (represented by grandparents' income and education), the mother's high school preparation and cognitive skills, and also her psychological orientation regarding mastery.[9] Beyond these, race also affects chances for children's educational success.

The model we have presented implies that intergenerational advantage and disadvantage operate in an additive or cumulative fashion across three generations: from the grandparents to the mother to the grandchildren. Each dimension of background has its independent effect and these accumulate to provide a certain advantage or disadvantage. However, also implied by this model is that a family disadvantage in one dimension may be partly or fully offset by an advantage on some other family aspect. So, for example, the advantage of having a high-IQ mother more than balances out the disadvantage of having less-educated or low-income grandparents. The process is not "one strike and you're out."

Does Maternal Education Affect Children's Success?

These regression analyses have demonstrated the extent to which social privilege on the one hand and social disadvantage on the other are able to reach across the generations and affect the life chances of new generations. This occurs not through impermeable barriers of caste or class—for at any moment many individuals are moving upward and a few fortunate individuals are rising from the very bottom to the top of the social pyramid—but rather through a multistep process that stacks the odds against those from poorer backgrounds and in favor of children of privilege.

Although the transmission of privilege and disadvantage is an omnipresent ongoing phenomenon, it is not the only social force that determines social mobility. There are influences that lessen the influence of family class background. The game of chutes and ladders will alter according to the numbers of ladders on the board. Policies that affect access to higher education are the real-world analogue to those ladders—from the numbers of student slots in two- and four-year colleges to the affordability of tuition and the availability of financial aid. And since this game of chutes and ladders spans multiple generations, we discover that providing ladders for one generation changes the odds of success for the next generation.

It is straightforward to show that on average, the children of college-educated women fare much better educationally than children whose mothers did not go to college. The first column in Table 4.7 reports the effect of having a mother who earned a B.A. on a range of child outcomes, for the CUNY sample. For every child outcome—from vocabulary scores before entering school, to academic track and test scores in high school, to college entrance—we find associations between mother's education and child's educational progress. The bivariate effects are statistically significant and large in magnitude.

However, this evidence is insufficient for assessing the impact of maternal education as a social intervention, because we know that women who attend college differ from those who don't on numerous dimensions, not only in their race and family class background and their high school preparation but also in IQ and self-esteem and various psychological predispositions. The bivariate coefficients incorporate those background differences into the B.A. effect. We want to know instead whether maternal college education makes a difference in children's educational outcomes even after removing all those underlying differences.

For this purpose we use the propensity-score matching technique that we explain in the methodological appendix to this book. In table 4.7, the column titled "Propensity Score Model" reports the effect of a mother's having a B.A. degree on a child's educational outcomes, after matching and controlling for mother's age, whether she started college in a two- or four-year college, the number of academic courses she took in high school, her high school record, her GPA as of her last semester in college, her race, the mother's parents' highest degree, and her parents' household income.

Table 4.7   Effect of Mother's Earning a B.A. on CUNY Children's Educational Outcomes

Child's Outcome	Bivariate	Propensity Matched Sample[a]
Elementary school		
Effect size (z score)	.290***	.035
Predicted value when mother earned B.A.	.2403984	.0159993
Predicted value when mother did not earn B.A.	−.0500075	−.018844
High school performance		
Effect size (z score)	.388***	.129***
Predicted value when mother earned B.A.	.3342682	.046109
Predicted value when mother did not earn B.A.	−.0538919	−.0828978
High school trouble		
Effect size (z score)	−.363***	−.154***
Predicted value when mother earned B.A.	−.2934788	−.0593257
Predicted value when mother did not earn B.A.	.069128	.0950347
College track		
Effect size (logistic coefficient)	.744***	.129
Predicted value when mother earned B.A.	.7362	0.5890
Predicted value when mother did not earn B.A.	.5703	0.5575
Attended college		
Effect size (logistic coefficient)	1.368***	.414**
Predicted value when mother earned B.A.	.9605	.9388
Predicted value when mother did not earn B.A.	.8609	.9103
Completed college		
Effect size (logistic coefficient)	1.063***	.477***
Predicted value when mother earned B.A.	.9182	.8690
Predicted value when mother did not earn B.A.	.7951	.8046
Earned a B.A. degree		
Effect size (logistic coefficient)	.885***	.525***
Predicted value: mother earned B.A.	.8742	.8199
Predicted value: mother did not earn B.A.	.7415	.7293

Source: CUNY Women File.

[a]Matched on mother's propensity to earn a B.A. Controls include mother's age, whether she started college in two-year or four-year school, the number of academic courses she took in high school, her high school record, her GPA as of her last semester in college, her race, her parent's highest degree, and her household income before enrolling at CUNY.

*p < .05; **p < .01; ***p < .001

For five out of the seven CUNY child outcomes, the effect of a mother's having a B.A. was a highly statistically significant predictor of the child's educational performance. (The exceptions were child's academic performance in elementary school, and whether a child entered a college track in high school.) As might be expected, the effects of maternal B.A. in the propensity models are considerably smaller in magnitude than the bivariate effects. Children of B.A. mothers are .13 standard deviation higher on a measure of high school performance, and .15 standard deviation lower on a measure of getting into trouble in high school. Children of mothers with a B.A. have a 94 percent probability of attending college, compared to 91 percent of those whose mothers did not obtain a B.A. They have an 87 percent probability of completing college, compared to 80 percent for those whose mothers did not obtain a B.A. Finally, 82 percent of the children of B.A. mothers earned a B.A. themselves, compared to 73 percent of children with a non-B.A. mother. These are not large effects; however, it should be born in mind that "the effect of a mother earning a B.A." in the CUNY sample involves a contrast between the children of women who did go to college but earned ten or fewer credits and did not earn a B.A. and the children of women who also went to college and completed a B.A.

Table 4.8 reports similar analyses for the broader NLSY national sample. The NLSY controls are more extensive than those available for the CUNY sample. They include the mother's IQ (AFQT score) and mastery score, as well as several measures of family background. The NLSY analyses show statistically significant effects of maternal college attendance, measured in two ways. The first part of the table compares mothers who earned a B.A. degree with women who were high school graduates but had no college experience. The second half of the table contrasts women who attended college (whether or not they graduated) with high school graduates.

In the first half of table 4.8 we find that the mother's B.A. has a statistically significant effect on five of the seven children's educational outcomes.[10] Looking at the right-hand column, we see that children of B.A. mothers scored on average .23 standard deviations higher on early vocabulary, and .15 standard deviations higher on early tests of reading and math. The child of a B.A. mother had a 52 percent probability of going into a college-preparatory track in high school, compared to 41 percent for the child of an otherwise identical woman without a B.A. Children of B.A. mothers score .10 standard deviations higher on reading and math after age thirteen. These significant effects of a mother's B.A. are measured after controlling statistically for the mother's class background, IQ, high school preparation, and mastery score. Thus, they reflect the impact of completing a college education itself, and not differences in the social background or intelligence of those who obtain B.A.s and those who do not.

Table 4.8   **Effect of Mother's College Education on NLSY Children's Educational Outcomes**

Educational Outcome	Bivariate	Propensity Matched Sample
B.A. versus no B.A.		
Vocabulary		
Effect size (z score)	.979***	.232***
Predicted value when mother earned B.A.	.8137	.3057
Predicted value when mother did not have B.A.	−.1658	.5374
Reading and Math (under age seven)		
Effect size (z score)	.693***	.152***
Predicted value when mother earned B.A.	.5615	.3701
Predicted value when mother did not have B.A.	−.1385	.2182
Behavior Problems Index (age six to ten)		
Effect size (z score)	−.546***	−.184***
Predicted value when mother earned B.A.	−.6404	−.6030
Predicted value when mother did not have B.A.	−.0949	−.4188
Held back in school		
Effect size (logistic coefficient)	−1.922***	.236
Predicted value when mother earned B.A.	.0567	.0751
Predicted value when mother did not have B.A.	.2911	.0602
College track		
Effect size (logistic coefficient)	1.071***	.432**
Predicted value when mother earned B.A.	.5588	.5203
Predicted value when mother did not have B.A.	.3026	.4132
Reading and math (age thirteen to sixteen)		
Effect size (z score)	.886***	.100*
Predicted value when mother earned B.A.	.7528	.5401
Predicted value when mother did not have B.A.	−.1332	.4398
Attended college		
Effect size (logistic coefficient)	1.121***	.479
Predicted value when mother earned B.A.	.7047	.7645
Predicted value when mother did not have B.A.	.4821	.6679

(Table continues on p. 76.)

Table 4.8   *Continued*

Educational Outcome	Bivariate	Propensity Matched Sample
Any college versus no college		
Vocabulary		
Effect size (z score)	.542***	.077***
Predicted value: college mother	.3542	.0761
Predicted value: no college mother	−.1881	−.0011
Reading and Math (under age seven)		
Effect size (z score)	.416***	.111***
Predicted value: college mother	.2683	.1053
Predicted value: no college mother	−.1481	−.0053
Behavior Problems Index (age six to ten)		
Effect size (z score)	−.290***	.003
Predicted value: college mother	−.2113	−.0934
Predicted value: no college mother	.0789	−.0962
Held back in school		
Effect size (logistic coefficient)	−1.258***	−.269***
Predicted value: college mother	.1041	.1045
Predicted value: no college mother	.2901	.1325
College track		
Effect size (logistic coefficient)	.609***	.194***
Predicted value: college mother	.4393	.4410
Predicted value: no college mother	.2988	.3938
Reading and math (age thirteen to sixteen)		
Effect size (z score)	.433***	.078***
Predicted value: college mother	.2843	.1803
Predicted value: no college mother	−.1492	.1019
Attended college		
Effect size (logistic coefficient)	.751***	.509***
Predicted value: college mother	0.6146	0.6065
Predicted value: no college mother	0.4293	0.4808

Sources: NLSY Child File; CUNY Child File.
Note: N on matched regression model = 359.
*p < .05; **p < .01; ***p < .001

The second half of table 4.8 shows the effect of mother's college attendance on a child's success, compared to children of similar background whose mothers never attended college. It looks at a broader group of women than previously, by including women who went to college but did not graduate and those who received A.A. and B.A. degrees. The propensity-score column in table 4.8 indicates that attending college has a significant effect on early vocabulary, reading and math scores around age seven, being kept back a grade, entry to a college-prep track in high school, reading and math ability at age thirteen or older, and college going. College attendance did not affect behavioral problems, however.

How large are these effects of maternal education for children's academic outcomes? How important an advantage does maternal higher education provide? One way to evaluate this is to compare the size of the effect of having a mother with a B.A. to the size of the negative effects of having a mother who grew up in a poor or less-educated family, or a mother with a weak high school background. In other words, we can compare the advantage for her child of having a B.A. mother against the disadvantages of other family-background characteristics, statistically controlling for class, race, maternal IQ, and so forth.[11]

In general, having a mother with a B.A. balances out the disadvantage to a child's academic success of the mother's coming from low social-class origins, but it does not fully balance the disadvantages associated with minority race. On two of the three outcome measures, a mother's B.A. provides the equivalent benefit to that of a large increase in maternal IQ (that is, one standard deviation increase in IQ). If a mother goes to college but does not get as far as a bachelor's degree, there is still a clear benefit in terms of improved children's educational outcomes, but it is not as large. The benefit of having a mother with some college but less than a bachelor's degree is about one-third to one-half as large as the benefit of having a mother with a B.A. degree.

As we noted earlier, a mother's psychological orientation, her greater sense of mastery and self-esteem, were also associated with better child outcomes. But in multivariate models we used, it is clear that these effects of psychological orientation on children are considerably smaller than the benefit gained by a mother's having a B.A. Likewise, the effects on a child of growing up with a mother who had a weak high school background are smaller than the boost provided by a B.A.

The statistical models show that on average, a mother's college education is associated with significantly better educational outcomes for her children, and that this benefit persists over and above advantages or disadvantages of family background, high school preparation, psychology, and IQ. But does this hold true for minority women and for women from poorer backgrounds? To examine this we ran models predicting child academic outcomes for college and noncollege mothers, separately for whites, blacks, and Hispanics. When we look at bivariate relationships (those without controls) we find, for all three racial and ethnic groups, that children of college-educated women have considerably better outcomes than children of less-educated mothers for all educational outcomes. When we control for background differences between high school graduates and college graduates, a somewhat weaker picture emerges. Nevertheless, we find for each racial group that in four out of six child outcome measures, maternal college education confers a statistically significant educational advantage upon children.[12]

We also looked at whether the size of the educational benefit derived from mother's education was smaller or larger for each racial and ethnic group. The findings were not consistent across outcome measures. In some cases, black or Hispanic children benefited more than white children from having a college-going mother; on other outcome measures, there was no difference, or maternal education had less of an effect for minority children. We conclude from these additional analyses that maternal college education has a significant impact on children's educational success for all ethnic and racial groups, and that there are no clear differences between racial groups in the size of this impact.

Finally, we examined whether maternal college education depends upon the gender of the child. It is widely supposed that mothers have a stronger influence over daughters than sons. When we included interaction terms to model differential effects for sons and daughters we found little or no gender differences: boys and girls benefited equally from having a mother go to college. There was one clear exception: maternal education had a significantly larger effect on reducing the Behavioral Problems Index for young boys than it did for girls. On all other outcome measures, there was no child gender effect.

Conclusion

We began this chapter by observing that socioeconomic advantage and disadvantage can reach across the generations. The income and education of grandparents clearly affect the educational chances of their grandchildren, for good or for ill. Beyond this, maternal characteristics, including IQ and psychological "optimism" as measured by scales of self-esteem and mastery, clearly influence children's academic development. Moreover, disadvantage based on one's race is very strongly transmitted from generation to generation. This pattern is consistent with a large body of prior research on intergenerational persistence, best summarized by the aphorism "The apple does not fall far from the tree."

This picture changes in interesting ways, however, after we consider maternal access to college. If a mother goes to college, and especially if she earns a B.A., her child's chances of educational success receive a significant boost. That benefit is apparent even when the mother was a member of an ethnic minority, grew up in a lower-class family, had a poor high school preparation, or was otherwise disadvantaged. Since the 1970s, increased access to higher education among women from disadvantaged backgrounds has clearly weakened the negative side of the intergenerational transmission of status. Our analyses are unequivocal that the cycle of disadvantage is not yet broken—class and race continue to influence children's life chances. But we also find that increased entry to higher education weakens the cycle of disadvantage.

═ Chapter 5 ═

How College Changes a Mother's Parenting and Affects Her Children's Educational Outcomes

WHY DO some children develop into successful adults, while others struggle through childhood or adolescence and find the transition to adulthood challenging? From antiquity to the present, thinkers have contended that the manner in which parents raise a child is critical for the child's ultimate success.[1] When social scientists consider this issue, they often focus on different styles of parenting that coexist in our society, with the idea that some styles of child rearing or certain parenting behaviors are more effective than others in developing independent, self-motivated, or resilient children and that these traits pay off in children's educational success.

This formulation quickly leads to the question of why some parents raise their children differently than others; what are the origins of divergent approaches to child rearing? One answer common among sociologists has been that styles of parenting are associated with the social class of parents: upper-, middle-, and working-class families have somewhat different values and practices around raising their children (Bronfenbrenner 1958; Gans 1962; Kohn 1969; Lareau 1989, 2003; Lynd and Lynd 1956).

For our purposes, this well-established view that links parenting to social class is problematic because it tends to lump together three distinct factors under its notion of adults' social class: their education, their occupation, and the kind of family they were born into. Scholars have not found this to be a problem, because in many families there is a great deal of overlap among these three factors: middle-class families are often headed by college-educated parents who hold professional or complex jobs. Working-class parents tend to have less education and hold routine jobs. The focus of this book, however, is on women who grew up in less-educated, often economically disadvantaged, families but who nevertheless were able to make it to college. In such cases, there is a clear disjuncture between the class of the family a woman grew up in and her educational and occupational attainment in adulthood.

This disjuncture leads us to ask whether higher education in itself is associated with certain styles of raising children, or whether one's social class background is key. Our goal is to distinguish the effect of a mother's going to college upon her parenting practices from several other potentially confounding factors: not only the mother's social-class background, but also her race and ethnicity, her IQ and high school preparation, her age, and her psychological attributes such as self-esteem and mastery. We achieve this separation using the propensity score–matching techniques described in the methodological appendix. In this way we determine whether college-going per se is associated with a certain approach to raising children.

In this chapter we examine a series of parenting activities or behaviors that previous research has suggested are important predictors of children's success. For each particular activity, our presentation occurs in three stages. First, we review past theory and research about that particular parenting activity. In some cases our analyses have led us to modify or reconceptualize some of these parenting concepts, and we explain when and how our formulations differ from those found in previous research. Second, we determine whether mothers who attend college engage in that particular parenting practice to a greater or lesser extent than less-educated mothers. Our regression and propensity score analyses then indicate whether this observed difference in a given parenting activity is really due to college attendance or whether it reflects the college-educated mothers' intelligence, class, race, or other background characteristics. In other words, we isolate the effect of college going or obtaining a degree on that parenting activity.

Third, we estimate how much each particular parenting activity improves a child's educational progress, using a set of child-outcome measures from early vocabulary acquisition to the child's enrollment in college. In this step we focus on the effect of a given parenting approach on the child, while controlling for maternal education and several other factors. We also estimate how much of a difference several parenting activities taken as a whole can make on children's educational prospects. Finally, we check whether the most effective parenting practices function equally well for mothers of different races and ethnicities, for mothers from different class backgrounds, and for mothers with varying amounts of education.

Overall, this chapter builds a case that going to college does indeed affect the ways mothers from disadvantaged backgrounds raise their children, and that this shift in child-rearing practices is one reason (though not the only one) that maternal access to college improves educational chances for the second generation. In a later chapter we will look at some of the other mechanisms besides parenting behaviors by means of which college going improves child outcomes.

Parenting Behaviors and Children's Outcomes

Scholars have studied many aspects of parenting in their attempts to understand what forms of adult control help children to develop into well-balanced and capable individuals. In our research we focused on about a dozen parenting behaviors that we thought might be linked to the amount of education that a mother had completed. In the following sections we will review each of them.

Cultural Capital

Two French scholars, Pierre Bourdieu and Jean Passeron (1977), employed the concept of cultural capital to describe differences in the educational prospects of children from different social classes, and to explain the reproduction of class inequality in society. Cultural capital has taken on a range of different meanings (Lamont and Lareau 1988), but in part the term refers to knowledge of art, literature, classical music and history, which is seen to be the prerogative of the middle and upper classes.[2] A family's cultural capital does not have a utilitarian purpose; rather, it mainly reflects the lifestyle, tastes and manners of the family's social class.[3] However, according to Bourdieu and Passeron, cultural capital has very important consequences for educational attainment, even if these are unintended.

Schools use the knowledge-base and communicative style of the affluent classes as their medium of expression, according to Bourdieu and Passeron. Schools do not teach cultural capital; they assume that pupils already have it. Consequently, students who have been brought up in families with plentiful cultural capital draw on this resource in the classroom. Children of less-privileged families find themselves listening in class to topics and terms that are foreign to them. A lack of cultural capital therefore leaves students from less affluent families at a chronic disadvantage in middle- or upper-class educational institutions. When children with plentiful cultural capital excel in schoolwork, their success is misrecognized as superior intellect or academic ability rather than attributed to their family's cultural capital. Thus, cultural capital disguises, legitimates, and reproduces class inequality in education by handicapping and excluding children of the working and lower classes (Bourdieu 1986).

Paul DiMaggio (1982), DiMaggio and Michael Useem (1982), DiMaggio and John Mohr (1985), and Mohr and DiMaggio (1995) have applied Bourdieu's framework to studies of children's educational success in the United States. DiMaggio (1982) found that cultural capital—a child's interest and participation in classical music, art, and literature—predicted school grades in a number of subjects for eleventh graders, net of parental education and of the student's ability as measured by academic test scores. The size of the cultural capital effect in predicting grades was of roughly the same magnitude as that of measured ability, which underlined the considerable importance of this form of advantage. These educational benefits of cultural capital, including intergenerational benefits, have been replicated in several subsequent studies (reviewed in DiMaggio 2001).

Bourdieu painstakingly avoided any language that might suggest that schooling itself creates cultural capital in the student. Instead he referred to "the best hidden and socially most determinant educational investment, namely the *domestic transmission* of cultural capital" (Bourdieu 1986, 244, authors' emphasis), and repeatedly emphasized "the scholastic yield from educational action depends upon the cultural capital previously invested by the family."[4]

Our own research agenda differs from Bourdieu's, and reflects an American sensibility. We aren't interested only in *inherited* cultural capital accrued during childhood and reflecting the class of the family one grew up in. We also want to consider the possibility of *achieved* cultural capital, obtained through access to a college education, and to assess the consequences of a college student's achieved cultural capital for her children (see DeGraaf, DeGraaf, and Kraaykamp 1998; DiMaggio 1982). We do not assume that inherited and achieved cultural capital are the same, or that the latter is reducible to the former, as Bourdieu seems to have assumed.

We speculate that access to university might promote the acquisition of cultural capital beyond that inherited from one's family in several different ways. First, higher education may directly develop cultural capital among lower-class (as well as more affluent) students by raising students' interests in and knowledge of history, literature, music, theater, and the arts while in college. (The same may be true for K-through-twelve schooling also.)

Second, our interviews suggest that going to college may spur disadvantaged women to provide culturally enriching experiences for their children, even if these college-going mothers don't themselves develop interests in high culture. Proximity to middle-class peers during college may sensitize disadvantaged students to the cultural advantages that more affluent families enjoy. So, when these college-educated women from lower-class backgrounds have children, some take their offspring to museums and theaters, and purchase music or dance lessons for them, in a deliberate attempt to cultivate the children beyond the parent's own level. This can be termed a *lagged* acquisition of cultural capital. Driven by their experiences in higher education, the upwardly mobile college generation perceives the importance of cultural capital, but organizes it for their children rather than for themselves.

A third possibility is that college going may increase a family's cultural capital via marriage: disadvantaged women who get to college may marry men who come from a higher socioeconomic background and who have more cultural capital than their wives (DiMaggio and Mohr 1985). (We will consider marriage effects in chapter 6.)

Our concept of achieved cultural capital informs the way we think about parenting activities and cultural activities.[5] Bourdieu would never have characterized cultural capital as a "parenting activity." For him, cultural capital is "acquired effortlessly as a by-product of socialization" in a privileged family (DiMaggio 2001, 544). This may be true to some extent, but in the United States, cultural capital is often associated with goods and services that are purchased with a deliberate end in mind (books, newspapers and magazines; dance, music or art lessons; family trips to museums, concerts, and performances; foreign travel; after-school programs and summer camp). In the United States, cultural and aesthetic skills and tastes are acquired by children not simply by learning from their parents but sometimes as a result of a rather earnest effort organized by parents for their children as a form of intergenerational investment and personal improvement (Lareau 2003; Seeley, Sim, and Loosley 1956).

Even among the upper classes, where many parents have plentiful cultural capital, getting their children into the right school with the right kind of curriculum (Cookson and Persell 1985; Powell 1996) and enrolling them in the right kind of after-school activities and cultural lessons are matters of great importance. At later ages, elite colleges offer (and sometimes require) courses in art history, music appreciation, and contemporary civilization, which offer students a smorgasbord of cultural capital.[6] In sum, even among privileged families, rearing cultivated children is much more than "an effortless by-product" of family socialization; it's a family project that depends on the purchase of outside cultural expertise.

The acquisition of cultural capital is not always limited to the affluent. In his book *The Color of Water*, the African American writer James McBride (1996) provides a vivid memoir of growing up in a large poor black family in a ghetto neighborhood of New York City. He was raised in a world of hand-me-down clothes and chronic hunger. This is not the soil that usually yields professionals and scholars, yet McBride informs us that he and all eleven of his siblings went to college. His mother manipulated the New York City school bureaucracy to get her children into superior public schools far away from their home in the projects. As McBride (1996, 90–96) recalls:

> Music arrived in my life around that time, and books. I would disappear inside whole worlds comprised of *Gulliver's Travels*, *Shane* and books by

Beverly Cleary. I took piano and clarinet lessons at school, often squirreling myself away in some corner with my clarinet to practice, wandering away in Tchaikovsky or John Philip Sousa. . . . We thrived on thought, books, music and art which [Mother] fed to us instead of food. At every opportunity she loaded five or six of us onto the subway, paying one fare and pushing the rest of us through the turnstiles while the token-booth clerks frowned and subway riders stared, parading us to every free event New York City offered: festivals, zoos, parades, block parties, libraries, concerts.

In sum, we argue that it makes sense to examine cultural capital in terms of specific parenting activities, as the deliberate provision of cognitive stimulation and cultural resources to children, in addition to (and separate from) the passive inheritance of parental class attributes.

In our statistical analyses, we employed two measures of cultural parenting. For the CUNY survey, we asked how frequently a mother took her child to a zoo, museum, or library. For the NLSY analyses, we employed an established battery of items, the Home Observation and Measurement of the Environment–Short Form, called the HOME-SF scale. Information for this scale was obtained by observers' visiting respondents' homes. This measure was constructed in two versions, one for children under six years old and another for children six and over. The former included items on how many books a child has, how many magazines the family buys; how often a mother reads to the child and how often a family member helps the child learn the alphabet, or numbers, shapes and colors; how many cuddly, role-playing, and push- or pull-toys the child owns; how often the child gets out of the house and whether the child accompanies mother to the grocery; frequency of visits to museums and other outings. This ensemble is intended to measure the cognitive stimulation a family provided to the child.

The items for children over six included whether the family subscribes to a newspaper; the number of books in the home; how often the child goes to museums and theaters; whether there is a musical instrument in the home and whether the child gets special lessons of any type; whether the family encourages hobbies; and other similar questions. These are reasonable proxies for parental efforts at offering cultural enrichment.

In the national NLSY study, we found there was a substantial difference on average between mothers who attended college and mothers who did not attend college in the amount of cultural activities they undertook with their children: the two groups differed by .57 standard deviations in cultural stimulation for younger children and .54 standard deviations for older children, which are large differences (see table 5.1). Even after controlling for the mother's family's class background, race and ethnicity, age, race, and other characteristics, and using propensity score matching, this college-based difference in cultural capital parenting

Table 5.1   Effect of Mother's Educational Attainment on Cultural Parenting Activities (Measured in Standard Deviation Units)

Mother's Education (Years)	Bivariate	Regression	Propensity Matched Sample
NLSY sample			
HOME cognitive stimulation scale (less than ten)			
Any college	.571***	.198***	.199***
B.A.	.765***	.115***	.232***
HOME cognitive stimulation scale (over ten)			
Any college	.545***	.197***	.206***
B.A.	.879***	.267***	.309***
CUNY sample			
Cultural capital scale			
B.A.	.155***	.097***	.092***

Sources: NLSY79 and CUNY Women File.
*p < .05; **p < .01; ***p < .001

remained significant but was reduced in magnitude to .20 standard deviations for younger and .21 standard deviations for older children, an effect of moderate or medium size.[7]

Even larger statistical differences in cultural parenting were found in the NLSY survey when the contrast was between women who received a B.A. degree and those who did not: the average gap in cultural-parenting activities for younger children was .77 standard deviation and for older, .88 standard deviation. With propensity score controls these were reduced to .23 and .31 standard deviation, respectively—still significant differences. Similar but smaller contrasts were observed in the CUNY survey, which compared women who earned a B.A. or higher with women who went to college but did not obtain a B.A.

In summary, women who go to college infuse their parenting with significantly more cultural activities than women who don't go to college, and women who receive a B.A. or higher degree do more of this activity than women who attend college but do not earn a B.A. A substantial portion of these gaps in cultural parenting appear to be due to the mother's college experience or possession of a degree, over and above the influences of her family class background, income, race, and other factors that are associated with college attendance.

Do these cultural-parenting activities have an impact on children's educational outcomes?

In the CUNY survey, cultural-parenting activities were associated with better children's outcomes at several points in a child's education, even after controlling for many family characteristics. Cultural parenting was associated with better elementary school performance and higher school grades, with a higher likelihood of being in the college track, and a lower likelihood of getting into trouble during high school. These were statistically significant effects of small to medium size (see table 5.2).

Similar findings were found for the NLSY, where the cultural-parenting measure was associated with children's higher test scores in reading and math. These effects were statistically significant; after propensity score matching and controls, cultural-parenting activities resulted in student test scores .25 to .27 standard deviation unit higher.

The NLSY survey included PIAT measures of reading and math achievement repeated around ages seven and thirteen. Consequently, we could estimate a longitudinal model in which a child's score at thirteen was predicted by his or her score at age seven, plus cultural parenting and controls. This is equivalent to predicting the change in reading and math ability over six years. In table 5.2 we see that when greater cultural resources are provided, the child shows significantly greater improvement in reading and math over time. On average, early cognitive stimulation is associated with a higher PIAT of .12 standard deviations, after controlling for other factors, including the child's initial PIAT score, in a propensity score matched sample.

In conclusion, when parents provide their children with forms of cultural enrichment such as books in the home or visits to museums and zoos, it has a measurable impact on children's academic performance, even after controlling for parents' education and many other family resources and advantages. We wish to underline the implications of the statistical controls we used: cultural and cognitively enriching activities undertaken with or provided by parents have a substantial influence on children's educational outcomes over and above the effects of parental education itself and beyond social-class background. This diverges considerably from Bourdieu's theory: he viewed cultural parenting and social class as inextricably intertwined, whereas we have separated them, as well as parental education, and we find that all three factors separately and in combination provide an advantage for children.

Moreover, we found that when women get to college, and again when they obtain a B.A., they provide more cultural-parenting activities for their children than mothers with less education. This is the case after controlling for the mother's family class background, IQ, and high school preparation. Thus, maternal college attendance appears to have a significant influence on this parenting practice. We conceptualize this as acquired or achieved cultural capital, and distinct from Bourdieu's concept of inherited cultural capital. Overall, the benefit of maternal education for children's educational success operates partly through the mechanism of increased cultural parenting.

Table 5.2 Effect of Cultural-Parenting Activities on Children's Educational Outcomes (Measured in Standard Deviation Units)

Child's Outcome	Parenting Variable (Child's Age)	Bivariate	Regression	Propensity Matched Sample
CUNY sample				
Elementary school success	Cultural capital scale	.2284***	.1707***	.1858***
High school success	Cultural capital scale	.3829***	.2086***	.2100***
High school trouble	Cultural capital scale	–.3603***	–.2278***	–.2456***
Probability of college track placement	High cultural capital	.7136***	.6668***	.6850***
NLSY sample (age)				
Early PIAT score (under seven)	HOME cognitive stimulation[a]	.5804***	.2730***	.2499***
Behavior Problems Index (six to ten)	HOME cognitive stimulation (under ten)	–.4012***	–.2762***	–.3176***
Probability of grade retention	High HOME cognitive (under ten)	.1625***	.1655***	.1488***
	Low HOME cognitive (under ten)	.3206	.1989	.1894
Late PIAT score (over thirteen)	HOME cognitive stimulation (under ten)	.6449***	.2014***	.2721***
	+ control for early PIAT score	—	.1206***	.1198***
	HOME cognitive stimulation (over ten)	.6139***	.2243***	.2331***
	+ control for early PIAT score	—	.1435***	.1494***

(Table continues on p. 88.)

Table 5.2 *Continued*

Child's Outcome	Parenting Variable (Child's Age)	Bivariate	Regression	Propensity Matched Sample
Probability of college prep track placement	High HOME cognitive (under ten)	.4070***	.3554***	.3788**
	Low HOME cognitive (under ten)	.2883	.3175	.3342
	High HOME cognitive (over ten)	.4263***	.3836***	.3957***
	Low HOME cognitive (over ten)	.2623	.2844	.2706
Probability of college enrollment	High HOME cognitive (under ten)	.5850***	.5464***	.5261***
	Low HOME cognitive (under ten)	.3934	.4403	.3674
	High HOME cognitive (over ten)	.5716***	.5335***	.5099***
	Low HOME cognitive (over ten)	.4101	.4585	.3908

Sources: CUNY Women File and NLSY79.

[a]These analyses use a dichotomized version of the HOME cognitive stimulation scale, for the purposes of propensity score matching. This dummy variable is coded as 1 if the score rated in the top half of the HOME scale and 0 if the score rated in the bottom half.

*p < .05; **p < .01; ***p < .001

Social Capital

Individuals live in networks of social relationships that link each person to family and close friends and, moving outward, to acquaintances, friends of friends, and people in the community. The sociologist James Coleman (1988, 1990) suggested that each person's social network be viewed as a resource that helps that individual achieve his or her goals. He termed this resource social capital (Coleman 1988, 100–101; see also Bourdieu 1986; Lin 2001; Porter 2002):

> If physical capital is wholly tangible, being embodied in observable material form, and human capital is less tangible, being embodied in skills and knowledge acquired by an individual, social capital is less tangible yet, for it exists in the *relations* among persons. Just as physical capital and human capital facilitate productive activity, social capital does as well.

Coleman (1990, 304–10) identified several kinds of social capital within interpersonal networks: information; structures of obligations, expectations, and trust; and sanctioned norms of behavior. Information, for example, helps people to hear about job openings or find out which are the best schools to apply to. Obligations, expectations, and trust also inhere in social networks: a parent feels confident having her child play at a friend's house because she has ties to the other child's parent, knows what kinds of behavior that parent would tolerate, and can be sure that adult supervision will be provided. Norms, customs, or social rules are similarly embedded in networks: group members use gossip, sarcasm, complaints, shunning, and denunciation to inflict punishment on rule breakers within their networks in order to assert shared norms. Strong, dense social networks more effectively compel conformity to community norms and values than weak networks do.

This concept of social capital implies that some people or groups may have superior interpersonal networks or more social capital than others. William Julius Wilson (1987), Peter Marsden (1987), Katherine Newman (1999), and Sandra S. Smith (2000) are among those who have looked at race and class differences in social capital, examining whether poor minority residents of the inner city are socially isolated or have interpersonal networks populated with fewer employed people or with less occupationally and economically diverse contacts. Poorer people may have less dense networks, meaning fewer numbers of connections per person or fewer links between persons in the network than affluent whites have. The concern among these researchers is that reduced social capital will handicap poor people, leading to greater inequality and lower employment or incomes.

Coleman (1990) was especially interested in the implications of social capital for rearing children. He viewed children as embedded in adult networks. To the extent that adults spend time with their children and know their children's friends, parents can keep a collective eye on the younger generation and can enforce norms either through surveillance and sanctions or by socializing children to internalize norms. Single parents, Coleman (1990, 585–96) believed, cannot carry out this intergenerational surveillance and socializing as effectively as two-parent families can; nor can working mothers do it as successfully as stay-at-home moms. In a similar vein, Suzanne M. Bianchi and John Robinson (1997) found that social capital and dual-parent families play important roles in getting kids to read instead of watching TV at home, to do their homework, and stay out of trouble.

In his consideration of social capital in child raising, Coleman (1990, 318–19) particularly emphasized the importance of intergenerational social closure. For adults to be maximally effective in influencing children's behavior, not only strong bonds between each child and her or his parents but also tight-knit relations between the adults in the community are needed, so the adults can collectively reinforce one another's child-raising efforts and share information and monitoring, sometimes in opposition to children's desires. A high degree of intergenerational social closure exists "in a community in which neighbors know one another, children go to the same school, and teachers are part of the community" (Coleman 1990, 596). Hillary Clinton's book *It Takes a Village* was a popular expression of this idea of intergenerational social closure.

In our surveys, the measure we used to capture this idea were questions that asked a parent how many of a child's friends the parent knows by name, and how many of the parents of one's child's friends one knows. These are indicators of intergenerational social closure. Coleman (1990, 595) lists several additional factors that he views as related to social capital: the effect of a single- versus two-parent family structure; mother's work outside the home; number of siblings; college aspirations; and talking about personal matters with one's child. We chose to consider them separately, and they will be considered in due course.

Focusing for the present on social capital as intergenerational closure, however, we find in the NLSY and in the CUNY surveys that maternal college going is indeed significantly associated with greater social capital, even after social class, income, race, and other family background variables are controlled. Table 5.3 shows that there are large significant differences in social capital between college goers and those who never attended college, and also between B.A. recipients and those who did not get as far as a B.A. Social closure remains greater among college-educated women, even after controlling for social class, IQ, and other background measures, as shown by the regression and propensity analyses.

Table 5.3   Effect of Mother's Educational Attainment on Social Capital (Closure)

Mother's Education	Bivariate	Regression	Propensity Matched Sample
NLSY: Probability that mother knew most of child's friends and their parents			
Entered college	.5528***	.4918***	.4787***
No college	.4352	.4542	.4391
Earned B.A.	.6600***	.5715***	.5330***
No B.A.	.4516	.4545	.4323
CUNY: Probability that mother knew most of child's friends and their parents			
Earned B.A.	.4142***	.3396***	.3655***
No B.A.	.3422	.3032	.3001

Sources: NLSY79 and CUNY Women File.
*p < .05; **p < .01; ***p < .001

Showing that college-educated parents are a lot more likely to know their children's friends and their parents (that is, to possess greater social closure) is only the first step, however. We also need to determine whether this higher social closure is associated with better educational outcomes for children, as Coleman asserted. In table 5.4 we observe that, when we look at bivariate effects for the NLSY, children do on average fare better educationally if their families have greater social capital. However, after we control for factors such as family income, mother's education, and occupational prestige, race, and so forth, or use a matched sample based on propensity scores, this effect of social capital on children is reduced to nonsignificance for several outcomes. Social capital remains significant for four outcomes: a Behavior Problems Index, the probability of grade retention, math and reading scores measured after age thirteen, and the probability of the child's going to college. Thus, the support for Coleman's theory is mixed.

The effects of social capital were more consistent for the CUNY analyses (see table 5.4): greater social closure was associated with better outcomes for children on all five educational-outcome measures, and these effects persist after controls and propensity score matching. We cannot explain why the effects of social capital or closure were stronger in the CUNY study.

Parents' Talking with Children

Many purposes are served when a parent takes time to talk with her or his child, and listens to a child's opinions and views. Some are indirect

Table 5.4   Effect of Social Capital on Children's Educational Outcomes (Measured in Standard Deviation Units)

Child's Outcome	Parenting Variable (Child's Age)	Bivariate	Regression	Propensity Matched Sample
NLSY				
Early PIAT score (under seven)				
	High social capital	.1106***	−.0161	−.0203
Behavior Problems Index (six to ten)				
	High social capital	−.2455***	−.1553***	−.1585***
Probability of grade retention				
	High social capital	.2198***	.1847*	.1596**
	Low social capital	.2803	.1935	.1735
Late PIAT score (over thirteen)				
	High social capital	.1696***	.0461***	.0501***
Probability of college prep track placement				
	High social capital	.3670***	.3424	.3496
	Low social capital	.3324	.3328	.3499
Probability of college enrollment				
	High social capital	.5353***	.5215*	.5232**
	Low social capital	.4798	.4937	.4622
CUNY				
Elementary school success				
	High social capital	.1207***	.0637***	.0720***
High school success				
	High social capital	.2759***	.1898***	.1638***
High school trouble				
	High social capital	−.2146***	−.1351***	−.1176***
Probability of college prep track placement				
	High social capital	.7496***	.6639***	.7010***
	Low social capital	.6052	.5446	.5826
Probability of college enrollment				
	High social capital	.9538***	.9632***	.9744***
	Low social capital	.8813	.9289	.9549

Sources: NLSY79 and CUNY Women File.
*p < .05; **p < .01; ***p < .001

and symbolic: such communication expresses the parent's interest in the child's activities and regard for the offspring's opinions and individuality. Others are emotional: these can be expressions of affection or solidarity—or perhaps disparagement. Some parent-child conversation is more instrumental, for example, when a parent monitors what a child is doing so that the parent may give direction, or attempts to provide encouragement or increase self-esteem. Extended conversation also communicates parental expectations, priorities, interests, and values to the child as well as providing knowledge. As a by-product, conversation also imparts vocabulary, grammar, and diction.

Researchers have discovered that the amount and tenor of parent-child communication vary a lot from family to family. Betty Hart and Todd R. Risley (1995, 1999) observed infants and toddlers in their homes, where they coded adult-child interactions; they found that parent-child communication differs systematically in amount and kind according to a family's class or socioeconomic status. They acknowledged idiosyncratic as well as class variation: some families are taciturn and others are loquacious, but their most striking finding was that on average a family's socioeconomic status (SES) had a huge effect on parent-child communication.

Annette Lareau (2003), observing nine- and ten-year-old children at home with their families, found a strong class contrast in language use. Middle-class parents of all races talked to their children a lot; they reasoned and bargained with their children, solicited their views, gave impromptu lessons in grammar and vocabulary while conversing; enjoyed wordplay, and talked at length with their child about school assignments and current events. By contrast, in the poor and working-class families she observed, Lareau (2003, 146) found that sentences were short, vocabulary was simple, and conversation was to the point. There were long periods of silence. Adults seldom sought children's opinions or drew children out verbally. Working-class adults told children what to do rather than reason with them, and their children rarely if ever argued back. Children tended to remain silent around adults for extended periods of time, though they were much more voluble with their siblings and around peers.

Surveys are not well suited to capture the amount of conversation or the nuances of parent-child interaction. Instead, in the CUNY survey, we focused on how frequently parents reported talking to their children about school, specifically how often they discussed what courses to take or how well their child was doing in class, or talked about the topics or ideas the child was studying in a class. We reasoned that these kinds of communications might be most important to children's educational outcomes. In the NLSY, the children reported whether they spoke with their parent(s) about school activities, topics the student was studying in class, their grades, community or world events, going to college, choosing courses, and things that were troubling them. For propensity analyses we dichotomized this scale, indicating students who sometimes or often spoke with parents on these topics.

Our analyses of NLSY data, reported in table 5.5, revealed statistically significant average differences between college-going women and

Table 5.5   Effect of Mother's Educational Attainment on Communicative Parenting

Mother's Education	Bivariate	Regression	Propensity Matched Sample
NLSY: Effect of mother's education on standardized communicative parenting scale			
Entered college	.118***	.024	.123***
Earned B.A.	.133***	.097***	.100***
CUNY: Probability that mother frequently discussed school subjects with child			
Earned B.A.	.9629	.9593	.9560
No B.A.	.9651	.9667	.9627

Sources: NLSY79 and CUNY Women File.
*p < .05; **p < .01; ***p < .001

women who never attended college, and between B.A. and non-B.A. women, on the frequency of parent-child discussions about school. More-educated women talked more often with their children about these matters. These educational differences remained small in size but statistically significant in the NLSY after controlling for the women's family background, race, and other factors, and after using a sample matched on propensity scores. However, the effects were weaker among the CUNY sample, where the contrast was between college women who failed to obtain a B.A. and those who earned that degree. For this CUNY contrast, there was not a statistically significant difference in communicative parenting.

Our next step was to determine whether parent-child communication was associated with better child-educational outcomes. On all four NLSY child-outcome measures (see table 5.6), more parent-child communication was significantly associated with better child educational outcomes. The size of the effect was small for grade retention and behavior problems, but was considerably larger for PIAT reading and math scores, after statistical controls were added. The picture was more mixed for the CUNY data, where significant parent-child communication effects were observed for only two outcomes after controls were added.

Table 5.6 includes a longitudinal, or change, model, in which we estimated the effect of parent-child conversation on a child's reading and math score around age thirteen, controlling for the child's score at age seven. Communicative parenting had a significant positive effect on math and reading scores at age thirteen (.38 of a standard deviation) even after controlling for a child's math and reading score at age seven and

Table 5.6   Effect of Communicative Parenting on Children's Educational Outcomes (Measured in Standard Deviation Units)

Child's Outcome	Parenting Variable (Child's Age)	Bivariate	Regression	Propensity Matched Sample
NLSY				
Early PIAT score (under seven)				
	Communicative parenting	.2061***	.1587***	.1436***
Behavior Problems Index (six to ten)				
	Communicative parenting	−.1102***	−.0658***	−.0511**
Probability of grade retention				
	High communicative parenting	.1166***	.0877***	.0859***
	Low communicative parenting	.1551	.1078	.1055
Late PIAT score (over thirteen)				
	Communicative parenting	.4295***	.3993***	.4592***
	+ control for early PIAT score	—	.3225***	.3809***
CUNY				
Elementary school success				
	Communicative parenting	.1589***	.1178***	.2007***
High school success				
	Communicative parenting	.0767**	.0198	.0241
High school trouble				
	Communicative parenting	−.0984***	−.0176	−.0194
Probability of college prep track placement				
	High communicative parenting	.6613***	.5844***	.5626**
	Low communicative parenting	.5417	.5037	.4727
Probability of college enrollment				
	High communicative parenting	.8586**	.8657	.8499
	Low communicative parenting	.8147	.8735	.8750

Sources: NLSY79 and CUNY Women File.
Note: Because the communicative parenting questions were only asked of relatively young children in recent NLSY surveys, we have no NLSY findings on the effect of communicative parenting on high school track placement and college enrollment.
*p < .05; **p < .01; ***p < .001

other family variables, using a propensity score matched sample. This would be considered a medium-size effect (Rosenthal and Rosnow 1991).

In sum, even though survey research is not well suited to measuring interpersonal communication, our analyses indicated that maternal education does affect the amount of parent-child communication and that this communication in turn is reflected in better educational outcomes for the child.

Parental Involvement in School

Parents get involved in their children's education in various ways. At home, parents may discuss schoolwork, help supervise or organize homework, and sometimes drill or tutor their children in specific skills. Beyond the home, many parents visit the child's school in order to attend parent-teacher conferences to discuss their child's educational progress, or participate in parent-teacher association (PTA) meetings where school policies and initiatives are often discussed. Going to school to attend student performances or sports events is another, somewhat different, kind of involvement, as is volunteering in the classroom. All these school-based activities constitute "parental involvement in school."

For several decades social scientists claimed an association between parent involvement in schools and children's success, without detailing how, exactly, parental involvement works: whether attendance at school events yields direct benefits (such as useful information), or whether parental involvement at school signals to the child that the parents view education as important and expect the child to devote their full effort. Most commonly, scholars have noted that children whose parents were uninvolved in their schooling tended to be less successful educationally. Policymakers have interpreted this research literally: if the level of parental involvement in school could be increased, children's academic performance would improve. This belief has led to new federal legislation encouraging schools to increase the scope and extent of parental involvement. In response, open houses, back-to-school nights, scheduled parent-teacher conferences, and other events aimed at drawing parents closer to their children's schools have become nearly universal features of American public education.

When researchers have tried to prove that parental involvement results in better academic performance for children, their findings have been mixed. Several studies found that parental involvement is related to improved child outcomes (Epstein and Sanders 2000; Hoffer, Greeley, and Coleman 1985; Lareau 1989; Miedel and Reynolds 1999; Stevensen and Baker 1987; Useem 1992). However, others have found no association between involvement and children's performance (Fine 1993; Singh et al. 1995), and a few have even reported negative effects of parental involvement on student performance (McNeal 1999; Milne et al. 1986; Muller 1993).

These apparent inconsistencies may be partly explained by the fact that when students have academic or behavioral problems at school, school officials often contact parents and invite them to the school to discuss the issue, so children facing educational difficulties are more likely to have their parents visit school. Conversely, some parents of strong students may decide that they don't need to participate a lot in school, since their students are managing fine without their intervention (Crosnoe 2001; Lareau 1989; McNeal 1999; Muller 1998; Sanders 1998). In such cases, parental involvement is likely to be associated with low student success, but the causal direction is that poor school performance is causing parents to become involved.

Another theme in this literature concerns demographic differences in parental involvement with schools. David L. Stevenson and David P. Baker (1987) found that highly educated mothers were more likely to be involved in their child's school than less-educated mothers. Other scholars have shown that higher socioeconomic status and income go hand in hand with more involvement in children's schools (Fehrmann, Keith, and Reimers 1987; Ho and Willms 1996; Lareau 1989; McNeal 1999; Muller 1993).

This relationship between parents' SES and school involvement overlays observed racial differences in school involvement. Initial findings that African American parents were, on average, less involved in schools than white parents were reconsidered after scholars realized that, after controlling for SES, African American and Hispanic parents were *more* likely than whites of the same SES to be involved with their children's schools (Muller and Kerbow 1993; Schneider and Coleman 1993). However, this effect is not uniform: involvement is highest among minority parents whose children attend predominantly minority schools; involvement is lower among minority parents whose children attend predominantly white schools (Ho and Willms 1996; Kerbow and Bernhardt 1993).

John Ogbu (2003) provided an ethnographic picture of this issue, looking at affluent African American families in a wealthy racially integrated suburb. His conclusions (Ogbu 2003, 260–61) concerning these upper-middle-class black parents and students were harsh:

At school, parents' participation or involvement was dismal, even when the main objective of the expected participation was to enhance their children's academic success. . . . Parents involvement with their children's education at home was equally dismal. They did not supervise their children's homework closely; neither did they teach their children appropriate use of their time. Many did not shield their children enough from negative peer pressures, and their methods of motivating their children to engage in schoolwork were not usually effective.

Table 5.7   Effect of Mother's Educational Attainment on Her Involvement in Child's School

Mother's Education	Bivariate	Regression	Propensity Matched Sample
NLSY			
Parent highly involved in child's school			
Entered college	.4087***	.3385*	.3468*
No college	.3320	.3689	.3731
Earned B.A.	.5504***	.4483***	.5339***
No B.A.	.3320	.3442	.4357
CUNY			
Parent intervened to get child placed in particular class or program			
Earned B.A.	.4537	.4674	.4852
No B.A.	.4405	.4425	.4552
Parent made a special request to get child placed with particular teacher			
Earned B.A.	.4028***	.3126***	.2918***
No B.A.	.2081	.2609	.2438

Sources: NLSY79 and CUNY Women File.
*p < .05 **p < .01 ***p < .001

Using survey data, Thurston Domina (2005) reported that the children of minority parents get less of an educational advantage from parental involvement than whites do, in part because minority parents tend to emphasize attendance at meetings at school, whereas whites were more likely to volunteer at school. Domina found that volunteering at school has a considerably greater impact on one's children's academic progress than attending school meetings does. (The survey data don't speak to why this is the case.) Thus, on average, minority parents may be expending effort on less productive types of school involvement.

We included two measures of parental school involvement in the CUNY survey. Following Lareau (1989), we focused on parent activities aimed at gaining a particular advantage for one's child: (1) contacting a school to get the child a place in a particular class or program; (2) contacting the school to get the child assigned to a particular teacher. For the NLSY, we built a scale from several NLSY items that highlighted the kind of school involvement a parent undertook: 0 for parents with no school involvement; 1 for attending parent-teacher conferences; 2 for attending PTA meetings; and 3 for volunteering (Domina 2005).

The effects of maternal education on parental school involvement are not straightforward (see table 5.7). In the NLSY, on average mothers with some college did have higher school involvement than mothers with no college, and mothers with a B.A. or higher degree had greater school involvement than mothers without a B.A. The B.A. effect remains when controls are added and when propensity score matching is used, supporting the notion that earning a B.A. degree is associated with greater involvement in one's child's school. However, when comparing mothers who attended college with those who did not attend (ignoring whether they earned a B.A. or not), the effect is reversed after controlling for family background, income, race, and so on. Mothers who had some college are *less* involved in their child's school than mothers who never attended college. We cannot explain this anomalous result.

In the CUNY survey, maternal education was not associated with the first of our two measures: whether a parent intervened to get a child placed in a particular program or class. However, having a B.A. was positively and significantly associated with making a special request to get one's child placed with a particular teacher, a result that persisted after adding controls and propensity matching.

The analyses reported in table 5.8 examine whether school involvement was associated with better child-educational outcomes. In the NLSY, this school-involvement measure—volunteering and attending school events—was measured in 1996. For the PIAT test of reading and math, the NLSY employed the test in 1996 and again in 2000, enabling us to examine whether children whose parents were more involved in school in 1996 made more improvement in their math and reading over the following four years than children of less-involved parents. In both OLS regression models with controls and in a propensity score matched sample, children with highly involved parents improved significantly more in reading and math than children with less-involved parents, although the size of the effects was quite small.

A similar longitudinal analysis was performed for the Behavior Problems Index, but the results were not consistently significant. Nor was there a significant effect of parental involvement in the NLSY on the probability of a child's being retained in grade.

The questions about parental involvement in the CUNY survey were quite different from those in the NLSY. While the NLSY looked at degree of parental involvement, from PTA to volunteering, our CUNY questions asked whether parents ever requested a specific class or program for their child, or if they ever asked for a specific teacher. In the CUNY survey, these parental requests were associated with significantly *worse* educational outcomes in elementary school, in high school, in college-track placement, and in probability of college enrollment. Those effects remain after controls and propensity matching were used. These findings are consistent with earlier research that found that certain kinds of parental school involvement occurred when children were having academic troubles (Lareau 1989; McNeal 1999; Muller 1998). Parents who requested a special teacher or class or program tended to have

Table 5.8   Effect of Parental School Involvement on Children's Educational Outcomes (Measured in Standard Deviation Units)

Child's Outcome	Parenting Variable	Bivariate	Regression	Propensity Matched Sample
NLSY				
PIAT score (2000)				
	Highly involved parent	.2929***	.0746***	.0718***
	+ control for 1996 PIAT	—	.0278**	.0272*
BPI score (2000)				
	Highly involved parent	−.2022***	.0964***	−.0827***
	+ control for 1996 BPI	—	−.0324*	−.0222
Probability of grade retention				
	Highly involved parent	.0601***	.0434	.0373
	Less involved parent	.0803	.0456	.0423
CUNY				
Elementary school success				
	Requested class or program	−.2448***	−.2323***	−.2430***
	Requested teacher	−.1011***	−.1766***	−.1662***
High school success				
	Requested class or program	−.4355***	−.4080***	−.4114***
	Requested teacher	−.1688***	−.2984***	−.2928***
High school trouble				
	Requested class or program	.3885***	.3702***	.3742***
	Requested teacher	.0987***	.22087***	.2145***
Probability of college prep track placement				
	Requested class or program	.6158***	.5790***	.5776***
	Never requested class or program	.6874	.6774	.6879
	Requested teacher	.6914***	.5979*	.6085
	Never requested teacher	.6395	.6342	.6338
Probability of college enrollment				
	Requested class or program	.8759*	.9072*	.9174***
	Never requested class or program	.9326	.9233	.9410
	Requested teacher	.8678	.8910***	.8827**
	Never requested teacher	.8525	.9239	.9273

Sources: NLSY79 and CUNY Women File.
*p < .05; **p < .01; ***p < .001

children with worse academic outcomes than parents who did not make these requests.

In conclusion, our findings reinforce previous warnings from other scholars that parental involvement is too broad a concept, and that researchers need to distinguish the different contexts of parental involvement in school. Some kinds of parental involvement are reactions to children's academic problems, so that more involvement follows academic problems. Intervening to try to influence a child's track placement or course assignment appears to be this negative, reactive, type. On the other hand, parental volunteering at school, in class, or on field trips or school committees is positively associated with improvements in children's scholastic performance. The latter type of involvement is associated with higher-SES parents, but it is also associated with greater maternal education, even after controlling for SES.

Educational Expectations

Students' educational expectations in elementary, middle, and high school—whether they expect to complete high school, and to obtain an associate's, B.A., or graduate degree—are known to be positively associated with their subsequent performance in school and their later college enrollment (Ainsley, Foreman, and Sheret 1991; Conklin and Dailey 1981; Entwisle and Alexander 1990; Mickelson 1990). The predictive power of expectations remains after controlling for SES and other family-background characteristics and also for academic skills. At first impression, then, it appears that student expectations, especially about going to college, make an independent contribution to academic success, perhaps by increasing motivation or effort.

Parents' educational expectations for their children are also related to the family's SES, with poorer families having lower expectations for their children, on average. Moreover, higher parental expectations predict better educational achievement by their children, even after controlling for family SES. Robert Crosnoe, Rahsmita Mistry, and Glenn Elder (2002) suggest that parental efficacy mediates the relationship between economic advantage and disadvantage and expectations: some adults are pessimistic about their ability to control their lives, whereas others remain optimistic even when facing material deprivation. Thus, two families with similar material resources may have different educational expectations for their children as a result of their differing levels of parental efficacy. Crosnoe, Mistry, and Elder (2002) also report that lowered educational expectations reduce parental motivation to invest money, time, and energy in their adolescent children's education, leading to lower chances of college enrollment. Diane S. Kaplan, Xiaoru Liu, and Howard B. Kaplan (2001) look at parental self-esteem as a moderator between parental academic expectations for their children and children's educational performance.

Many questions remain unanswered about the origins of educational expectations. Some students appear to have expectations about college attendance from an early age that do not change much during the school years. We know that children's expectations are strongly associated with their parents' expectations for them, as well as with their family SES (Trusty and Pirtle 1998). Other students' expectations change during the school years, for some reflecting the development or erosion of educational self-esteem, probably in response to their classroom experiences and the grades they earn, and to teacher and peer-group expectations (Dauber et al. 2002).

One puzzling finding that has emerged both from ethnography (MacLeod 1987) and survey research (Hanson 1994; Kerckhoff and Campbell 1977; Morgan 1998) is that on average, African American students have *higher* educational expectations and aspirations than whites, after controlling for SES. Despite these high expectations, black students on average do not do as well in school as whites. Roslyn Mickelson (1990) views this as a disjuncture between attitudes and behavior among many black students: their high aspirations do not translate into high academic effort (see Ogbu 2003). Stephen Morgan (1998), however, has proposed a rational-choice argument to explain the racial difference in expectations. He argued that since the earnings returns to a college education were greater for blacks than for whites during the period from 1976 to 1985, it was rational for African Americans to have higher college expectations than whites. James Rosenbaum (2001) also advances a rational-choice argument, but to very different effect. He suggests that poor students have high expectations of enrolling in college and believe they can go to college irrespective of their high school performance, and this leads many of these students to slack off during high school. However, their poor high school performance comes back to haunt them, because very few low-performing high school students graduate from college, despite those high expectations. Rosenbaum argues that these students do not realize that their chances of graduating from college are so low and suggests they should be informed of this by school counselors and colleges.

Some scholars question the meaningfulness of educational expectations and aspirations. After noting the near uniformity of college aspirations among current high school students, Grace Kao and Jennifer Thompson (2003, 422–23) caution:

> It is unclear that modern survey instruments actually capture the difference between students who are seriously and actively thinking about college and those who simply report lofty goals. . . . Although aspirations are correlated with grades, test scores, and eventual attainment, it is unclear what having high educational aspirations actually implies for today's youth.

Our first goal in examining educational expectations as an aspect of parenting practices is to determine whether mothers who went to college

Table 5.9   Effect of Mother's Educational Attainment on Her Expectations for Her Child's Educational Attainment, NLSY Women

Mother's Education	Bivariate	Regression	Propensity Matched Sample
Probability that mother expected child to attend college (when child was six years old)			
College	.9032***	.8636***	.8792***
No college	.6980	.7852	.8134
Earned B.A.	.9718***	.9189***	.9750***
No B.A.	.7446	.8024	.9208
Probability that mother expected child to attend college (when child was fourteen years old)			
College	.8934***	.8683***	.8799***
No college	.6739	.7677	.7894
Earned B.A.	.9566***	.8872***	.9620***
No B.A.	.7391	.8027	.8993

Source: NLSY79.
*p < .05; **p < .01; ***p < .001

develop higher educational expectations for their children than otherwise similar mothers who did not go to college. We suspect that after family members in one generation make it to college, college education becomes a family commitment for future generations. Education becomes a trophy, a symbol of success that upwardly mobile parents feel obliged to pass on to their children. Second, we examine whether higher parental expectations for children lead to greater educational success on the various child-outcome measures. We hypothesize that educational expectations will increase the likelihood of children's educational success, since they reflect a level of motivation on the part of the parent and of the child, over and above the family's material and cultural resources, to get as far as college.

In the NLSY survey (but not in the CUNY study) we have data on parental expectations for their children to go to college. Mothers were asked at two points in time whether they expected their child to go to college: when the child was about six years old, and again when the child was about fourteen. Both when children were six and when they were fourteen, mothers' college education was very strongly related to mothers' expectations about their child's attending college (see table 5.9). The size of this effect diminishes very little when we control for family background and other potentially confounding variables, or use a propensity matched sample. This suggests that college going itself affects educational expectations for the next generation, rather than class, race, and other background differences between college goers and less-educated women; when women from disadvantaged families do make it to college, they raise their ambitions for their children's education.

In our second step we find that a mother's early expectation that her child will go to college proves to be a significant predictor of how well the child does academically in later years. Even the expectations that were reported when the child was six years old—well before a child's prowess in school is readily apparent—turn out to predict every child educational outcome up to the child's college enrollment. We would expect some of this to be due to selection bias: mothers who expect their children to go to college are different from mothers who have lower expectations. However, even after adding several controls and using a propensity-matched sample of women, we still find statistically signif- icant effects from maternal expectations. For example, we see from table 5.10 that in a matched sample and after controls, children age six whose mothers expected them to go to college have a .23 standard devi- ation advantage on early vocabulary and a .26 standard deviation lower score on a Behavior Problems Index. Those children are also con- siderably more likely to get into a college track in high school and are substantially more likely to enroll in college.

In the NLSY, skills tests were repeated after several years, enabling us to examine whether parental college expectations predict a student's PIAT reading and math score around age thirteen, after controlling for the student's score at age seven. This is equivalent to asking whether parental college expectations affect a child's change in academic skills between age seven and thirteen. The middle row of table 5.10, the late PIAT score, indicates that parental college expectations at age six pre- dict improvement in reading and math between ages seven and thirteen, after controlling for family background and several other factors in both traditional regression models and using a propensity-matched sample. Overall, parental expectations about a young child's education provide a moderately strong predictor of children's educational success, over and above class background, race, and other factors.

Private and Parochial Schooling

Janet Swallow, the African American mother we met earlier, had heard so may bad things about the quality of local public schools that she and her husband went to the expense of enrolling their children in Roman Catholic parochial schools. Her perception that private schools pro- vide a superior education is supported by a stream of research, initi- ated by James Coleman and his collaborators, who found that students in parochial schools make greater academic progress (Bryk, Lee, and

Table 5.10   Effect of Early College Expectations on Children's Educational Outcomes, NLSY Women

Child's Outcome	Parenting Variable (Child's Age)	Bivariate	Regression	Propensity Matched Sample
Early PIAT score (under seven)				
	Expects college attendance (six)	.5028***	.2548***	.2331***
Behavior Problems Index (six to ten)				
	Expects college attendance (six)	−.4408***	−.2226***	−.2600***
Probability of grade retention				
	Expects college attendance (six)	.1940***	.1733***	.2751***
	No college expectations (six)	.4420	.2608	.3643
Late PIAT score (over thirteen)				
	Expects college attendance (six)	.6628***	.3767***	.3500***
	+ control for 7-year-old PIAT	—	.2801***	.2605***
	Expects college attendance (fourteen)	.8249***	.4972***	.4675***
	+ control for 7-year-old PIAT	—	.3871***	.3632***
Probability of college prep track placement				
	Expects college attendance (six)	.4022***	.3760***	.3480***
	No college expectations (six)	.2169	.2355	.2216
	Expects college attendance (fourteen)	.4096***	.3831***	.3255***
	No college expectations (fourteen)	.1764	.2049	.1897
Probability of college enrollment				
	Expects college attendance (six)	.5811***	.5683***	.4930***
	No college expectations (six)	.3014	.3323	.2636
	Expects college attendance (fourteen)	.5860***	.5680***	.4793***
	No college expectations (fourteen)	.2497	.2957	.2103

Source: NLSY79
*p < .05; **p < .01; ***p < .001

Holland 1993; Coleman and Hoffer 1987; Coleman, Hoffer, and Kilgore 1982; Hoffer, Greeley, and Coleman 1985; Morgan 2001) than those in public schools. The Catholic school advantage appears to be large; Anthony Bryk, Valerie Lee, and Peter Holland (1993, 247) reported, "By senior year, lower middle-class students attending Catholic schools are achieving 4.5 years ahead of their counterparts in the public sector."

Authors of other studies using similar data, however, dispute the superiority of private and parochial schooling or find minimal differences (Alexander and Pallas 1983; Goldberger and Cain 1982; Noell 1982; Willms 1985). Disputes such as these are often methodological and hinge on whether the kinds of people who send their children to parochial schools differ from those who do not, and whether those selection biases are adequately controlled for in statistical models (see Lieberson 1985; Morgan 2001).

We are particularly interested in finding out whether mothers who attended college are more likely to send their children to private school, net of the mother's family background, and whether children who attend private school are more successful on the various educational-outcome measures that span the period from elementary school to college, net of family income and parental characteristics. In neither the CUNY nor the NLSY do the data distinguish between parochial schools and other kinds of private schools. Our contrast is therefore between attending private school of any type and attending public school.

Table 5.11 shows that mothers who go to or complete college are indeed much more likely to send their child to a private school. In the NLSY, 33 percent of mothers with a B.A. sent their children to private school compared to 9 percent of mothers without a B.A. After controlling for other characteristics of the mother, using propensity score matching, 29 percent of the children of B.A. mothers went to private school, compared to 18 percent of children of non-B.A. mothers.[8] Similar but smaller statistically significant differences were found in the CUNY sample. Mothers who go to college are significantly more likely to send their children to private schools.

In both the CUNY and NLSY surveys, we find that children who attended private schools had better educational outcomes from elementary age through college than otherwise equivalent children who did not attend private school (see table 5.12). These differences remain significant after controlling for family characteristics such as race and class, mother's education and IQ, and several other potentially confounding factors, whether in conventional regression models or in propensity score–matched samples. The estimate of the advantage from private school (in a propensity-matched model) suggests that 74 percent of children from private schools go on to college, compared to 61 percent of otherwise similar children who attended public schools.

Table 5.11   Effect of Mother's Educational Attainment on Private
School Attendance

	Mother's Education	Bivariate	Regression	Propensity Matched Sample
NLSY				
Probability that child attended private school				
	Entered college	.2093***	.1354***	.1261***
	No college	.0720	.0867	.0916
	Earned B.A.	.3326***	.1135***	.2898***
	No B.A.	.0930	.0790	.1835
CUNY				
Probability that child attended private school				
	Earned B.A.	.2559***	.2410***	.2463*
	No B.A.	.1987	.1990	.2130

Sources: NLSY79 and CUNY Women File.
*p < .05; **p < .01; ***p < .001

We were also able to examine the effect of attending a private school
on a child's educational progress over time. In the middle section of
table 5.12, we predict a child's PIAT score (reading and writing) at
around age thirteen, including as a predictor his or her score on the test
around age seven. Children who attended a private school increased
their PIAT scores between age seven and thirteen by .1883 standard
deviation more than students who did not attend a private school, after
controlling for PIAT score at age seven and for class, race, and other
background factors.

To summarize: Mothers who went to college are more likely to send
their children to private or parochial school, irrespective of their class
background. On average, children who are sent to private school have
better educational outcomes and also show bigger improvements in
reading and math skills over time. This payoff to private schooling is not
simply a reflection of the higher incomes and higher educations of parents whose children attend private school; the benefits persist even after
controlling for those influences.

Residential Moves

The United States has a highly mobile population. In the year 2000,
about 15 to 18 percent of school-age children moved.[9] In most cases,
when a child moves home, he or she also changes schools. Other children change schools without changing their residence. Russell W.
Rumberger and Katherine A. Larson (1998) estimated that between 30

Table 5.12   Effect of Private School Attendance on Children's Educational Outcomes

Child's Outcome	Parenting Variable (Child's Age)	Bivariate	Regression	Propensity Matched Sample
NLSY				
Early PIAT score (under seven)				
	Private school attendance	.4729***	.2179***	.1440***
Behavior Problems Index (six to ten)				
	Private school attendance	−.4501***	−.2046***	−.1515***
Probability of grade retention				
	Private school attendance	.1030***	.1725*	.0704
	Public school attendance	.2727	.1946	.0718
Late PIAT score (over thirteen)				
	Private school attendance	.6490***	.2500 ***	.2172***
	+ control for seven-year-old PIAT	—	.1892***	.1883***
Probability of college prep track placement				
	Private school attendance	.5795***	.4973***	.5948***
	Public school attendance	.3305	.3249	.4291
Probability of college enrollment				
	Private school attendance	.7206***	.6446***	.7407**
	Public school attendance	.4874	.4930	.6066
CUNY				
Elementary school success				
	Private school attendance	.1033***	.0341	.0638*
High school success				
	Private school attendance	.2674***	1893***	.2163***
High school trouble				
	Private school attendance	−.2420***	−.1879***	−.2089***

(Table continues on p. 109.)

Table 5.12   *Continued*

Child's Outcome	Parenting Variable	Bivariate	Regression	Propensity Matched Sample
Probability of college prep track placement				
	Private school attendance	.7128***	.6224**	.6467**
	Public school attendance	.6370	.5675	.5787
Probability of college enrollment				
	Private school attendance	.8965***	.9070***	.9233***
	Public school attendance	.8425	.8519	.8834

Sources: NLSY79 and CUNY Women File.
*p < .05; **p < .01; ***p < .001

and 40 percent of unscheduled school moves are not accompanied by shifts in residence.[10] Combining these two kinds of mobility suggests that roughly one in five schoolchildren make unscheduled school moves each year (see also Swanson and Schneider 1999). Inner-city children in poorer families tend to change schools more often than others; in New York City, for example, inner-city schools report annual student mobility rates of 30 percent or higher.

Changing schools, especially in the middle of the school year, can disrupt a student's learning. Students who change are likely to miss material that their classmates have already learned and so are out of sync with other students in the class. They also have to adapt to new teachers and peers. The schools face the added paperwork burden of enrolling new students throughout the school year. Furthermore, teachers in high-turnover schools cannot be sure what their students have already been taught, meaning that children who have not moved but who attend schools where there is a high rate of student turnover are likely to be negatively impacted, too.

There is considerable evidence (summarized in Educational Resources Information Center 1991, 2002) that student mobility depresses the academic achievement of the students who moved. However, some analyses of longitudinal surveys also indicate that, on average, mobile students had lower academic performance even *before* they moved, so it may be that already-weak students move more and thereby depress their academic skills even further (Alexander, Entwisle, and Dauber 1996; Nelson, Simoni, and Adelman 1996; Pribesh and Downey 1999).

The long-term consequences of geographical mobility on children's outcomes can be very striking. Robert Haveman and Barbara Wolfe (1994, 102–3) found that when contrasting students with zero household moves to those with five residential moves between the ages of six and fifteen, the students' high school graduation rate drops from 91 to 68 percent, their college attendance rate drops from 46 to 25 percent, their out-of-wedlock birth rate goes from 8 to 15 percent, and their likelihood of being out of the labor force at age twenty-four rises from 18 to 26 percent.

The literature on the effects of moving on children sounds unremittingly negative, but we are concerned that previous research may have overlooked class or SES differences (or interactions) in moving. Moving may be especially harmful for the education of children from poor or disorganized families who repeatedly change homes (Long 1992; South, Crowder, and Trent 1998; Speare and Goldscheider 1987), and moving following divorce is clearly costly for children (South, Crowder, and Trent 1998; Speare and Goldscheider 1987). But for some other families, moving home may be associated with better occupational and educational opportunities. Some families move into wealthier neighborhoods as they grow more affluent; others deliberately move to places where the public schools are superior. These types of move are unlikely to have the same effect on children as moves from one poor neighborhood to another poor neighborhood. Our analyses probed for such contextual differences.

In the CUNY survey we had information about changing schools, as opposed to changing residences, and we created a variable to indicate whether a child had changed elementary school two or more times. (A single move seems not to matter.) The NLSY survey lacked an equivalent variable. However, because the NLSY has geographical codes, we were able to determine whether a family had moved from one county to another (either within or between states) while the child was between zero and ten years old. Children of mothers with a B.A. are more likely to move across county lines than children whose mother had no B.A. (55 percent versus 47 percent in the propensity matched models in table 5.13); thus, education is positively associated with changing residence. When we shift to the CUNY data, which examines whether a child changes school twice or more, however, the picture is the opposite: children whose mothers have a B.A. were significantly less likely to change school twice or more: 37 percent compared to 30 percent in the propensity matched models. We don't read these as contradictory findings, because we believe the two moving variables describe different phenomena.

When we turn to the correlates or consequences of moving, shown in table 5.14, we find, for the NLSY measure of moving one's residence, that moving is modestly positive for children's outcomes. On average, children who moved home showed greater improvement between seven

Table 5.13   Effect of Mother's Educational Attainment on the Probability That Children Moved While Growing Up

	Mother's Education	Bivariate	Regression	Propensity Matched Sample
NLSY				
Probability that child had any intercounty move between zero and ten years old				
	Entered college	.4746***	.4633***	.4541
	No college	.4379	.4417	.4464
	Earned B.A.	.5533***	.5289***	.5571***
	No B.A.	.4393	.4406	.4774
CUNY				
Probability that child moved twice or more in elementary school				
	Earned B.A.	.2179***	.2710***	.3015***
	No B.A.	.3397	.3397	.3707

Sources: NLSY79 and CUNY Women File.
*p < .05; **p < .01; ***p < .001

and thirteen on the math and reading battery than children who did not move. We also discovered that this positive effect of moving residence to another county was greater for higher-income families; children in the lower half of the income distribution did not show a significant improvement on test scores after changing their residence.

By contrast, in the CUNY survey that measured changing schools twice or more during elementary school, this was associated with significantly worse educational outcomes. This negative outcome was found for all levels of income. Children who experience multiple changes in the elementary school they attend clearly fare worse academically.

In sum, our analyses provide a complicated but interesting picture of the effects on children of moving or changing schools. College-educated mothers are more likely to move across county lines during their children's upbringing than less-educated women (net of other background characteristics). Moving home is associated with better educational outcomes for their children, but this depends on one's income: moving home has a payoff for more affluent families but not for poorer ones. (We speculate that when more affluent families move, they deliberately move to places with superior schools, but that poorer families are unable to move to take advantage of better schools.) Mothers who had not earned a B.A. are more likely than more educated women to have their children change schools twice or more during the elementary years, and that kind of school move is associated with worse educational outcomes for children at all income levels.

Table 5.14   Effect of Moving on Children's Educational Outcomes

Child's Outcome	Bivariate	Regression	Propensity Matched Sample
NLSY			
PIAT age thirteen and older			
All children	.0722***	.0030	.0491**
Bottom income quartile	−.0202	−.7994**	−.0141
Second income quartile	.0372	−.0455	.0083
Third income quartile	.1400***	.0856**	.1307***
Top income quartile	.0775***	.1132***	.1360***
PIAT thirteen and older (controlling for earlier PIAT)			
All children	—	.0406**	.0505***
Bottom income quartile	—	−.0008	−.0025
Second income quartile	—	.0370	.0346
Third income quartile	—	.0819**	.1134***
Top income quartile	—	.0968**	.1160***
CUNY			
High school success			
All children	−.5547***	−.3903***	−.3760***
Bottom income quartile	−.4608***	−.2961***	−.2011***
Second income quartile	−.6158***	−.5014***	−.4736***
Third income quartile	−.5754***	−.3527***	−.3404***
Top income quartile	−.4116***	−.3333***	−.3527***

Sources: NLSY79 and CUNY Women File.
*p < .05; **p < .01; ***p < .001

Organizational and Community Involvement

In their book *Managing to Make It: Urban Families and Adolescent Success,* the sociologist Frank Furstenberg and his colleagues (1999) explored why some adolescents were psychologically and academically successful despite growing up in poor communities. They studied a sample of adolescents ten to fourteen years old and their parents, drawn from sixty-five census tracts in Philadelphia. Previous research had led Furstenberg and colleagues to anticipate a substantial relationship between neighborhood characteristics and child outcomes, but they did not find this. Socially and academically competent children were not overrepresented in financially better-off neighborhoods (Furstenberg et al. 1999, 67–68). Nor was there evidence of greater family dysfunction in poorer high-risk neighborhoods (99). This drew the researchers to examine differences between families rather than between neighborhoods in order to explain youths' outcomes.

Although Furstenberg and colleagues argued that even in the poorest neighborhoods, most parents did a good job of raising their children (Furstenberg et al. 1999, 217); nevertheless they linked successful child outcomes to effective parenting, especially what they called "family management practices" and "promotive" and "preventive" strategies by parents. These included some factors we have discussed earlier: parent-child communication, shared child-adult decisionmaking, parental school involvement (97), and choice of private schools (88–89, 97). In addition, they found that parents who were very involved in community organizations, including but not limited to church groups, had more successful adolescents (117, 127–31, 133).

When parents become involved in community organizations, they contribute to and draw upon the social capital of a particular part of the community. They socialize with other adults who are in those organizations, and gain access to information about the community and about opportunities for themselves and their children. Participants often obtain social or emotional support from fellow organization members. Some organizations also provide special activities for members' children; in other cases, informal socialization among members' children creates peer groups. In addition, parents who are organizational joiners are more likely to enroll their children in other organizations and activities, from sports to Scouts. The children of organizational joiners therefore experience a more structured environment for leisure and for extra-curricular activities and a more selective group of peers than the typical adolescent, and this pays off psychologically and academically.

Furstenberg's notion of organizational joiners provides a method for looking at social capital at the community level. Not social capital as intergenerational closure, which we considered in an earlier section, but social capital as membership in organizations. We incorporated items about parent involvement in organizations, drawn from their Philadelphia study, into our CUNY survey. The measure counted parent participation in a crime-watch group, in a tenants' or neighborhood council, in any political organization, in a church or congregation, or the local library, in youth or sport clubs or in community health organizations, or in any other kind of community-based group. We combined these different items into a scale that has a maximum value of 12.

We found (reported in table 5.15) that maternal college education is associated with higher levels of community involvement by the mother, after controlling for several aspects of family background, including class and race.

Table 5.16 shows that community involvement is significantly associated with better children's educational outcomes through high school. (One exception is that we did not find an effect of parents' organizational membership on children's probability of going to college.) These

Table 5.15   **Effect of Mother's Educational Attainment on Her Community Involvement, CUNY Women (Measured in Standard Deviation Units)**

Mother's Education	Bivariate	Regression	Propensity Matched Sample
Mother's community involvement			
B.A.	.2066***	.1573***	.1646***

Source: CUNY Women File.
*p < .05; **p < .01; ***p < .001

Table 5.16   **Effect of Mother's Community Involvement on Children's Educational Outcomes, CUNY Women (Measured in Standard Deviation Units)**

Child's Outcome	Parenting Variable	Bivariate	Regression	Propensity Matched Sample
Elementary school success				
	Mother highly involved in community	.0826***	.1472***	.1539***
High school success				
	Mother highly involved in community	.1156***	.0712***	.1328***
High school trouble				
	Mother highly involved in community	−.1195***	−.0754***	−.1358**
Probability of college prep track placement				
	High community involvement	.7359***	.7032***	.6705***
	Low community involvement	.6129	.5824	.5701
Probability of college enrollment				
	High community involvement	.9282***	.8814*	.9586
	Low community involvement	.8981	.8584	.9610

Source: CUNY Women File.
*p < .05; **p < .01; ***p < .001

child outcomes do not reflect differences in income or education or class background between parents who are invested in community organizations and those who are not. Our propensity score analyses controlled for such forms of selection. They are consistent with Furstenberg's finding that when parents are more involved in the community, their children have better educational outcomes, but the effects are small.

Church Attendance

Membership in a church or religious congregation provides not only a locus for spiritual matters but also a community for members' children. Churches provide important help in child rearing, not just through prayer groups and Bible study but also by organizing activities that members view as positive for children and by ensuring that kids associate with like-minded youngsters. Involvement in church also provides adult and peer role models and opportunities for mentoring and counseling. Previous research has documented that children of churchgoing families have superior academic achievement on average than children who do not attend church (for example, King et al. 2001; Resnick et al. 1997; Wagener et al. 2003; Youniss, McLellan, and Yates 1999). Obviously, there are selection issues at play in this: families who attend church regularly are likely to be different from non-church-going families on many dimensions besides religious belief. Our analyses below are designed to minimize selection effects and to identify the influence of church attendance itself.

Both the NLSY and CUNY surveys contained questions about the frequency with which a child attended church or another religious institution with his or her parent(s) or guardian. So the construct involves a joint family activity. In the NLSY, the church attendance measure was available only for a late cohort of children, limiting the kinds of outcome measures that we could use.

In both the CUNY and NLSY surveys, we found that maternal higher education is positively associated with taking one's child to church, net of family background (see table 5.17). In the NLSY, on average 82 percent of B.A.-achieving mothers took their children to services, compared to 56 percent of mothers without a B.A. After minimizing effects of background factors such as race and income, this effect of having a B.A. on church attendance shrinks to 78 percent, compared to 58 percent—still a big difference. The findings for the CUNY survey were still significant but were smaller, perhaps because all the women were college goers.

We also confirmed the findings of earlier studies in observing that positive child educational outcomes are associated with family churchgoing, net of family income, education, race, and other factors. These educational differences associated with church attendance were small

Table 5.17   Effect of Mother's Educational Attainment on Child's
Church Attendance

Mother's Education	Bivariate	Regression	Propensity Matched Sample
NLSY			
Probability that child regularly attended church when ten to fourteen years old			
Entered college	.6799***	.6801***	.6771***
No college	.5647	.6201	.6037
Earned B.A.	.8174***	.7913***	.7839***
No B.A.	.5647	.6271	.5857
CUNY			
Probability that child regularly attended church			
Earned B.A.	.6026	.6395***	.6390**
No B.A.	.5808	.5944	.5894

Sources: NLSY79 and CUNY Women File.
*p < .05; **p < .01; ***p < .001

in size. In table 5.18, the sole exceptions to this positive picture were college track placement (in the NLSY) and college attendance (in the CUNY survey), where there were no significant effects of church attendance.

Emotional Support from Parents

The NLSY survey includes two well-established scales that measure parents' emotional support for the child (Caldwell and Bradley 1984). These scales are age-specific: the scale for younger children emphasizes physical punishment and mother-child interaction. For children over six, the NLSY HOME emotional support scale includes information on how often a child cleans her or his own room; how often a child picks up after self; how often the family gets together with friends or relatives; how often a child spends time with the father or a father figure; how often a child spends time with a father figure in outdoor activities; how often a child eats with both parents; how a mother responds to a child's tantrum; how often the child was spanked in the last week.

Some items included in this authoritative scale may seem only indirectly related to gauging parental emotional support.[11] We are concerned that children from homes with no father present are bound to score lower on this scale. We believe that single and dual parenting are better analyzed in their own terms, rather than single parenting being interpreted as a dearth of emotional support. Items such as cleaning up one's room and picking up after oneself also seem to measure dimensions

Table 5.18   Effect of Church Attendance on Children's
Educational Outcomes

Child's Outcome	Parenting Variable (Child's Age)	Bivariate	Regression	Propensity Matched Sample
NLSY				
Late PIAT score (over thirteen)				
	Regular church attendance	.1318***	.0449***	.0578***
Probability of college prep track placement				
	Regular church attendance	.3670***	.3424	.3496
	No church attendance	.3324	.3328	.3499
Probability of college enrollment				
	Regular church attendance	.5353***	.5215*	.5232**
	No church attendance	.4798	.4937	.4622
CUNY				
Elementary school success				
	Regular church attendance	.1207***	.0637***	.0720***
High school success				
	Regular church attendance	.2759***	.1898***	.1638***
High school trouble				
	Regular church attendance	−.2146***	−.1351***	−.1176***
Probability of college prep track placement				
	Regular church attendance	.3868***	.3635***	.3524***
	No church attendance	.2904	.2982	.2941
Probability of college enrollment				
	Regular church attendance	.5305***	.5195	.5131
	No church attendance	.4739	.4922	.4910

Sources: NLSY79 and CUNY Women File.
*p < .05; **p < .01; ***p < .001

Table 5.19   Effect of Mother's Educational Attainment on HOME Emotional Support Scale, NLSY Women (Measured in Standard Deviation Units)

Mother's Education	Bivariate	Regression	Propensity Matched Sample
HOME emotional support scale (less than ten)			
College	.343***	.088***	.122***
B.A.	.514***	.033*	.098***
HOME emotional support scale (over ten)			
College	.175***	−.019	−.013
B.A.	.437***	.086***	.163***

Source: NLSY79.
*p < .05; **p < .001; ***p < .001

other than emotional support. The scale also has a strong built-in assumption that emotional support and physical punishment are incompatible. That view may be dominant among academic experts on child development, but many of the world's cultures (including many working-class Americans) view occasional physical punishment as a normal aspect of life in an emotionally warm family. The home emotional support scale has been widely used by researchers, so despite these reservations, we examined its relationship to child outcomes.

We observed that maternal college education is significantly associated with higher values (greater support) on the home emotional scale. In table 5.19 significant differences exist between college goers and non–college goers, and between B.A. holders and non–B.A. mothers, for two age groups of children (under ten and over ten years old). In size these are moderate to large differences. When controls are added for family class background, high school preparation, IQ, and so on, and when samples are matched on propensity scores, these differences are considerably reduced, but they remain statistically significant for three of four comparisons, indicating that higher maternal education per se is associated with somewhat higher emotional support levels.

Our analyses also indicate that an emotionally supportive home environment has a positive effect on children's educational outcomes, from early vocabulary to probability of college enrollment (see table 5.20). These differences remain statistically significant, though small, after extensive sociodemographic controls were added and after propensity score matching was done to reduce selection bias. Of the effects, that of early emotional support on a child's later college enrollment is the most striking: otherwise equivalent children with a high home emotional score before age ten have a 50 percent likelihood of attending

Table 5.20   Effect of Emotionally Supportive Parenting on Children's Educational Outcomes, NLSY Women

Child's Outcome	Parenting Variable (Child's Age)	Bivariate	Regression	Propensity Matched Sample
Early PIAT score (under seven)				
	HOME emotional support (under ten)	.3966***	.1318***	.1363***
Behavior Problems Index (six to ten)				
	HOME emotional support (under ten)	−.3970***	−.2582***	−.2720***
Probability of grade retention				
	High HOME emotional (under ten)	.1634***	.1613***	.1447***
	Low HOME emotional (under ten)	.3168	.2017	.1888
Late PIAT score (over thirteen)				
	HOME emotional support (under ten)	.5867***	.1732***	.1938***
	HOME emotional support (over ten)	.4287***	.0739***	.1086***
Probability of college prep track placement				
	High HOME emotional (under ten)	.3958***	.3513***	.3706***
	Low HOME emotional (under ten)	.3021	.3224	.3169
	High HOME emotional (over ten)	.3851***	.3535***	.3626***
	Low HOME emotional (over ten)	.2991	.3168	.2931
Probability of college enrollment				
	High HOME emotional (under ten)	.5507***	.5077	.5036**
	Low HOME emotional (under ten)	.4366	.4865	.4237
	High HOME emotional (over ten)	.5541***	.5120	.5055*
	Low HOME emotional (over ten)	.4435	.4907	.4587

Source: NLSY79.
*p < .05; **p < .01; ***p < .001

college, compared to a 42 percent likelihood for children with a low emotional score.

Effect of All Parenting Activities on Children's Outcomes

Thus far, we have identified a set of parenting activities, each of which is associated with child educational outcomes, independent of parental education, income, and social-class background. The activities:

- Cultural enrichment
- Social capital (intergenerational social closure)
- Extended discussions with children (communicative parenting)
- Parental involvement in school
- Educational expectations
- Private schooling
- Residential moves
- Parental involvement in community organizations
- Church attendance with children
- Parental emotional support

It would be very convenient if all these parenting activities reflected one underlying dimension, so that one could simply talk about "effective parenting." Unfortunately, our attempts to build a scale combining these activities failed.[12] This implies that these activities are really independent or alternative strategies, each one contributing something to the likelihood of a child's doing well educationally.

Nevertheless, we would like to know how much of a difference parenting activities, taken together, can make to children's outcomes, if only to compare parenting activities' importance to other possible mechanisms that transmit advantage, such as family income, or two-parent families, or occupational prestige. To gain such an estimate, we calculated the effect of a family's having a value of one standard deviation unit above the sample mean on each parenting variable, while including control variables. This procedure is equivalent to imagining two hypothetical families: one is completely average on each of the parenting variables; the other has values one standard deviation unit higher on each parenting activity.

The two families are otherwise identical. For the CUNY analyses, the controls included child's gender and race; family income; mother's personal earnings and work time; family economic well-being; parental occupational prestige; mother's educational attainment; family composition;

mother's high school record; college grades and level of entry; the median income and racial composition of neighborhood child grew up in; mother's family background; and the timing of the child's birth relative to mother's college enrollment. For this analysis, these variables are all set at the population mean. For the NLSY analysis the controls included current family-income-to-needs ratio; early childhood poverty exposure; family home ownership; maternal SEI (socioeconomic index) score and education; family composition and stability; the mother's age; mother's parents' income, SEI, and highest degree (measured when mother finished high school); mother's armed forces qualification test (AFQT) score; high school performance, mother's self-esteem and self-mastery scores; and child's gender and race.

We can now ask: How would the children of these two families fare educationally?

In table 5.21, for the NLSY, the child of a family with higher parenting scores on average .29 standard deviation higher on early vocabulary, has a .42 standard deviation advantage in math and reading scores measured before age seven; a .45 standard deviation better score on the Behavior Problems Index, and a .54 standard deviation advantage in reading and math measures after age thirteen. The same higher parenting score reduces the likelihood of repeating a grade from nearly 17 percent to about 10 percent, and increases the probability of a child's entering a college track from about 35 percent to 62 percent. Several of these are large effects; parenting activities do make a substantial difference to children's educational outcomes.

In conclusion, parenting activities make a significant difference for children's educational chances, net of other family advantages or disadvantages. They are a mechanism whereby parental education is translated into better educational chances for children. But do these parenting activities work equally well for whites, African Americans, and Hispanics? Do they pay off equally for women with less education, as they do for college-educated women? Do they make as much of a difference for children of women from lower-class backgrounds as they do for women from affluent families?

To answer these questions we estimated the effects of parenting separately for each racial and ethnic group, separately by maternal education, and separately by mother's class background, with other factors controlled. The answers can be observed in table 5.21, where we see positive statistically significant payoffs to these parenting activities for women of all races, for mothers with various levels of education, and for mothers who grew up in poor, in middle-income, and in affluent families. Some of these parenting activities, such as cultural parenting, may be linked in most people's minds with a middle-class lifestyle, but our analyses show that these parenting activities still

Table 5.21   Effect of One Standard Deviation Change of Parenting Activities on Children's Educational Outcomes, by Race, Maternal Education, and Income, NLSY Survey

By race

	All Races	White	Black	Hispanic
Vocabulary	.2938978	.3853709	.1875876	.2726257
Early PIAT	.416442	.485231	.379096	.346077
Behavior Problems Index	.453786	.557979	.40378	.326825
Late PIAT	.539756	.705681	.4229	.53954

By maternal education

	All	No College	Some College or A.A. Degree	B.A. or Higher
Vocabulary	.2938978	.266256	.345405	.407372
Early PIAT	.416442	.394251	.494722	.275519
Behavior Problems Index	.453786	.466216	.458277	.575271
Late PIAT	.539756	.557282	.503333	.762432

By income of mother's family of origin

	Poor (Bottom Quartile)	Middle-Income (Middle Quartiles)	Affluent (Top Quartile)
Vocabulary	.1871	.3123	.4068
Early PIAT	.3784	.4838	.3454
Behavior Problems Index	.3217	.4863	.5409
Late PIAT	.4698	.5643	.6377

Source: NLSY79.

improve children's educational progress when less affluent or less-educated parents employ them.

At the same time, in table 5.21 we do find differences in the influences in parenting between women of different ethnic groups, education levels, and class backgrounds. The payoff from parenting activities—represented by the coefficient for parenting—is not equal across races, education levels, or class backgrounds. In the NLSY, the payoff for parenting, measured as the effect of a one standard deviation increase in parenting upon a given child outcome, is consistently larger for whites than for African Americans. In most but not all cases, the size of the parenting effect for Hispanic mothers lies between the white and black values. The payoff of these parenting activities also varies by social-class origin: the children of women who grew up in affluent families tend to gain more from these parenting activities than do children of women from poor families. On most child-outcome measures, parenting has a greater payoff for children of college-educated women than for those with no college.

This pattern is consistent with a cumulative model of social advantage. The parenting activities we have identified are associated with better child outcomes no matter who deploys them, but the children of already-advantaged families gain a somewhat bigger boost from these child-raising activities than do minority children and children with mothers who were raised in lower-class families.

In the CUNY survey reported in table 5.22, which is limited to women who attended college, a different picture emerges. Parenting activities among these college-educated women pay off more for the children of Hispanic and Black women than for white women, in terms of children's outcomes. Parenting also pays off more for women who come from poor families than for women who grew up in affluent families, and parenting pays off at least as much for women who don't have B.A. degrees as for women who did not get as far as a B.A. We do not have a simple explanation for this difference between the two surveys. However, in both the NLSY and the CUNY surveys, the combined elements of parenting are associated with better outcomes for all race, class, and educational levels. The surveys diverge only on the secondary issue of differences in the size of the parenting advantage.

Summary and Conclusion

Several generations of sociologists have demonstrated a link between the social class of parents and the ways those parents tended to raise their children. Instead of looking at class background and parenting, we examined the relationship between a mother's educational attainment and her parenting behaviors and the effect of these on child outcomes, while controlling for the mother's social-class origins. We identified about ten different parental behaviors. For each of these dimensions of parenting, we discovered that when a mother has attended college or received a B.A., she engages in these positive parenting behaviors more often. We felt confident attributing increases in these kinds of parenting to mother's college attendance, because our models controlled for social-class background and for other forms of family advantage, including income. We also employed techniques intended to minimize selection bias. There is something about the college experience, beyond class origins or differences in background, that affects how women later raise their children.

We documented that nine of these parenting practices were associated with better outcomes for children at various stages of the child's education, from elementary school to college entrance. These nine practices

Table 5.22   Effect of One Standard Deviation Change in Parenting Style on Children's Educational Outcomes, by Race, Maternal Education, and Income, CUNY Survey

By race

	All Races	White	Black	Hispanic
Elementary	.210165	.200476	.38942	.314486
High school	.360546	.414187	.613785	.483034
High school trouble	.3815581	.378222	.608182	.445754

By mother's education

	High School	Some College or A.A.	B.A. or Higher
Elementary	.333549	.30626	.225816
High school	.418377	.422128	.363712
High school trouble	.524782	.454513	.267645

By income of mother's class origin

	Poor (Bottom Quartile)	Middle-Income (Middle Quartiles)	Affluent (Top Quartile)
Elementary	.3429	.2414	.2668
High school	.4847	.4045	.3283
High school trouble	.5129	.3063	.3181

Source: CUNY Women File.

are cultural enrichment; social capital (intergenerational closure); extended discussions with children (communicative parenting); parental involvement in school; educational expectations that one's child will go to college; private schooling; residential moves; parental involvement in community organizations; church attendance with children; and parental emotional support. Changing schools was associated with worse child educational outcomes.

Again, care was taken to estimate the effects of each parenting practice on children's educational progress separate from confounding influences such as parental income, education, and class background. These parenting behaviors, even when isolated from families' other attributes, improve children's educational outcomes.

The various parenting behaviors appear to be independent of one another; it is not the case that parents who undertake one tend also to undertake all the others. It would be misleading to think of these activities as manifestations of one underlying construct, such as "effective parenting." Instead they seem to be a repertoire of distinct behaviors, a toolkit, each of which affects to a modest extent a child's chances for success. Parents who invest in several of these activities provide a substantial boost to their child: the combined effect sizes for the NLSY survey were in the range of .3 to .55, which are conventionally considered moderate to large effects.[13] Those effects in the CUNY survey were somewhat smaller.

Differences in parenting behaviors partly explain why some children thrive educationally, while others do not. These parenting behaviors are efficacious no matter what the educational level of a mother: less-educated parents who utilize them also advantage their children. But college-educated mothers are more likely to engage in these kinds of parenting behaviors than less-educated mothers. These parenting behaviors are therefore a mechanism whereby maternal education pays off for the next generation.

Parenting is only part of the puzzle, however. In the next chapter we consider other factors, turning to the importance of fathers for children's success and delving into family structure and family stability. We will also determine what money buys and cannot buy in terms of children's educational progress. And we will tease the effects of job complexity as distinct from those of social class and education. When these additional pieces are fitted into the puzzle, we will be able to assess the overall importance of educational opportunity in one generation for the prospects of successive generations.

═ Chapter 6 ═

Dads and Neighborhoods: Their Contributions to Children's Success

The central concerns of this book are the role that college plays in increasing women's chances of success, and the spillover from a mother's college education to her children's achievement. In pursuing these topics, however, we need to remain aware of what other factors besides maternal education affect children's well-being: matters such as marital stability and family structure, household income, and neighborhood. These other factors might become confused or conflated with the effect of education, but by separating out the influence of each one through statistical techniques, we can better grasp its role. Equally important, some of these variables, such as marital stability and neighborhood, may be mechanisms whereby increased maternal education improves children's outcomes, so we need to assess their importance as boosters of maternal education.

In this chapter we focus on two factors that are commonly believed to be very important for children's success: whether a child is raised jointly by the mother and father or by a mother alone, and whether the child is raised in a good residential neighborhood. Although common sense and the mass media assert that living with both parents as well as living in a safe and supportive neighborhood advantage children, social scientists are far from unanimous on the importance of these factors. Some scholars suggest that children manage just fine in mother-headed families. Other researchers question how much of a difference neighborhoods make in how kids turn out. We will discuss each of these scholarly controversies in turn, adding our own contributions, drawing upon the CUNY (City University of New York) and NLSY (the U.S. Department of Labor's National Longitudinal Survey of Youth) surveys.

How Important Is Dad?

Posing this question would have been unthinkable thirty years ago. Back then, research on social mobility dwelled almost exclusively on the father's characteristics—his education, income, and the complexity of his job. Scholars linked those factors to his children's educational prospects and their occupational attainment in adulthood. It was considered self-evident that a family's future depended on the father as the primary wage earner and "head of household." Even though the responsibility for raising children was left almost entirely to mothers, a father's status was considered central to children's mobility prospects.

Families, and researchers' perspectives on them, have undergone major shifts in recent decades. In families with children under one year old, 60 percent of mothers now work for pay, double the rate of the 1970s (U.S. Census Bureau 2001). In households where both parents work, women's earnings now constitute a bigger part of a family's income than in years past: about one-quarter of working wives now earn more than their working husbands (U.S. Census Bureau 2004). Given this increased economic clout of women within two-parent households, it is no longer reasonable to assume that a husband's income or occupation defines the socio-economic status (SES) of a family, let alone determines the educational prospects of the children.

Other demographic trends have drawn us even further away from a father-centered view of the family and social mobility. Divorce rates in America hit a high in the 1970s: about 40 percent of women born in the 1970s will divorce during their lifetime. In addition, 34 percent of births are currently to unwed women (Martin, Park, and Sutton 2002). Divorce plus out-of-wedlock births jointly contribute to large numbers of children being raised solely by their mothers: about one in four American children under eighteen (and nearly half of all African American children) currently live with their mother without a father present (Fields 2004). Even more children live in a mother-headed household at some time in their formative years.

Given these trends, we decided to reverse the father-centered perspective on intergenerational mobility, and instead ask: How important are fathers for their children's success, over and above the contributions of the mother? What is the value added of having a father in the home? After examining whether a two-parent family structure improves children's chances of success, we next ask what it is about a father's presence that makes a difference for children. Do dual-parent families rear their children differently than families headed by a single mother? Is it the added income that a father contributes to the household that matters? Or are the father's occupational complexity, and education the important influences on children's chances?

College Improves a Woman's Chances of Marriage and Her Marital Stability

As a preliminary matter, we should note that quite aside from its educational impact, attending college increases a woman's chances of getting

Table 6.1   Effect of Women's Educational Attainment on Her Marital History, NLSY Women

Outcome	Mother's Education	Bivariate	Propensity Matched Sample
Probability mother was married or partnered when first child born	Entered college	.8757***	.8492***
	No college	.6013	.6707
	Earned B.A.	.9209***	.8967***
	No B.A.	.7148	.8235
Probability mother was married or partnered entire time child was zero to eighteen years old	Entered college	.6248***	.5796***
	No college	.2827	.3368
	Earned B.A.	.7414***	.6824***
	No B.A.	.4163	.6012
Probability mother was married or partnered most of the time child was zero to eighteen years old	Entered college	.8746***	.8422***
	No college	.7085	.7610
	Earned B.A.	.9193***	.9111***
	No B.A.	.7767	.8560

Source: NLSY79.
*p < 0.05; **p < .01; ***p < .001

married and her chances of staying married. Attending college is also associated with a lower likelihood of having a child out of wedlock.[1]

Using the nationwide NLSY sample, we estimate the effect of college on the probability that a woman was married (or had a live-in partner) when her first child was born (see table 6.1). Table 6.1 also shows the probability that a woman was married for most or all of the time between her child's birth and the child's eighteenth birthday. The column labeled "Bivariate" provides probabilities without any statistical controls. Here we see, for example, that 87 percent of women who entered college were married when their first child was born, compared to only 60 percent of women who never entered college. Likewise, 92 percent of women who earned a B.A. had their first child when married, compared to 71 percent of women who never earned a B.A. This tells us that on average, both college going and getting a degree are associated with getting married before having children.

Similarly, we find that women who enter college are very much more likely to remain married the entire time their kids were growing up (62 percent versus 28 percent). So on average, children of educated mothers not only enjoy any cultural benefits that their educated mothers bring to the family, they also have a much higher chance of being raised by two parents—a double dividend, so to speak. Completing a B.A. adds further to marital stability: 74 percent of B.A. holders remained married for the entire time up to their child's eighteenth birthday, compared to only 42 percent of women who failed to get a B.A.

Moreover, college is associated with a longer-lasting marriage even for those women whose marriages do ultimately break up. The bottom panel of table 6.1 shows that 87 percent of women who entered college stayed married (or partnered) for most of the time while their children were growing up, compared to 70 percent of women who never entered college. Ninety-two percent of women who completed a B.A. stayed married for most of the time their children lived at home, compared to 78 percent of women who didn't complete a B.A.

All these differences are statistically significant and are very large in magnitude. However, they overstate the causal effect of higher education on marriage and marital stability, because they don't control for the myriad of background differences between women who do go to college and those who don't, or between B.A. recipients and women who attend college but do not earn a B.A. Following our previous methodology, we addressed such selection biases by creating a sample matched on the propensity of entering college (in the second instance, the propensity for getting a B.A.).[2] The second column in table 6.1, "Propensity Matched," reports the effects of maternal education on marriage and marital stability, now controlling for many background characteristics, including mother's class origin, high school preparation, age, race, IQ, and her psychological levels of mastery and locus of control, using propensity matching. This gives us a better estimate of the causal impact of a college education on marriage and marital stability.

The effects of college education on a woman's marriage and marital stability remain important after adding these controls. The differences are smaller than before, but in all cases but one they remain statistically significant and quite large. The most striking finding, given our focus on children, is that, all else being equal, 58 percent of college women stayed married until their child reached eighteen, compared to only 34 percent of noncollege women. Marital stability is a powerful and unexpected side effect of maternal education and of educational opportunity.

Table 6.2 presents similar analyses for the CUNY sample, where the contrast is limited to that between B.A. holders and women with some college short of a degree. For five of the six comparisons, the more-educated women were, again, advantaged on these marital and stability measures.

Together, these analyses of NLSY and CUNY data indicate that, other factors being equal, having a mother with a college education substantially increases the likelihood that her child will grow up in a two-parent family, that is, that a father will be in the household while a child is growing up. But how consequential is the presence of this father? Do children raised by a single or divorced mother do less well in their

Table 6.2   Effect of Educational Attainment on Marital History of Women with Children, CUNY Women

Marital History	Mother's Education	Bivariate	Propensity Matched Sample
Ever married or partnered	Earned B.A.	.9794***	.9710
	No B.A.	.9543	.9652
Currently married or partnered	Earned B.A.	.8252***	.7741***
	No B.A.	.6909	.6947
Ever a single parent	Earned B.A.	.2368***	.3011***
	No B.A.	.4229	.4455

Source: CUNY Women File.
*p < 0.05; **p < .01; ***p < .001

educational and occupational careers? Since scholars lack consensus on these questions, we will first explain why they disagree, and then add our own analyses.

Do Children Raised by a Single Mother Fare Worse Educationally?

Efforts to study the impact of different family forms on children's development began in earnest in the 1960s, led by Daniel Patrick Moynihan's (1965) controversial report, *The Negro Family: A Case for National Action.* Moynihan was disturbed by the increasing numbers of African American children born out of wedlock and by an escalating rate of marital breakdown within the black community. Moynihan identified high levels of unemployment, poverty, and racial discrimination as causes of these changes in family structure, but he was adamant that in addition to these factors, the increase in families headed by a single mother constituted a major social problem in its own right. He talked about a "tangle of pathology" associated with a black "matriarchal" family structure, and emphasized the deleterious effects on children of absent fathers. Moynihan's report provoked a torrent of criticism, much of which accused him of blaming the victim, but by the 1970s, divorce rates among whites had also climbed to new highs, leading scholars to extend his critique of mother-centered families to the American population in general.

Two sociologists, Beverly Duncan and Otis Dudley Duncan (1969), employed large-scale surveys to show that, on average, men raised in single-parent households attained fewer years of education and were employed in jobs of lower prestige than men who grew up in two-parent households. Since then, as more multigenerational data sets have become available, evidence has accumulated supporting the claim that growing up in a single-parent family is disadvantageous for children. The most wide-ranging compilation of this research can be found in *Growing Up with a Single Parent*, by Sara McLanahan and Gary Sandefur (1994); it summarized prior studies and presented new analyses using the Panel Study of Income Dynamics, the High School and Beyond Study, the NLSY, and the National Study of Families and Households. Their findings were consistent and unambiguous: on average, children who grew up in single-parent families were more likely to drop out of high school, had lower grade-point averages, and were less likely to go to college than children who grew up in two-parent families. Within single-parent families, children raised by unwed mothers fared worse than those raised by divorced mothers.

Despite these studies' findings, a few scholars have dissented from the view that single-parenthood per se disadvantages children (see, for example, Biblarz and Raftery 1999; Biblarz, Raftery, and Bucur 1997; Lang and Zagorsky 2001). At the surface, this disagreement appears to hang on technical issues, but deeper scrutiny shows that the dispute centers on how causal processes are conceptualized. To explain what is at stake requires some discussion of terminology and other technical issues to distinguish variables according to their positions along a causal chain.

Consider the following, an oversimplified causal sequence among four variables:

A		B		C		D
growing up in a poor family	→	single motherhood	→	lower income	→	worse child outcomes
Exogenous variable		*Treatment, or "cause"*		*Endogenous, or mediating, variable*		*Outcome dependent variable or "effect"*

In the diagram, an arrow implies that the factor to the left causes or influences the factor or variable to the right of the arrow. So growing up in poverty increases the likelihood of becoming a single mother, which in turn typically leads to lower family income, which in turn leads to worse child educational outcomes, on average. In this schema, being a single mother may be considered to be a "treatment" (variable B), and assessing the influence of this treatment on the child outcome D is our main intellectual task. Of particular importance is C, the family income that the child experiences while growing up with the mother. C is called an "endogenous variable" because lower family income is caused in part by the treatment: as the sole earner in the household, single mothers tend to have lower household incomes than two-parent families. C is also called an "intervening variable" because it stands between the treatment or cause and the outcome.

In a regression model, the coefficient for the treatment variable indicates how large the effect of the treatment is upon the child outcome: how much of a difference growing up in a single parent family makes for a child. However, this treatment coefficient will increase or decrease, depending on what other predictor variables the researcher includes or leaves out of the regression model. This inclusion or exclusion of predictors other than the "treatment" is what fuels researchers' conflicting interpretations of single parenting.

If a regression model fails to include exogenous variables such as mother's growing up in poverty, then the coefficient for the treatment variable (being a single mother) may overstate the true effect of the single mothering. Using this logic, the sociologists Timothy Biblarz and Adrian Raftery (1999, 328) fault studies that omit the SES of the single mother's parents (their income, education, and occupation—indicators of the mother's socioeconomic origins) and argue that this omission artificially increases the apparent negative effects of having a single mother. When these socioeconomic variables are omitted, the effects of a mother's class origins erroneously become bundled into the regression coefficient for single mother. Hence, leaving exogenous variables out of an analysis creates what is known as "omitted-variable bias," which researchers on both sides of the argument acknowledge as a fault and try to avoid.

How to deal with the endogenous, or intervening, variables is more contentious. In the absence of any intervening variables in a statistical model, the coefficient for the treatment variable represents the total effect of having a single parent on the child's outcome. However, when intervening variables are included in a regression model, the coefficient for the single-mother variable represents something different: it estimates only the direct effect of having a single mother on the child's outcome, after subtracting any indirect effects of having a single mother that occur via the intervening variables. In the example above, when mother's income is included, the coefficient measures the direct effect of being raised by a single mother, after subtracting that part of the effect of single parenting that works via lower income.

In practice, including intervening variables like C in a regression model reduces the magnitude of the single-mother effect, sometimes to zero. That creates the impression that single parenting does not adversely affect children. But *should* one include intervening variables? The conventional view (which we share) is that intervening variables should *not* appear in a regression if one's purpose is to estimate the total effect of a treatment, such as being raised by a single mother. Unfortunately, some scholars do include intervening variables into regression models; when this causes the treatment effect to be greatly reduced or become zero, they then interpret this as implying that the intervening variable is the "true cause" of the outcome, and that the treatment (single mothering) is not really consequential.

For example, Biblarz and Raftery (1999, 322) write: "Other studies . . . show that once other factors are taken into account, children from single-mother families do approximately as well as children from two-biological-parent families"; "All else being equal (including number of siblings and so on), a single mother family has no effect on children's occupational attainment" (348); and "We find that there is no effect of growing up in a single-mother family once family head's socio-economic location (employment, occupation) is taken into account" (535). In each of these instances, the "all else being equal" and the "other factors" being taken into account are intervening endogenous variables. It is not surprising that the single-mother effect "disappears" after one has controlled for intervening variables. These "other factors" are influenced by single-parent status and are the mechanisms through which the single-parent family has a deleterious impact on children. They do *not* negate the fact that on average children of single parents will be disadvantaged because of the form of family in which they grew up.

Another example of (erroneously) controlling for intervening variables can be found in an article by two economists, Kevin Lang and Jay Zagorsky (2001), titled "Does Growing Up with a Parent Absent Really Hurt?" Their initial analyses indicate that children from two-parent families score significantly higher on cognitive-skills tests, complete more years of education, are more likely to be married, and enjoy significantly higher incomes in adulthood than children who grew up in single-parent households. This makes a strong case that family structure affects children's prospects, and that children of a single parent are at a considerable disadvantage.

However, these researchers then add to their models the offspring's highest grade completed and his or her cognitive-skills test score. Including these two variables is unfortunate, because they are endogenous intervening variables: Lang and Zagorsky's own analyses showed that both were predicted by single parenting. After those intervening variables were added to the regression model, the coefficient for single parenting ceased to be statistically significant, leading Lang and Zagorsky (2001, 253) to conclude, "Econometric tests . . . show little evidence that a parent's absence affects economic well-being in adulthood." On the contrary, single parenting was a statistically significant predictor of the offspring's economic well-being in adulthood, until intervening or downstream variables were included in the model. Once again, controlling for endogenous variables results in a misleading interpretation of single parenting.[3]

To summarize: Past disagreements among scholars over the effects of single parenting were caused by researchers' treatment of endogenous intervening variables as control variables in regression models. This decision reduces the apparent effect of growing up in a single family. Whenever this conceptual mistake is avoided, the evidence is clear and convincing that children who grow up in single-parent families experience worse educational outcomes that are attributable to growing up in a single-parent family. That conclusion is supported by numerous analyses involving several high-quality national data sets.

Previous debates about single-mother families, and arguments over what variables to omit or include, nevertheless failed to address one additional problem in ascertaining the true effect of family configurations. They did not speak to selection bias: the idea that single mothers might differ systematically from married mothers in terms of background characteristics, such as IQ or self esteem or social class, that predate the marriage breakup. It is possible that scholars' current understanding of single-parent effects would change if we were able to remove selection bias. Biblarz and Raftery (1999, 326) note that this problem remains unresolved: "One of the unanswered questions in family structure research is whether the observed negative effect of alternative families on children represents a selection effect."

One way to examine selection bias has been to examine how children were doing before the marital breakup, as well as afterward. For example, Andrew Cherlin and his colleagues (1991) found that boys whose parents divorced had been having behavioral difficulties for years before the divorce, suggesting that the boys' problems after divorce should not be attributed entirely to the divorce itself. However, in a later study with a much larger sample, Donna Morrison and Cherlin (1995) found that the negative impact of divorce on boys was not reduced, after controlling for predivorce attributes of the children and their families. Gary Painter and David Levine (2000) took a similar approach, controlling for family characteristics prior to divorce. They observed that divorce during a child's high school years had roughly the same deleterious effects even after controlling for predivorce attributes. On balance, this research has tended to support the idea that divorce has negative consequences for children, and to suggest that selection effects are not a major issue.

We will address the selection issue employing the counterfactual model of causal inference (propensity matching), whose details are discussed in the methodological appendix. This is a recent and powerful technique for reducing selection bias, and for estimating the true effect of a treatment like single parenting on children's outcomes.

Table 6.3 shows the effects of various family configurations on educational outcomes, for all children and then separately, by race. Each panel in this table examines a different aspect of family structure or stability. The top panel in the table is limited to children who were born into two-parent families. Within this group, it contrasts those children who lived with both their mother and father from birth till age eighteen (labeled "Two-Parent Family") with other children where the parents later split up or one parent died, labeled "Disrupted Family." This comparison reveals how family stability affects children.

We first report bivariate effects, which indicate the overall or average effect of having a stable two-parent family throughout childhood, and we then estimate the effect of a stable two-parent family, after propensity-score matching for maternal differences such as class, race, age, education, psychological attributes, and IQ, as well as for family income measured in the year prior to the child's birth.

The NLSY staff visited children's homes to observe interactions between mothers and children and to measure the cognitive environment provided to children under seven years old. In panel A of table 6.3 we examine this cognitive stimulation in the home as a possible outcome of family stability. The column labeled "Bivariate" shows a large significant difference in the home cognitive environment of children who grew up in intact two-parent families as compared to that of children in disrupted families: a .4 standard deviation difference. After controlling for background differences (including income) and selection, we still find a substantial, though smaller, effect: children in stable two-parent families grew up in a more cognitively stimulating environment (.176 standard deviations more). Evidently, undisrupted two-parent families are able to provide, on average, a richer, cognitively more stimulating environment for their young children. This finding was also evident in separate analyses for black, white, and Hispanic families.

Panel A of table 6.3 also shows each child's reading and math ability, measured on several different occasions between ages four and seventeen. Preliminary analyses indicated that these assessments were relatively stable from year to year, so we averaged each student's scores over all the occasions. Children who grew up in a stable two-parent family from birth to age eighteen had higher test scores and were more likely to go to college than similar children who started life in a two-parent family but later faced a family disruption. The bivariate effects are large, .42 standard deviation, but the size of that effect shrinks after controlling for selection biases to a .09 standard deviation lead in test scores. This is a small effect. The picture is very similar for white and Hispanic children. Looking at African American children separately, the effect of a stable two-parent family is not as statistically significant as for whites and Hispanics. This lack of statistical significance is likely due to small

Table 6.3 Effects of Family Disruption and Structure on Children's Outcomes, NLSY Children

Panel A

Treatment variable: Child lived with mother and her spouse or partner all the time growing up (children born into two-parent families only)

Dependent variables: Children's educational outcomes

	All Children		Black Only		White Only		Hispanic Only	
	Bivariate	Matched	Bivariate	Matched	Bivariate	Matched	Bivariate	Matched
Home cognitive								
Treatment effect size	.4078***	.1760***	.3977***	.2711***	.3209***	.2094***	.1821***	.0837*
Predicted value: two-parent family	.3512	.1941	.0840	.0238	.5445	.4475	-.1765	-.2578
Predicted value: disrupted family	-.0566	.0182	-.3137	-.2472	.2236	.2381	-.3585	-.3415
	N = 4,810	N = 2,886	N = 760	N = 428	N = 2,706	N = 1,562	N = 1,012	N = 704
Math and reading								
Treatment effect size	.4204***	.0922***	.3505***	.0739+	.3156***	.1113***	.2090***	.1340***
Predicted value: two-parent family	.3610	.1327	-.0443	-.1772	.5594	.3832	-.1194	-.2040
Predicted value: disrupted family	-.0594	.0405	-.3948	-.2511	.2437	.2719	-.3284	-.3380
	N = 4,922	N = 2,938	N = 796	N = 436	N = 2,750	N = 1,586	N = 1,034	N = 714
College going								
Treatment effect size	.4988***	.2967**	.1302	—	.7250***	.6255***	.3881*	—
Predicted value: two-parent family	.5976	.5862	.4885	—	.6715	.6587	.5484	—
Predicted value: disrupted family	.4742	.5129	.4561	—	.4975	.5080	.4517	—
	N = 648	N = 430	N = 154	—	N = 299	N = 242	N = 151	—

Panel B

Treatment variable: Child lived with mother and her spouse or partner most of the time growing up
Dependent variables: Children's educational outcomes

	All Children		Black Only		White Only		Hispanic Only	
	Bivariate	Matched	Bivariate	Matched	Bivariate	Matched	Bivariate	Matched
Home cognitive								
Treatment effect size	.5661***	.1918***	.4441***	.2596***	.4700***	.2350***	.1808***	.0118
Predicted value: most or all of time	.1560	−.1292	−.0820	−.1465	.3760	.1597	−.2634	−.4252
Predicted value: less than half	−.4101	−.3210	−.5261	−.4061	−.0940	−.0753	−.4443	−.4370
	N = 9,372	N = 3,378	N = 2,640	N = 1,704	N = 4,312	N = 801	N = 1,851	N = 725
Math and reading								
Treatment effect size	.5002***	.0692**	.2297***	.0649**	.3011***	.0577+	.1491***	.0506+
Predicted value: most or all of time	.1462	−.1886	−.2546	−.3201	.4083	.1652	−.2208	−.3161
Predicted value: less than half	−.3541	−.2578	−.4843	−.3850	.1073	.1075	−.3699	−.3667
	N = 8,153	N = 3,520	N = 2,505	N = 1,774	N = 3,542	N = 833	N = 1,633	N = 756
College going								
Treatment effect size	.2301***	−.0639	.1520+	.0557	.3222*	.1892	−.2375+	−.3921**
Predicted value: most or all of time	.5205	.4762	.4792	.4781	.5685	.5356	.4949	.4560
Predicted value: less than half	.4631	.4922	.4414	.4642	.4884	.4884	.5541	.5537
	N = 1,329	N = 656	N = 559	N = 366	N = 430	N = 114	N = 270	N = 148

(Table continues on p. 138.)

Table 6.3 *Continued*

Panel C
Treatment variable: Child lived with single parent the entire time
Dependent variables: Children's educational outcomes

	All Children		Black Only		White Only		Hispanic Only	
	Bivariate	Matched	Bivariate	Matched	Bivariate	Matched	Bivariate	Matched
Home cognitive								
Treatment effect size	-.6137***	-.1423***	-.3023***	-.1261***	-.5055***	—	-.4830***	-.1812**
Predicted value: ever two-parent	.0501	-.4121	-.2769	-.4426	.3574	—	-.2934	-.5929
Predicted value: single parent only	-.5636	-.5544	-.5792	-.5687	-.1481	—	-.7764	-.7741
	N = 7,883	N = 1,442	N = 2,379	N = 1,196	N = 3,466	—	N = 1,582	N = 124
Math and reading								
Treatment effect size	-.5359***	-.0473*	-.1958***	-.0676**	-.1945**	—	-.1957***	.0852
Predicted value: ever two-parent	.0504	-.4315	-.3422	-.4632	.3754	—	-.2480	-.5262
Predicted value: single parent only	-.4855	-.4787	-.5380	-.5308	.1809	—	-.4436	-.4410
	N = 8,153	N = 1,522	N = 2,505	N = 1,263	N = 3,542	—	N = 1,633	N = 130
College going								
Treatment effect size	-.4496***	-.1834	-.3255***	-.1663	—	—	-.0380	—
Predicted value: ever two-parent	.5110	.4455	.4739	.4363	—	—	.5095	—
Predicted value: single parent only	.4000	.4008	.3942	.3959	—	—	.5000	—
	N = 1,328	N = 290	N = 559	N = 260	—	—	N = 269	—

Panel D

Treatment variable: Child lived in stable two-parent family versus child lived with single mother for all of childhood

Dependent variables: Children's educational outcomes

	All Children		Black Only		White Only		Hispanic Only	
	Bivariate	Matched	Bivariate	Matched	Bivariate	Matched	Bivariate	Matched
Home cognitive								
Treatment effect size	.8544***	.2462***	.5510***	.2524***	.6621***	—	.5640***	.2206**
Predicted value: two-parent family	.2909	-.1600	-.0282	-.1240	.5140	—	-.2124	-.5573
Predicted value: single parent	-.5636	-.4062	-.5792	-.3764	-.1481	—	-.7764	-.7780
	N = 4,006	N = 792	N = 1,012	N = 554	N = 2,056	—	N = 691	N = 118
Math and reading								
Treatment effect size	.7785***	.1048***	.4022***	.1458***	.3376***	—	.2897***	.0067
Predicted value: two-parent family	.2931	-.2383	-.1358	-.2523	.5185	—	-.1539	-.4439
Predicted value: single parent	-.4855	-.3431	-.5380	-.3981	.1809	—	-.4436	-.4506
	N = 4096	N = 822	N = 1,058	N = 572	N = 2,079	—	N = 703	N = 122
College going								
Treatment effect size	.7840***	.0779	—	—	—	—	—	—
Predicted value: two-parent family	.5935	.4962	—	—	—	—	—	—
Predicted value: single parent	.4000	.4767	—	—	—	—	—	—
	N = 428	N = 108	—	—	—	—	—	—

Source: NLSY79.
†< p < .10; *p < 0.05; **p < .01; ***p < .001

sample sizes: far fewer black children were born into two-parent families than children in other ethnic groups, and fewer still of those families remained intact for the eighteen years in which the child grew up, making these comparisons problematic in terms of statistical power: we don't have enough cases.

Our third outcome variable in panel A measures whether a child attended college at any point after high school. This variable only applies to students aged eighteen or older who have graduated from high school, so the sample size shrinks compared to that used in the previous skills tests measure. Nevertheless, we observe a statistically significant difference in the proportion of children from stable two-parent families who enter college compared to children from disrupted families. The effect size is initially about half a standard deviation in the bivariate and shrinks to .29 in the propensity model, which controls for family income and many aspects of parental family background. Growing up in a two-parent family, separate from having higher income or other advantages, benefits children in terms of college going. Small sample sizes again prevent us from determining whether this effect is linked to race and ethnicity. For whites, the effect seems larger than for all races taken together.

To recap, looking only at children who were born into two-parent families, those whose parents remained together throughout a child's upbringing enjoyed a clear advantage in terms of the cognitive environment in the home, in math and reading test scores, and in likelihood of entering college, over otherwise similar children whose parents separated, divorced, or were widowed. These advantages were associated with the two-parent family structure itself, and are evident even after removing effects of income, parental education, and other factors.

There are two different explanations for why growing up in a two-parent family proves advantageous for children. According to one, which emphasizes the number of caregivers, two parents can more easily provide materially for children than one, and two people are more effective in providing nurturance and guidance or control than one single parent. According to the second explanation, which emphasizes the emotional upheavals that occur when a two-parent family breaks up and the harm that the breakup itself does to children, it is the stability of a family that is important, rather than the number of parents. Both explanations are plausible, and it is possible that both may be operating when we see that children in single-parent families show worse developmental outcomes. We can tease apart these alternative explanations by contrasting several different family configurations, some stable ones and others disrupted ones, and looking at the effects on children (see the remaining panels of table 6.3).

In panel B, we compare children who lived in a two-parent family for half or more of their childhood with children who lived in a two-parent family for less than half of the time between birth and eighteen years old. There are "disrupted families" in both groups. The findings indicate that children who were in two-parent families for most of their childhood years did better than those who were in such families for less than half of their childhood. The former experienced more cognitive stimulation in the home and had higher test scores in reading and math. The effects on a child's likelihood of going to college disappeared, however, after propensity-score matching.

In panel C of table 6.3 we compare children who grew up entirely with a single mother with children who ever lived with two parents. This is an important comparison because some scholars believe that children who grow up with a single parent throughout their childhood enjoy a stable family environment, and therefore do not suffer any disadvantage. However, the bivariate contrasts do not support that conclusion: there are large statistically significant differences in cognitive stimulation, test scores, and going to college. In each case, children who spent their whole childhood with a single mother are worse off than children who ever lived in a two-parent household.

Could this be an artifact of selection bias? The propensity-score matched analyses are intended to reduce that possibility. They indicate that children who always lived with a single mother had lower test scores and experienced a less cognitively stimulating environment than otherwise similar children who lived with two parents for part of their upbringing. The separate analyses for African American children are especially compelling. There were clear differences between black children raised by single mothers and those raised at least part of the time in two-parent families, even after background differences were controlled (including maternal IQ and income prior to the child's birth). The children of black single mothers fared worse in terms of cognitive environment and test scores, although college going did not seem to be affected. (Matched analyses for whites are missing from this table because there weren't enough cases of white children raised by single mothers for all of their childhood.)

Panel D of table 6.3 contrasts children who grew up in a single-parent family from birth to eighteen with other children who grew up in a two-parent family from birth to eighteen. None of these children experienced a marital disruption: they all grew up in a family structure that stayed the same throughout their childhood. The bivariate effects of growing up in a single- versus a two-parent family were huge: on cognitive environment, test scores, and college going, children in stable two-parent families averaged three quarters of a standard deviation or more than their counterparts in stable single-parent families. The matched analyses control for differences in race, class background, maternal IQ and psychological orientation, maternal education, and family income immediately before the child's birth. They indicate that children raised in intact two-parent families still enjoy substantial advantages in terms of cognitive environment and test scores (though not in college going). After propensity matching, we encountered inadequate sample sizes for white and Hispanic children, but the sample size for black children was sufficient for a separate analysis. Again, African American children who were raised in two-parent families scored significantly higher on tests and experienced a more stimulating home environment than their counterparts who were raised in single families, even after controlling for background differences, including family income and earnings prior to the child's birth.

The measures of family structure for the CUNY sample are less elaborate than those provided by the NLSY. Table 6.4 provides estimates for the effect of family structure for bivariate and matched models, on all children and then separately by race, for the CUNY sample. Panel A of the table focuses on family disruptions. For children as a whole, disruption is associated with worse educational outcomes at three stages of a child's life. The effects for high school and college were quite large: from .31 to .57 standard deviations in the matched analyses. Looking at the racial breakdowns, we see, for all three racial or ethnic groups, that children in disrupted families had significantly worse outcomes in high school and in terms of entering college. The results for elementary school were not statistically significant in the matched models for black and Hispanic children, however.

Panel B in table 6.4 compares children who were in two-parent families with all other children. When all racial groups were considered together, children who grew up with two parents for most of the time did significantly better in high school and were more likely to attend college (86 percent versus 80 percent in the propensity-matched model). When racial groups were examined separately, it was evident that the effects were significant for white and Hispanic children but not for black children.

Summarizing the NLSY and the CUNY results, these analyses indicate that children who grow up in an intact two-parent family have a clear advantage over children whose two-parent families break up. However, children who spend most of their preschool and school years in a two-parent family still do better in reading and math skills than children who spend no time or less than half their years in a two-parent family. Finally, children who grow up with a single parent all of the time have significantly lower skills-test results than children from two-parent families, even after controlling for maternal class background, race, IQ, high school preparation, and initial income, compared to children who are not raised continuously by a single mother. These deleterious consequences of growing up in a single-parent family are unlikely to be artifacts

Table 6.4 Effect of Family Disruptions on Children's Outcomes: CUNY Children

Panel A
Treatment variable: Child experienced no family disruptions
Dependent variables: Children's educational outcomes

	All Children		Black Only		White Only		Hispanic Only	
	Bivariate	Matched	Bivariate	Matched	Bivariate	Matched	Bivariate	Matched
Elementary school success								
Treatment effect size	.1929***	.0922***	-.0171	-.0391	.1335***	.1420***	.0903**	.0490
Predicted value: no disruptions	.1737	.1167	-.1304	-.1332	.2307	.2568	-.0825	-.1234
Predicted value: disrupted family	-.0192	.0245	-.1133	-.0941	.0972	.1148	-.1728	-.1724
	N = 2,632	N = 1,370	N = 460	N = 280	N = 1,877	N = 868	N = 295	N = 222
High school success								
Treatment effect size	.4634***	.3172***	.1577***	.1271**	.4416***	.3993***	.3166***	.2279***
Predicted value: no disruptions	.3237	.2351	-.0385	-.0436	.3981	.3932	.0321	-.0155
Predicted value: disrupted family	-.1397	-.0821	-.1962	-.1707	-.0435	-.0061	-.2845	-.2124
	N = 2,026	N = 1,116	N = 401	N = 238	N = 1,379	N = 692	N = 246	N = 186
Went to college								
Treatment effect size	1.414***	.5718***	.5669***	.3782**	1.247***	.5078***	1.247***	1.009***
Predicted value: no disruptions	.9563	.9302	.8679	.8670	.9724	.9571	.9305	.9214
Predicted value: disrupted family	.8416	.8826	.7885	.8171	.9102	.9308	.7938	.8103
	N = 1,346	N = 762	N = 316	N = 178	N = 857	N = 456	N = 174	N = 128

(Table continues on p. 144.)

Table 6.4 *Continued*

Panel B
Treatment variable: Child lived in two-parent family most of the time
Dependent variables: Children's educational outcomes

	All Children		Black Only		White Only		Hispanic Only	
	Bivariate	Matched	Bivariate	Matched	Bivariate	Matched	Bivariate	Matched
Elementary school success								
Treatment effect size	.2241***	.0152	-.0332	-.0658	.2172***	.0957	.1124**	.0375
Predicted value: two-parent family	.1310	-.0725	-.1379	-.1729	.2091	.0949	-.1037	.1653
Predicted value: disrupted family	-.0931	-.0877	-.1047	-.1071	-.0081	-.0008	-.2161	-.2028
	N = 2,477	N = 672	N = 437	N = 285	N = 1,753	N = 248	N = 286	N = 138
High school success								
Treatment effect size	.4309***	.1587***	.0522	-.0042	.5703***	.3586***	.1546***	.1614**
Predicted value: two-parent family	.2050	-.0609	-.1420	-.1949	.3228	.1140	.1041	-.0773
Predicted value: disrupted family	-.2259	-.2196	-.1942	-.1907	-.2475	-.2446	-.2587	-.2387
	N = 1,897	N = 580	N = 382	N = 256	N = 1,278	N = 206	N = 237	N = 118
Went to college								
Treatment effect size	1.153***	.4068***	.2426*	.1185	1.562***	.8093*	.7839***	.8195***
Predicted value: two-parent family	.9243	.8578	.8147	.8026	.9619	.9262	.8799	.8830
Predicted value: disrupted family	.7942	.8006	.7753	.7831	.8410	.8482	.7699	.7687
	N = 1,222	N = 424	N = 297	N = 204	N = 758	N = 132	N = 166	N = 86

Source: CUNY Women File.
*p < 0.05; **p < .01; ***p < .001

of selection bias, because they were also apparent in propensity-matched models.

We conclude that the presence of a father in the home is a positive force for a child's educational career. For child outcomes, having two parents in the home is better than having one, and avoiding a change in family structure during childhood, such as a divorce, is an additional positive for the child's successful development.

What Characteristics of Fathers Matter Most?

Having determined that children in two-parent families indeed enjoy educational advantages compared to children raised without resident fathers, we assess what it is about having a father at home that enhances children's educational chances. Prior research suggests a focus on three mechanisms: the father's education, the complexity of his job, and his monetary contribution to the household.

Table 6.5 shows our analyses of the national NLSY data. Models 1 and 3 are limited to children of stable two-parent families. The rationale is to hold family structure constant for this particular analysis. We focus on two outcome variables: the child's test scores and the cognitive environment of the home, as measured by visits by researchers.

The standardized coefficients in table 6.5 inform us about the relative importance of parents' education, occupations, and earnings for these children's outcomes. We find that mother's education, father's education, mother's occupational complexity, father's occupational complexity, and family income are each separate statistically significant predictors of children's academic test scores. It is noteworthy that father's education has a much greater effect on children than his occupational complexity and a slightly larger effect than his earnings. This is especially striking, given that this model only estimates the direct effect of parental education on children's outcomes in the coefficients for education. Since education results in higher occupational complexity and higher earnings, some considerable additional influence of parents' education operates indirectly via income and job complexity, but these indirect consequences are not captured by the educational coefficients in table 6.5. These regressions therefore understate, or provide a conservative picture of the relative importance of education vis-à-vis occupational complexity and earnings.

Comparing the size of the coefficients (which are standardized), we also discover that a given amount of maternal education has a larger effect on children's scores than the equivalent amount of paternal education does, whereas the opposite is true for earnings.

Mothers seem to influence their children more through their education; fathers through their earning power. Nevertheless, the overall

Table 6.5 The Relative Effect of Maternal and Paternal Education, Occupational Complexity, and Earnings (Standardized Coefficients or Betas)

	Model 1 Test Scores, Children Raised in Stable Two-Parent Families	Model 2 Test Scores, Children Raised in Disrupted Two-Parent Families	Model 3 HOME Cognitive Stimulation, Children Raised in Stable Two-Parent Families	Model 4 HOME Cognitive Stimulation, Children Raised in Disrupted Two-Parent Families
Mother's educational attainment	.1597***	.1403***	.1619***	.1782***
Father's educational attainment	.1085***	.1653***	.1401***	.1409***
Mother's occupational complexity	.0796***	.0447**	.0629**	.1208***
Father's occupational complexity	.0299*	.0004	.0358*	.0209
Mother's earnings	.0516**	.0703**	.0527**	.0576**
Father's earnings	.1377***	.1489***	.1272***	.1125***
Black female	-.4814***	-.3515***	-.5640***	-.4023***
Black male	-.7704***	-.6121***	-.6842***	-.5174***
Hispanic female	-.6500***	-.5259***	-.3917***	-.3301***
Hispanic male	-.5595***	-.2988***	-.4036***	-.5221***
White male	-.1249***	-.1546***	-.0874**	-.0880**
Age	.0115***	.0440***	.0348***	.0408***
Mother's hours worked	.0835***	.1082***	.0259	.0281
Mother's X father's earnings	-.0223***	-.0264***	-.0572***	-.0172
Constant	.2295***	-.1958***	-.2585***	-.5033***
R-square	.2255	.2688	.1886	.2123
	N = 1,752	N = 1,749	N = 1,611	N = 1,599

Source: NLSY79–Children.
*p < .05; **p < .01; ***p < .001

picture is one where the resources that both parents bring to the family, both material and educational, contribute additively to the cognitive environment of the home and to children's academic performance.

Our analyses also indicate that the effects of all three parental resources—education, job complexity, and earnings—on children's outcomes are considerably smaller than the effects of race. Black male students, for example, have test scores that on average are .77 standard deviation lower than white female students (the reference group), even after controlling for parental education, income, and job complexity. This large racial gap in children's test scores is of great concern to social scientists and policymakers, especially since they are net of differences in income, education, and other resources. Recent studies show that a substantial racial skills gap has formed by the time children enter kindergarten (Fryer and Levitt 2004; Jencks and Philips 1998; Lee and Burkam 2002).

The implication of these findings, along with our own analyses, is that while maternal access to higher education is clearly associated with better outcomes for children, parental education in itself is not enough to compensate for the large disparity between black and white children in educational outcomes. In other words, higher maternal education and higher family income in the parents' generation attenuate but by no means eradicate race-based educational disadvantages for the next generation.

Consistent with previous research, our models also indicate that mother's work hours are related to children's academic test scores in the NLSY, net of race, earnings, and education (Parcel and Menaghan 1994). On average, children do better, the fewer hours their mother works, net of earnings and the other predictors, but fathers' hours worked has no significant effect. Such findings fuel ongoing debates about gender roles and child-rearing practices (see Barnett and Rivers 1998).

Models 2 and 4 in table 6.5 show equivalent regressions, but for a broader family type—children who grew up in two-parent families for only part of their childhood—and the results are very similar to those found for the previous models.

Summary of the Effects of Family Structure on Children

First, we found that women who went to college were more likely to marry or have a partner and their family relationships were considerably more likely to last than women who did not get to college. Thus, higher education influences family structure.

We reconfirmed previous research findings that children raised in two-parent families had better educational outcomes than children raised either in single-parent families or in two-parent families that break up.

Moreover, children from stable two-parent families were educationally better off than children of stable single-parent families. These advantages of growing up in a two-parent family were evident even after controlling for differences in family income, parental background, and so forth. Our analyses also minimized selection effects. Separate analyses examined the impact of family disruption, and found that disruption per se was associated with significantly worse child outcomes, net of income and parental background. These findings contradict those who argue that the apparent disadvantage of single parenting is just a reflection of single-parent families' having lower incomes. Both single parenting and disrupted two-parent families have deleterious effects on children's educational outcomes.

Among two-parent families, we looked for factors that improved children's chances, and we confirmed earlier research: family income, parental education, and parental job complexity separately contribute to better educational chances for children. The beneficial effects of parental education are larger than those of income and job complexity, but all three elements help children's educational chances. Mother's and father's contributions are additive in their effects on children's outcomes, which is why the presence of a father in the family home provides important advantages improving children's chances of success.

In the next section, we will examine an additional factor believed to influence children's educational progress: the kind of neighborhood a child grows up in.

Neighborhoods and Children's Prospects

"It takes a village to raise a child." Most sociologists would acknowledge the truth in this African proverb—the idea that people outside the immediate family play important roles in children's intellectual and moral development, and that where a child grows up influences the child's prospects. Teasing out the various ways that this occurs, however, has proved to be a major intellectual challenge. Over the last decade or so, hundreds of research articles have been published in the United States about "neighborhood effects." Some try to establish how much neighborhoods influence children's development. Others seek clarity about what features of a neighborhood matter: the presence of good schools, the amount of crime, the presence of strong social networks and trust among adult neighbors, the character of children's peer groups and the local teen culture, the incidence of unemployed adults in the community, the presence of affluent or educated neighbors. This literature is also fraught with contention. Some scholars note that what seem to be neighborhood effects could be illusory: statistical artifacts produced by measurement error in family characteristics. Proponents and critics alike agree that selection effects are a major problem in estimating the true effects of neighborhood. Finally, critics have pointed out that many reported neighborhood effects are really small in magnitude and therefore are not very important.[4]

Our main interest in considering neighborhoods is to find out whether access to higher education affects the kind of neighborhood that a woman raises her children in, and then whether the choice of neighborhood has an impact on children's educational prospects. In other words, we want to know whether neighborhood quality is a mechanism or route by which parental higher education is linked to children's success.

On the basis of preliminary analyses, we identified two variables in the NLSY survey that measured aspects of neighborhood quality. One asked mothers to rate how good a place their neighborhood was in terms of raising children. The second used census data to report the percentage of persons living in a census tract who had earned a B.A. degree or a higher educational credential. (The latter proved to be a better predictor of children's outcomes than alternatives such as mean household income in a tract, or percentage of tract population living in poverty, or percentage of minority residents.)

Analyses presented in table 6.6 indicate whether women who attended college lived in better neighborhoods than women who never entered college, and also whether women who earned a B.A. lived in better neighborhoods than those without a B.A. As expected, on average, more-educated women live in better neighborhoods, using both measures of neighborhood quality, looking simply at bivariate relationships. The less obvious finding is that regression analyses indicated that college-educated mothers lived in significantly better neighborhoods, even after controlling for their class background, race, high school preparation, household income, and psychological aspects of mastery and self-esteem. When we used propensity-score-matched samples, to minimize selection bias, the same picture emerged.

Given the high degree of residential segregation faced by African Americans, we undertook a separate regression analysis for blacks. The effects of maternal education upon neighborhood quality on children were, if anything, even stronger for African American women than for the NLSY sample as a whole.[5]

Evidently, college-educated mothers tended to raise their children in significantly better neighborhoods. But does living in a better neighborhood pay off in terms of better educational outcomes for their children? Does residential neighborhood matter for child outcomes, after controlling for the characteristics of the child's family: class background, income, parental education, and so on? We are looking for an independent contribution of neighborhood.

Table 6.6   Effect of Maternal Education on the Neighborhood in Which Children Are Raised

Maternal Education	Bivariate	OLS Regression	Propensity Matched Sample	Regression, Black Only
Mother's assessment of her neighborhood in standard deviation units				
Mother went to college	.48***	.14**	.06	.30**
Mother earned B.A.	.77***	.21***	.25***	.64***
Census tract percentage B.A. or higher				
Mother went to college	7.63***	3.07***	1.29*	n/a
Mother earned B.A.	14.81***	8.36***	4.74**	3.17**

Source: Authors' analyses of NLSY79, including restricted geocoded data.
Note: Census tract characteristics were measured when children were five to seven years old.
*p < .05; ** p < .01; *** p < .001

For this purpose, we focused on three children's outcomes: the home cognitive stimulation score for children aged three to five; children's PIAT math and reading scores, assessed when the child was between five and seven years old; and a Behavior Problems index, measured when children were between five and ten years old.

Table 6.7 shows how mothers themselves defined good neighborhood quality. Using that definition, we found that better neighborhood quality was associated with significantly higher cognitive stimulation scores and a lower frequency of child problems, but did not influence math and reading scores. The effect sizes were small to moderate. When we looked at racial and ethnic groups separately, the patterns held for blacks and whites but were less consistent for Hispanic families.

In table 6.8, looking at the influence of living in a more highly educated neighborhood, we found that growing up in a neighborhood with more college-educated residents was significantly associated with greater home cognitive stimulation and higher math and reading scores, but was not related to behavioral problems. Those effects remained statistically significant in propensity models that reduced selection bias, but the effects were quite small. The results were less clear when we looked separately at each racial and ethnic group; in particular, African American children seemed not to gain significantly from living in a more-educated neighborhood. This may be due to statistical power issues, although it is consistent with Mary Patillo-McCoy's (1999) ethnographic study that found that black families who moved to more affluent black suburbs were unable to isolate their children from negative influences and behaviors.

Table 6.7 Effect of Growing Up in a Neighborhood That Is Good for Raising Children

(Mother rated neighborhood as an "excellent" or "very good" place to raise children, measured before outcomes.)

Outcome	Bivariate	Regression	Propensity Matched Sample	Regression, Black Only	Regression, Hispanic Only	Regression, White Only	Regression, Boys Only	Regression, Girls Only
HOME cognitive stimulation score, ages three to five	.630***	.122***	.126**	.257***	-.009	.099**	.114**	.120**
PIAT math and reading, for ages five to seven	.416***	.063	.021	-.020	-.011	.042	.041	.017
Behavior Problems Index, ages six to ten	-.420***	-.206***	-.225***	-.188*	-.293**	-.199***	-.213***	-.218***

Source: NLSY79.
*p < .05; **p < .01; ***p < .001

Table 6.8 Effect of Growing Up in a Census Tract with a High Concentration of College Graduates

(Census tract percentage B.A. or higher, dichotomized at the median.)

Outcome	Bivariate	Regression	Propensity Matched Sample	Regression, Black Only	Regression, Hispanic Only	Regression, White Only	Regression, Boys Only	Regression, Girls Only
HOME cognitive stimulation score, ages three to five	.522	.111***	.089*	.045	.309**	.049	.111	.084
PIAT math and reading, ages five to seven	.339***	.096**	.091*	.076	.145***	.079*	.126**	.046
Behavior Problems Index, ages six to ten	−.252	−.049	−.043	.008	−.091	−.042	−.082	.019

Source: NLSY79.
*p < 0.05; **p< .01; ***p < .001

Chapter Summary: Dads, Neighborhoods, and Money

We began our inquiry expecting that family structure, neighborhood, and money would be important influences on children's chances of success, in addition to and possibly independent of parents' educational levels. To some extent they do have effects independent of parental education, but our analyses showed that these factors were also mechanisms by which maternal college education improves children's life chances.

Mothers who get to college, and mothers who complete a B.A., have better chances of getting and staying married while their children are growing up. Prior controversies notwithstanding, growing up in a stable two-parent family structure clearly pays off in terms of better educational outcomes for children. That empirical finding should not be taken as a moral or political condemnation of alternative kinds of families.

Mothers who get to college also have higher incomes, as was detailed in chapter 3, and higher income is associated with better child outcomes. However, money is neither the sole nor even the main reason that maternal college education benefits the next generation; in this chapter we showed that maternal education has strong effects on children's prospects even after controlling for household income.[6]

Finally, maternal higher education is associated with raising one's children in better neighborhoods, where the number of college-educated families is greater, and better neighborhoods are associated with modestly better outcomes for children, net of family characteristics. Like many previous studies, however, we find that neighborhood effects are relatively small, are less than consistent across ethnic and racial groups, and are not always robust statistically, leading us to be more tentative about the importance of neighborhood for children's outcomes than we are for the other factors we have examined.

═ Chapter 7 ═

Mass Higher Education
and Its Critics

In previous chapters we discussed whether going to college pays off financially for women, and whether a mother's college experience improves the educational chances of her children. We also traced out some of the mechanisms whereby maternal education benefited the children of the next generation. Along the way we considered whether racial minorities and poorer students also shared in the positive benefits of access to higher education, when they did make it as far as college. In those analyses, college going turned out to be a generally positive force, both for women and for their children.

For the last decade, however, public debate about higher education has had a different and much more negative tone than one would suspect from our largely upbeat findings. Some commentators are convinced that the United States made a terrible mistake in opening wide the doors to higher education. In their opinion, academe's efforts to become more inclusive have backfired, cheapening degrees and harming the institutions we cherish. They believe that colleges are awash with under-prepared students who have little chance of graduating or getting decent jobs. Are they right? In this chapter we will delve more deeply into those criticisms. We begin by reviewing the expansion of higher education, discussing the forces behind that growth, and noting how the demographic characteristics of undergraduates have changed over time. After providing this context, we turn to the specific criticisms of educational growth, assembling factual evidence that addresses several arguments against what has come to be called mass higher education.

The Development of Mass Higher Education

Americans have a seemingly insatiable thirst for education. Early in the twentieth century, more and more youths sought a high school diploma, at that time a mark of distinction. Over time, graduating from high school slowly changed from being something exceptional to the norm. As late as 1940, only a quarter of American adults had completed high school.

Figure 7.1   Percentage of High School Graduates Who Went to College

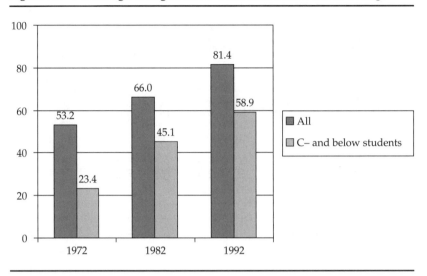

Sources: National Longitudinal Study of the High School Class of 1972 (2006), High School and Beyond (2006), National Education Longitudinal Study of 1988 (2006).

By 1970, about half were high school graduates, and this portion rose to roughly three-quarters of the nation by 1990.[1] According to the U.S. Census (U.S. Census Bureau 2005), nowadays only 12 percent of young people fail to graduate from high school.[2]

Enrollment in colleges and universities similarly grew throughout the twentieth century. Undergraduate enrollments doubled from 1970 to the present. By 2005, nearly 15 million Americans were enrolled as undergraduates.[3] Currently, almost two-thirds of all high school graduates begin college in the fall semester immediately after high school,[4] but this number understates how wide the doors to college have opened. As figure 7.1 shows, over 80 percent of a recent high school cohort had started college within about eight years of graduating from high school.[5]

Critics use the phrase "college for all" when they talk about this expansion of college access. The term is an exaggeration—not all youths go to college—but it vividly expresses the idea that the proportion of high school graduates entering college has sharply increased in recent decades, and suggests that more students with weak academic skills are attending college, as seen in figure 7.1. Unfortunately, the "for all" rhetoric also obscures substantial inequalities in college access and educational attainment associated with race and ethnicity and class and income. Recent evidence indicates that black students are about 27 percent more likely than whites to be retained in grade between kindergarten and twelfth grade[6] and that twice as many African American students, and four times as many Hispanic students, drop out of high school than whites.[7] Among students who do successfully graduate from high school, 69 percent of whites immediately transition to college, compared to 60 percent of blacks and 58 percent of Hispanics (National Center for Education Statistics 2005b).[8]

Racial and ethnic gaps in college attendance have fluctuated over time; the story is not one of uninterrupted progress. From 1972 to 1977, there was no measurable gap among whites, blacks, and Hispanics in the proportion of high school graduates going on to college immediately. After 1977 enrollments continued to climb, but minority enrollments fell behind those of whites. Around 1983, the gap began to narrow again. Currently, on this measure of immediate college going, the black-white gap is roughly 9 percentage points and the Hispanic-white gap is of similar size.[9]

Income or class-based inequalities in college attendance and educational attainment are much greater than those for race and ethnicity. In 2003, students from low-income families were 77 percent as likely to graduate from high school as students from affluent families. Among those high school graduates, youths from poor families were 67 percent as likely to continue into college. Overall, the chances of a youth from a poor family earning a B.A. by age twenty-four are only 22 percent of the chances for a youth from an affluent family.[10]

These very large class-based differences in access to higher education have not shifted much in the last thirty years. Clifford Adelman (2004, 23–24) finds "a consistent spread of 40 or more percentage points in access rates." David Ellwood and Thomas J. Kane (2000, 283) come to an even more pessimistic conclusion: "The role of family background . . . seems to have increased over time." Thomas G. Mortenson (2005b, 12) identifies "a sharp deterioration in bachelor's degree completion equity for students from the bottom family income quartile since the late 1970s." The important point is that there has been little or no progress in overcoming class-based educational disadvantage, despite decades of expansion in higher education. Although lower-class students are attending college in ever-greater numbers, students from more-privileged backgrounds are outpacing them (Karen and Dougherty 2005).

Notwithstanding these important class and ethnic disparities, each generation of Americans has accumulated more years of education than the preceding one, and projections suggest that the rate of college going will continue to increase in the decades ahead (Day and Bauman 2000; Wirt et al. 2004).[11] Most scholars have viewed this expansion of higher education in a positive light, crediting the prosperity of the United States to its high levels of human capital (for example, Goldin and Katz 2001).

There is less agreement about the causes of educational expansion. One standard explanation emphasizes the changing structure of the economy, which alters the demand for different kinds of labor. As production has shifted from agriculture to manufacturing to services, the dominant trend has been toward jobs with greater skills and complexity, necessitating more highly educated workers (Attewell 1987; Berman, Bound, and Machin 1998; Levy and Murnane 2004). College enrollments have responded to that need. A related thesis is that technological change is skill-biased: in particular, the recent spread of computer technologies increases demand for, and raises the relative wages of, more-educated employees, generating greater income inequality.[12]

Some sociologists have offered a different reading of the growth of education, one that stresses competition between different social strata over access to privileged jobs, and the importance of access to education for upward mobility, both for individuals and for groups. The German sociologist Max Weber (1922/1968, 1000) viewed educational credentials as certificates that guaranteed entrance to privileged occupations, sinecures whose superior pay was governed more by status than performance. Education, in Weber's view, allows certain groups to monopolize advantageous positions and to exclude potential competitors who cannot attain sufficient education. An American sociologist, Randall Collins (1979), has updated and extended those insights, arguing that the knowledge content of formal education is arbitrary and has little to do with the jobs that credentialed employees actually do. (Real skills are learned on the job.) However, education remains critical for personal mobility because so many jobs demand a college diploma or more specific credentials. Government colludes in and reinforces this credentialism, Collins argued, by issuing licenses requiring college course work for many occupations, from hair cutting to child minding to selling real estate.

From this sociological perspective, access to college is a key resource in a contest between more- and less-privileged strata for access to better-paid jobs. The expansion of higher education reflects increased demand from competing social strata, rather than the technical needs of the economy. In the nineteenth century, as the masses recognized that better jobs required a high school diploma and agitated for free public high schools for their children, more affluent families sent their children beyond high school, to college. A century later, when the masses pushed for affordable higher education in public universities, the affluent clamored for access to private colleges, and the more prestigious jobs began requiring higher degrees: M.B.A.s, M.A.s, L.L.B.s, and so on. This contest between classes continues today: affluent families can more easily live near superior high schools or pay for private schooling, prep courses, tutoring, extracurricular activities, or other forms of educational enrichment that provide an advantage to their children when they apply to selective colleges. They can better afford to pay tuition and support their children through the many years of higher education and graduate school. This dynamic generates a never-ending game of educational catch-up, fueling enrollment growth in higher education and status competition among colleges.

Viewed in this fashion, higher education on the whole reproduces or reinforces class inequality. However, at various points in time expanded access to higher education can also facilitate social mobility for some disadvantaged individuals and groups. After World War Two, the GI Bill paid the costs of attending college for veterans. More than 2 million young men, many of whom would not otherwise have been able to afford college, took advantage of that opportunity.[13] After graduation, they swelled the ranks of an expanding middle class. Veterans' benefits have been legislated after each war since then, most recently in 2004, drawing successive cohorts into higher education. The growth of the African American middle class has similarly depended on access to higher education.[14] Since the civil rights era, the number of black students entering college each year has risen to roughly 2 million; currently about 17 percent of African American adults are college graduates (Attewell et al. 2004).

One distinctive feature of America's educational system that is especially important for social mobility is its provision of "second chance" routes to educational attainment. Students who drop out of high school may later earn a high school equivalency, the GED. High school students whose weak grades preclude entry into a four-year college have the option of attending a community college, with possible transfer to a four-year institution. Students who lack academic skills can also take remedial courses in college. Finally, course credits earned in one college or university can usually be transferred to another. Taken together, these arrangements provide students who have performed poorly in high school, or who have interrupted their college studies, with the opportunity to go back and complete their education at a later time and in a different institution. This second-chance access to college keeps hopes of social advancement alive. As a result, "Educational attainment has ceased to be fixed in early adulthood, especially among members of racial and ethnic minorities" (Day and Bauman 2000, 4).

In recent decades, the expanding demand for higher education has also been fueled by the insecurity of private-sector employment. Employed adults respond to the precariousness of modern careers by returning to college to develop new skills or to increase their credentials. Displaced workers retrain in college for fields where employment is expanding. Consequently, higher education is no longer the preserve of eighteen-to-twenty-five-year-olds: more than half of today's undergraduates are older than the stereotypical college student (National Center for Education Statistics 1997).

In summary, going to college has become a key part of the American dream, the most important step on the road to a rewarding job and a comfortable life. Expanded access to college offers hope of advancement to people of all ages and backgrounds: a shot at upward mobility for young people from less-advantaged families, and a route of recovery for displaced and underqualified workers. It is also central for success among young people from affluent families, where college attendance has become almost universal.

Not everyone embraces this dream. Some critics have viewed this expansion of higher education as a nightmare, a plunge into intellectual mediocrity and institutional decline. In the opinion of other commentators, the dream is a harmful fantasy, a false promise of upward mobility made to disadvantaged students who are unlikely to succeed.

What the Critics of "College for All" Say

Criticism of mass higher education is far from monolithic. All parts of the political spectrum, from the Marxist left to the conservative right, are represented. Nor is politics necessarily the motivation; sometimes nostalgia seems to be the driving force behind criticism. Several commentators, for example, bemoan the erosion of the traditional curriculum. William Bennett (1994) complains about a retreat from the study of ethical and civic virtues, mainstays of the classical liberal arts curriculum. Allan Bloom (1988) decries the decline of the "great books" approach. Both dislike the emergence of new disciplines such as sociology, the spread of vocational majors in college, and the expansion of the literary canon to include what they view as less-distinguished works by women and members of ethnic minorities.

Unfortunately, it is a short step from nostalgia to condemning the new, and another short step to blaming educational changes on the kinds of students now attending college. A widespread complaint is that the college curriculum has been "dumbed down" because colleges have admitted students who lack the skills or intelligence to cope with a rigorous curriculum (Gray and Herr 1996; Harwood 1997; MacDonald 1997, 1998, 1999; Stanfield 1997; Traub 1995). In our opinion, blaming disadvantaged students for educational change is unfair. Many of the developments that traditionalists decry—from modifications in the canon of "great books" to the spread of preprofessional majors and majors in the social and behavioral sciences to the deemphasis on moral education and the spread of postmodernism—were pioneered at elite colleges. Several of these innovations emerged during decades when student applications to those institutions were increasing, and when top colleges were becoming more selective, demanding higher intellectual standards from applicants. Those educational changes therefore had nothing to do with a decline in student quality. Nevertheless, in the popular media, curricular changes, along with grade inflation, high dropout rates, and the prevalence of remedial course work, are all read as symptoms of a malaise in higher education and are often seen to be results of lower intellectual standards caused by wider access to public universities.

If intellectual standards have been debased, and if colleges routinely graduate students who cannot write a coherent sentence, as Stanley Fish (2005) asserts, one would expect the value of a degree to be undermined. That claim was made as early as 1971, when Vice President Spiro Agnew ("Bowker for Berkeley," *Time*, April 26, 1971, 81) talked disparagingly of "100,000 devalued diplomas." Others argued that the expanded production of college graduates exceeded the number of suitable job openings, leading to undervalued and underemployed degree holders (Berg 1970; Freeman 1976). Indeed, economic theory would lead one to expect a fall in the economic value of a degree from oversupply or from a drop in quality. We will examine whether that devaluation actually came to pass in a following section.

As college enrollments climbed, a quite different type of criticism from the left focused on equity issues, noting that students from disadvantaged backgrounds were disproportionately found in two-year associate's degree programs at community colleges. Associate's degrees are seen as inferior to bachelor's degrees. Thus, what at first seemed a democratization of higher education was arguably transformed into a kind of academic apartheid, whereby students from poorer backgrounds were relegated to a second-class education (Brint and Karabel 1989; Clark 1960; Dougherty 1994). According to such critics, students enrolled in two-year institutions might not have understood that they might get a lesser education. It takes students several semesters in a community college before some realize that they aren't going to get as far as a B.A. degree. By then, their aspirations have been lowered, in a process that Burton Clark (1960) terms "cooling out."

This notion that educators are systematically misleading disadvantaged students has been reiterated over the years. In a recent version, scholars charge that poorly prepared students in community colleges don't realize that their remedial courses carry no credit toward a degree, and that college staff members fail to alert them to this fact. Thus, weak students get bogged down taking multiple remedial courses that don't advance them toward a degree, leading many to give up and drop out. Remedial education, in this view, is a hoax perpetrated by educators upon academically weak students who will be unlikely ever to graduate (Deil-Amen and Rosenbaum 2002; Rosenbaum 2001).

One striking complaint about expanded access to college is that it has undermined the work ethic of students still in high school. If any high school graduate can gain admission into college, no matter how badly he or she performs in high school, then what incentive remains for students to study hard during their school years? "Many low-achieving high school seniors believe they can attain a college degree," James Rosenbaum has written (2001, 58). "Students who believe they can attain a college degree in spite of low achievement . . . exert little effort in high school." According to Heather MacDonald (1998), "But the greatest tragedy of open admissions occurred . . . in the city's public schools. CUNY's decision to admit any breathing human being with a record of occasional high school attendance proved a deathblow to the city's schools. Already underperforming in the 1960s, the schools had no incentive to strive."

Some of these criticisms about the expansion of higher education are too subjective or complex to evaluate empirically,[15] but we can extract five hard claims concerning American higher education that can be tested against the factual record:

1. Did the value of a college degree go down as student enrollments increased?

2. Are graduation rates abysmally low, especially for students with poor high school preparation?

3. Are community colleges a dead end, academically and occupationally?

4. Does remedial education imply a lack of academic standards in college?

5. Has increased access to college undermined the work ethic of students in high school?

We will marshal evidence to answer each of these questions in the following sections.

The Changing Payoff from College Attendance

There is a broad consensus among social scientists that college degrees have a substantial payoff in terms of annual and lifetime earnings (Boesel and Fredland 1999; Card 1999; Day and Newberger 2002). As we saw in chapter 3, college attendance paid off economically for the CUNY and NLSY populations. In this chapter we will document that college pays off for those entering college with weak high school backgrounds in addition to those who enter with straight A's; and for recipients of associate's as well as bachelor's degrees. College even pays off for students who attend but fail to graduate. As one reviewer of the literature put it, "While it is clear that investment in a college degree, especially for those students in the lowest income brackets, is a financial burden, the long-term benefits to individuals as well as to society at large, appear to far outweigh the costs" (Porter 2002).

Table 7.1   Mean Income by Educational Attainment for Male and Female Full-Time Year-Round Workers, 1974 to 2003

Education Level	Percentage Mean Income Change 1974 to 1990 (Inflation-Adjusted)	Percentage Mean Income Change 1991 to 2003 (Inflation-Adjusted)	Mean Income in 2003
Men Twenty-five Years Old and Over			
Less than ninth grade	−12.1	−4.6	$23,972
Ninth to twelfth grade	−16.1	−1.6	$29,100
High school graduate (includes GED)	−8.4	7.8	$38,331
Some college or associate's degree	−0.4	—	—
Some college, no degree	—	9.5	$46,332
Associate's degree	—	6.8	$48,683
Bachelor's degree	6.1	20.9	$69,913
Women Twenty-five Years Old and Over			
Less than ninth grade	3.0	28.6	$20,979
Ninth to twelfth grade	5.2	8.7	$21,426
High school graduate (includes GED)	10.1	13.5	$27,956
Some college or associate's degree	16.0	—	—
Some college, no degree	—	10.5	$31,655
Associate's degree	—	10.8	$36,528
Bachelor's degree	25.6	23.8	$47,910

Sources: U.S. Census Bureau, Historical Income Tables P-32, P-33, P-34, and P-35 (Derived from Current Population Survey, Annual Social and Economic Survey) (U.S. Census Bureau 2004b).
Note: Owing to changes in educational attainment questions in 1991, data from 1974 to 1990 are not completely comparable with data from 1991 to 2003.

Despite a steady growth in the proportion of high school students continuing on to college since the 1960s, and the burgeoning numbers of college students and graduates, the economic value of a B.A. degree has climbed over time. In table 7.1 we summarize a thirty-year span of education and income data, drawing upon the U.S. Census Bureau's annual Current Population Surveys (CPS). The data in this table are limited to full-time year-round workers, but we also analyzed data for the years 1963 to 2003 that included part-time and part-year employees, and the same patterns prevailed. Between 1974 and 1990 the incomes of men with B.A.s who worked full-time year-round grew by 6.1 percent, adjusted for inflation. Between 1991 and 2003, male B.A. incomes increased by another 20.9 percent. The incomes of full-time working women with B.A.s rose even more dramatically over the same periods, reflecting ever greater numbers of women college graduates who stay in the labor force through their childbearing years and hold professional jobs.

College students who enter college but don't go as far as a B.A. have also experienced income growth over the last three decades. Prior to 1990, the surveys classified persons with A.A. degrees along with those who had some college short of a B.A. degree. Between 1974 and 1990, the incomes of full-time year-round male workers in this category stagnated (−0.4 percent in real dollars), although those of women grew by 16 percent. Since 1990, real incomes for men with an A.A. degree and those with some college short of a degree have risen by 9.5 percent and 6.8 percent, respectively.

Full-time year-round employees who were high school graduates have fared less well than college goers over the last three decades. Male incomes for these high school graduates dropped by 8.4 percent, adjusted for inflation, between 1974 and 1990, and have risen by 7.8 percent since. However, the mean income for women high school graduates who work full-time year round has grown substantially over this period.

The largest drop in income over the last four decades has occurred among men who did *not* complete high school. As table 7.1 shows, the mean income for this group dropped by 16.1 percent in inflation-corrected terms between 1974 and 1990; it has declined another 1.6 percent since then. This plunge in the real income of the least-educated workers means that the gap between college-educated and the least-educated workers has widened considerably over time.

In sum, there is little empirical basis for the idea that college credentials have become devalued over the last four decades, either because more people, or less able students, were going to college. That idea emerged around the time the baby boom generation entered the labor market in the early 1970s, and indeed the earnings of college graduates did drop temporarily at that time. However, the incomes of college-educated employees recovered and they have been growing in the decades since then. Employees with college education earn considerably more today than their counterparts did in the 1960s and '70s, and the gap between the economic worth of a degree and that of a high school diploma has grown steadily wider.[16] Economic theory suggests that this pattern would not have developed if there had been a plunge in the quality of degree holders.

Nevertheless, critics of "college for all" remain convinced that many students currently attending college will not benefit economically from college. Rosenbaum (2001), for example, focuses on students with weak high school achievement, and argues vehemently that they are very

Table 7.2   Long-Term Payoff to College Attendance for Students With a C Average or Worse During High School

Earnings	Estimated Value from Conventional Regression	Estimated Value from Matched Sample
Effect of college attendance, including nongraduates (log earnings)	.1290***	.1284***
Mean personal earnings (high school only)	$24,851.91	$25,766.75
Mean personal earnings (college)	$28,273.61	$29,297.10
Number of cases	N = 2,598	N = 1,514
Effect of college attendance for nongraduates only (log earnings)	.0992***	.1071***
Mean personal earnings (high school only)	$23,537.97	$26,166.62
Mean personal earnings (incomplete college)	$25,992.66	$29,124.51
Number of cases	N = 1,814	N = 992
Effect of community college attendance, including nongraduates (log earnings)	.1346***	.1550***
Mean personal earnings (high school only)	$24,478.89	$25,900.05
Mean personal earnings (community college)	$28,006.39	$30,243.27
Number of cases	N = 2,027	N = 1,032

Source: NLSY79.
Note: The log coefficients may read as percentage differences, so a .129 coefficient implies that those attending college earned on average 12.9 percent more than those who did not attend, controlling for differences in family background and high school preparation.
*p < 0.05; **p < .01; ***p < .001

unlikely to gain from going to college. As evidence, he reports that the earnings of college graduates with weak high school GPAs trail those of college students who had strong GPAs in high school. That may be true, but this is not a good yardstick for assessing the value of college attendance. A better comparison contrasts weak students who went to college with classmates with identical high school grades who never went beyond high school. Did the weak students who continued into college fare better economically than their counterparts?

In table 7.2 we provide this contrast, analyzing national income data solely for people who graduated high school with a C average or worse. When evaluating the value of going to college, it is important to allow enough time elapse after college for people to establish their careers.[17] Fortunately, the NLSY surveys provide earnings data for full-time workers in the year 2000, by which time the people in the sample were all thirty-five or older.

These analyses assess the effects of college attendance after removing the influence of several confounding factors such as IQ, psychological orientation, race, sex, and family background.[18] In effect, we estimate the earnings of two students, both of whom had a C or below high school average and who were equivalent in intellectual and social respects, except that one went to college and the other did not.

The top panel compares academically weak students who went to college, including those who did not finish college, with otherwise-equivalent students who only completed high school. The ones who went to college earned about 13 percent more per year, on average. The middle panel of table 7.2 compares academically weak students who attended college but failed to obtain a degree with equivalent students who only completed high school. Even these college dropouts earned about 10 percent more than equivalent high school graduates. The bottom panel examines community college attendance separately, because some critics appear especially skeptical about the economic prospects of weak students who enter community college. This contrast includes all C or worse students who attended community college, whether or not they completed a degree. On average, the C or worse students who attended community college were earning between 13 percent and 15 percent more than their counterparts who only finished high school. All these annual earnings differences are statistically significant.

These longitudinal analyses that followed students until they were thirty-five or older document that, on average, there is a substantial economic benefit when students with weak high school records attend college. This payoff is evident even among those who failed to graduate with a degree. Critics' claims that students who are "not college material" would have been better off economically had they not attended college are contradicted by these analyses.

In providing these analyses, we do not mean to downplay the problem of poor academic performance in high school. Many students with low high school GPAs have to struggle to keep up with college work, and students would progress better in college if they improved their academic performance in high school. Nevertheless, academically weak high school students are correct in believing they will gain economically from going to college. Their average income gain is impressive. Thus, contrary to critics' assertions, career counselors in high school are not doing weaker students a disservice when they encourage them to aspire to college.

Some critics argue that our nation should build new systems of vocational education, revive the apprenticeship system, or build bridges from high school to work, to better serve the career needs of high school graduates who are not academically inclined. Those are sensible proposals. At present, however, those academically weak high school students who do go to college are gaining economically by attending college. It makes no sense to discourage them from continuing to college, and it is incorrect to assert that they are wasting their time there.

College Graduation Rates

A recent front-page headline in the *New York Times* trumpets a "college dropout boom." The governor of New York State proposes rewarding colleges according to the percentage of their students who graduate from the institution on time, and advocates withholding some aid until after students graduate to encourage speedy completion.[19] The authors of such policy initiatives and others like them justify the policies by citing alarming statistics: only 53 percent of B.A. students nationwide are graduating from their institution within five years, and 30 percent have dropped out of college in that time period (National Center for Education Statistics 2004, 64).

These numbers remind us of Benjamin Disraeli's complaint: "Lies, damned lies, and statistics." They are misleading because many of those college dropouts haven't actually dropped out, and those "on time" figures are meaningless. They simply fail to capture how college going works in the twenty-first century. First, students no longer stick with one institution for their whole undergraduate career, for "roughly 60 percent of bachelor's degree recipients have attended more than one school as undergraduates since the 1970s" (Adelman 2004, 45). It therefore makes no sense to reward or punish a college on the basis of the percentage of its entering students who ultimately graduate from that same institution. It's not the institution's fault if students move out of state or trade up to a more prestigious alma mater.

Second, as we demonstrated in our time-to-degree analyses in chapter 2, many students who complete their B.A. take much longer than four years. Some students cannot find the right courses to fulfill all their requirements in eight semesters. Others work part-time and compensate by taking a lighter course load each semester. They are willing to trade off an extended time-to-degree for earning money, which is not surprising in an era of skyrocketing tuition at public as well as private universities. Yet other students cycle in and out of college, alternating between work or family responsibilities and going to school. (In Adelman's [1999] phrase, these are "stopouts" rather than dropouts. Sara Goldrick-Rab [2006] describes poor and working-class students as "swirling" in and out of college.) Finally, certain majors—including engineering and architecture, health sciences, and education—take longer and require more credits than in previous decades (Adelman 1999, 117).

This leaves us with two questions: How long should researchers wait before counting graduates? And whom should we count as a student when we calculate success rates? If one decides these questions in one direction, college graduation rates will look atrocious; if one makes different choices, graduation rates will look much healthier.

The dismal numbers on graduation rates that the media and politicians are responding to tend to measure B.A. graduation rates four or five years after college entry. However, a recent government study reports that only two-thirds of college graduates complete their B.A.s within six years, and 19 percent of students complete their B.A.s more than ten years after their high school graduation (National Center for Education Statistics 2003a, 23). Thus, measuring graduation rates after five years overlooks a large number of people who do ultimately graduate. Moreover, these delayed graduates are disproportionately poorer and minority graduates, and women. Using a four- or five-year cutoff point, as most policymakers do, implies that these students have failed educationally, when they have simply graduated late.

The second issue—whom one counts as a student when calculating dropout rates—might seem straightforward, but it is not. One highly publicized claim is that only 14 percent of weak high school students ever graduate from college: an "86 percent chance of failure."[20] That remarkably high figure comes about by counting as college failures high school seniors with low grades who said they planned to attend college, but never actually enrolled. When most high school seniors report having college plans, there is a certain social pressure on the remaining seniors to say they are planning to go to college as well. But if those low-achieving seniors never set foot in an institution of higher learning, does it make sense to count them in a college failure rate? We don't think so.

At the other extreme, Adelman (2004) has argued against counting, for purposes of analyzing completion, "incidental students," those who enter college but fail to complete more than ten credits as college students. In his view, including in graduation statistics students who are just trying out college provides a misleading view of how well colleges are performing. Omitting those incidental students lifts the national B.A. graduation rate from 49 percent to 67 percent (Adelman 2004, 27). Evidently a lot of students briefly try out college and decide it is not for them.

In calculating college graduation rates for weak students, we have steered between these two extremes. We count only students who actually enrolled in college to get a degree; however, we include all college enrollees, even those whose stay in college was very brief. Use of that definition results in the graduation rates reported in table 7.3.

Each of these surveys indicates that the proportion of weak students who complete a college degree is much larger than the 13.9 percent graduation figure that critics cite. The survey data also show that graduation rates have increased in recent years: the most recent survey, which followed the high school class of 1992, suggests somewhere between

Table 7.3   Alternative Estimates of College Graduation Rates, by Survey; Percentage of Students Who Completed a College Degree (A.A. or Higher)

Survey		All Students	C Average or Below Students
NLSY79 survey—taken approximately twenty years after high school graduation around 1979.			
1. (Self-report)	College entrants	60.9	33.9
High School and Beyond survey—taken ten years after high school graduation in 1982.			
2. (Transcripts)	College entrants	58.0	25.2
3. (Self-report)	College entrants	60.7	30.3
NELS88 survey—taken approximately eight years after high school graduation in 1992.			
4. (Transcripts)	College entrants	64.4	39.3
5. (Self-report)	College entrants	68.2	51.6

Source: Authors' calculations.
Note: All analyses in this table are limited to high school students who indicated their intention to complete a degree and then attended college, if only briefly. "C and below" is defined as less than or equal to a 2.0 GPA or a 75 average in twelfth grade. The 1979 to 2000 waves of the NLSY are weighted by the normalized person weight for 1979. The NELS88 analyses use a normalized panel weight for base year and fourth panel.

39 percent and 52 percent of weak students who entered college earned a degree within about eight years of high school. However those figures are truncated: if those students were followed for more than eight years, their graduation rate would likely be higher. Our best estimate is that somewhere between 50 and 65 percent of C students in the class of 1992 will graduate with degrees in the longer run.[21] That strikes us as good news, especially when it is combined with the earnings data presented earlier that show that the students who fail to complete college still earn more than similar students who never entered college. Allowing academically weak students into college is therefore no "con game."

The Value of Community Colleges

Enrollment at public two-year institutions, often called community colleges, has grown even faster than at four-year colleges. Today about 42 percent of undergraduates begin their education at a community college (Dougherty 2002). These institutions are particularly important for the educational careers of poorer students. They are also the places

Table 7.4   Percentage of Community College Transfers Who Earned a B.A.

	Unadjusted Percentage with B.A.	Estimated Percentage with B.A., from a Conventional Regression	Estimated Percentage with B.A., from Propensity Matched Sample
Transferred from a two-year college	48.9***	56.9 n.s.	49.1 n.s.
Started at a four-year college	59.5	59.0	49.9
Number of cases	2,766	2,766	1,994

Source: NLSY79 cohort, Men and Women.
*p < .05; **p < .01; ***p < .001; n.s. = not statistically significant.

where most low-achieving students enroll after high school, if they enter college at all.

As mentioned previously, community colleges were roundly criticized in the 1970s and thereafter for shunting working-class students into associate of arts, or A.A., degree programs that led to less-rewarding occupations (Bowles and Gintis 1976; Brint and Karabel 1989, Dougherty 1987, 1994; Karabel 1972; Zwerling 1976). Although most community colleges provided an academic track as well as a vocational one, so that promising students could carry credits on to a four-year institution, critics argued that few students were actually following that route (Alba and Lavin 1981; Anderson 1984; Velez 1985). Some were also skeptical of the value of the sub-baccalaureate degrees that community colleges provided (Breneman and Nelson 1981; Monk-Turner 1990; Pincus 1986).

Community colleges have changed a lot since the 1970s, partly in response to earlier complaints. Many have expanded the academic channel that allows students to transfer into a B.A. program, urging more students to take the academic courses needed for transfer. Using national data, Adelman (2004, vi) reports that the transfer rate increased from 28 percent for the high school class of 1972 to 36 percent for the class of 1992. Once we control for demographic characteristics and high school preparation, we find that students who transfer from a community college into a four-year college fare just as well in terms of B.A. completion as similar students who started at four-year colleges (see table 7.4).

In addition, transfers from a community college who complete the B.A. earn as much as graduates who spent all their college career in a four-year college (see table 7.5). For this subgroup of transfers, there does not seem to be a disadvantage from starting at a two-year institu-

Table 7.5   Log Earnings for B.A. Recipients Who Transferred from a Two-Year College, Compared to B.A. Recipients Who Started at a Four-Year College for Full-Time Workers, NLSY Men and Women

	Unadjusted Percentage Gap in Earnings	Estimated Percentage Gap from Conventional Regression	Estimated Percentage Gap from Matched Sample
B.A. recipients who transferred from a two-year college	−13.1***	−3.4 n.s.	0.20 n.s.
N of cases	917	917	342

Source: NLSY79.
*p < .05; **p < .01; ***p < .001; n.s. = not significant.

tion, other than the important fact that it takes roughly two and a half years longer to get to the B.A. if one starts in a junior college than if one starts in a four-year college.

Community college students who transfer into B.A. programs are success stories, but what about the rest of the student body at two-year colleges? Most do not transfer. At first glance, it looks as though students at community colleges are much less likely to earn a degree than students enrolled in four-year colleges: in national NLSY data, only 24 percent of community college entrants receive a degree, compared to 60 percent of students who a entered four-year college. However, community colleges teach the most economically disadvantaged students, and those with the worst high school records. When we compare the progress of students at community colleges with those at four-year colleges after adjusting for students' family background and high school preparation, the differences in educational outcomes shrink. The adjusted percentage of students who earn any degree is 46 percent for community college entrants versus 52 percent for four-year college entrants (Levey 2005). This means that although dropout rates from community colleges are very high, they are not a lot different from the dropout rates one finds for students from similar backgrounds who go to four-year institutions.

Perhaps the most telling indicator that community colleges are fairly successful is that students who enter two-year colleges earn significantly more than equivalent students who only finish high school.[22] By our estimates, those who attend community colleges earn 7.5 percent more than equivalent students who only graduated from high school.[23] Other scholars, using alternative data sources, have previously documented the payoff to sub-baccalaureate degrees.[24]

Still, an A.A. degree is popularly viewed as worse than a B.A., and most of the time, a B.A. degree is indeed worth much more than an A.A. degree from a community college. For example, in 2003, the average male with an A.A. degree earned $48,683, working full-time, whereas the average male with a B.A. earned $69,913 (see table 7.1). That difference is what we would expect, given that a B.A. graduate takes many more college credits and therefore takes much longer than an A.A. to complete. However, when researchers calculate the economic benefit (in terms of earning power) per credit earned in a community college compared to per credit earned at a four-year college, they find that they are about the same (Kane and Rouse 1995a). Once again, the image of community colleges as second-class institutions seems overstated.

Many, though not all, of the programs of study offered at community colleges provide skills and credentials for particular jobs. Some of these vocational A.A. majors result in higher average earnings than some B.A. majors. As discussed in chapter 3, the field of study can greatly influence economic payoff (Jacobs 1986, 1995; Bauman and Ryan 2001). For example, A.A. degrees in business resulted in higher average earnings than B.A. degrees in education. After controlling for students' background characteristics, earnings for several A.A. degrees (business, natural sciences, math, computers, and health and social services) were not statistically significantly different from earnings for B.A. degrees in arts and humanities, social sciences, and education.

College Remediation and Academic Standards

Remedial, also called "developmental," course work in college has emerged as another highly contentious issue in higher education (Kozeracki 2002; Soliday 2002).[25] Some commentators view the existence of these courses in college as evidence that many of today's students are not academically strong enough to manage college-level work and should not have been admitted into college in the first place. The presence of remedial course work, in this view, is a demonstration of how low intellectual standards have fallen in academe (Harwood 1997; Marcus 2000; Trombley 1998). Remediation is also considered a shameful waste of money. Taxpayers paid high schools to teach skills in reading, writing, and basic math; now they are asked to pay colleges for teaching these skills all over again. Other critics focus on college students becoming bogged down taking multiple remedial courses in college, leading many to give up and drop out (Deil-Amen and Rosenbaum 2002; Rosenbaum 2001). Remediation is thus a waste of the student's time and resources as well as of taxpayers' money.

Arguments such as these have persuaded several state legislatures to remove remedial courses from public four-year universities and to redirect students in need of remediation into community colleges (Bettinger and Long 2004; Kozeracki 2002; Soliday 2002). That is insufficient, in the view of MacDonald (1999), who has argued that even community colleges should get out of the remediation business.

Many educators hold an opposite view, maintaining that remedial education is a necessary component of higher education, one with deep historical roots (Breneman and Haarlow 1998; Ignash 1997; Payne and Lyman 1996). Proponents note that many promising students combine strengths in certain subject areas with weaknesses in others, which can be addressed by skills courses. Moreover, many students enter college years after graduating from high school, and need to rebuild certain skills. Most important, proponents stress that most students who take remedial course work subsequently complete their degrees successfully (McCabe 2000; Merisotis and Phipps 2000).

Until recently, relatively little research existed about who was taking remedial courses and in what subjects, and how remedial students turned out in the long run. (The main exceptions are Adelman [1999, 2004] and Bettinger and Long [2004].) So policy debates have proceeded without much of an empirical grounding. Recently, the U.S. Department of Education remedied this by releasing college transcript data for a nationally representative sample of students in the high school class of 1992 and coding these data (in consultation with college registrars) to indicate which courses were remedial. Since we have published analyses of these data elsewhere,[26] the following section summarizes the main findings of our research. (Readers interested in the methodology, the prior literature, or who want to look at statistical results, should consult that paper.)

One theme in the controversy surrounding remediation is that students are taking many remedial courses. Our analyses show that such students do indeed exist, but they are a minority among those who take remedial courses. For example, at two-year colleges, 42 percent of students took no remediation, 44 percent took between one and three courses, and only 14 percent enrolled in more than three remedial courses. At nonselective four-year colleges, 68 percent took no remediation, 26 percent enrolled in between one and three courses, and 5 percent took more than three. At selective four-year colleges, only 2 percent of students took more than three remedial courses, and at highly selective four-year institutions almost no one attempted multiple remediation courses.

These data represent the situation that existed *before* many states adopted new policies that moved remediation out of four-year public colleges, reducing or eliminating its presence there. Our analyses found, however, that students who were taking more than three remedial courses (and were allegedly "bogged down") constituted at most 5 percent of traditional undergraduates at nonselective four-year colleges. That is a much smaller figure than anyone would have imagined from listening to the public debates over remedial education in four-year colleges.

The commonsense impression—that remedial courses are taken by students with poor high school preparation or very weak academic skills—has also proved inaccurate. Our analyses show that many college students with limited academic skills do *not* take remedial course work, whereas substantial numbers of students with strong high school backgrounds nevertheless do take some remedial courses. For example, among students who took the most advanced curriculum in high school (the top quartile), 14 percent took some remedial course work in college. In addition, 32 percent of students in the second highest quartile, who took fairly demanding courses in high school, enrolled in some remedial classes in college.

Nor is remedial course work the preserve of disadvantaged inner-city students: large proportions of students who graduated from suburban and rural high schools take remedial course work in college, as do many students from high-socioeconomic-status (high-SES) families (Adelman 1998). These empirical findings contrast with public stereotypes of remediation as a preserve of a small group of academic incompetents who have no hope of achieving success in higher education.

Critics have accused public colleges and universities of abandoning their commitment to academic standards, of granting diplomas to undeserving students. Implicit is the claim that these colleges have done this in order to accommodate academically unprepared minority students. Our analyses of national data show that public colleges are more likely than private colleges to require remedial course work for equivalently skilled students. In this context, public institutions appear to have created higher hurdles than their private-sector counterparts. In addition, black students are more likely to take remediation than white students with identical test scores and high school preparation. This is the opposite of the "soft bigotry of low expectations" that critics have claimed operates in public education.

Critics of remedial education suggest that students who need remediation will not be able to graduate. There is indeed a gap in graduation associated with taking remedial courses: 28 percent of remedial students in two-year colleges graduate within 8.5 years, compared to 43 percent of nonremedial students, and 52 percent of remedial students in four-year colleges finish B.A. degrees, compared to 78 percent of students who have not taken remedial course work. However, looked at another way, nationwide 50 percent of African American B.A.s and 34 percent of Hispanic B.A.s graduate after taking remedial course work. If those students had been deemed unsuited for college and had been denied entry to four-year institutions—as some critics have recommended—then a large proportion of the minority graduates in the high school class of 1992 would never have received degrees. (These graduation numbers would probably be considerably larger if the survey followed students beyond eight and a half years out from high school.)

Our analyses were able to distinguish the effects of a poor high school academic preparation from the effects of taking remedial courses in college, and we found that most of the gap in graduation rates has little to do with taking remedial classes in college, but instead reflects pre-existing skill differences carried over from high school. In two-year colleges, we found that taking remedial classes was not associated at all with lower chances of academic success, even for students who took three or more such courses. Contra Regina Deil-Amen and James Rosenbaum's (2002) thesis, in multivariate analyses, community college students who took remedial courses were no less likely to graduate than nonremedial students with similar academic backgrounds.

In sum, students with weaker high school backgrounds are less likely to graduate from community college, but remedial courses do not pose an additional barrier for students. On the contrary, we found evidence that community college students who successfully passed remedial courses were more likely to graduate than equivalent students who never took remediation, suggesting that such courses did help those students who completed them.

The remediation situation was different among entrants to four-year colleges. At four-year institutions, taking some remedial courses did lower student chances of graduation, even after taking prior academic preparation and skills into account. Student chances of graduation were reduced between 6 and 7 percentage points. This should be a matter of concern, but this is far from saying that students in four-year colleges who take remediation are unable to graduate. In four-year colleges, the graduation rate for students who took remedial course work was about two-thirds the graduation rate of students who took no remediation. As was the case for two-year college students, these lower graduation rates predominantly reflected skill problems that students brought from high school—specifically in reading—rather than a negative consequence of taking remedial courses per se. Taking remedial course work in reading at a four-year college had a clear negative effect on graduation, even after controlling for academic skills and background. This did not occur for remedial writing courses.

The majority of colleges in the United States are nonselective: they admit any high school graduate who applies and can pay tuition. Many colleges combine open access with requirements that weaker students take remedial or college prep courses in academic areas where they have problems. Thus, remedial education acts as both a gatekeeper and as a quality control in higher education, though this function is rarely acknowledged. Students who can successfully pass these courses continue into regular college-level courses. Students who can't make it through remediation either drop out or are academically terminated. Ironically, when, in an effort to maintain academic standards, colleges require their students to demonstrate proficiency in basic skills by passing remedial courses, they are criticized for wasting the time of the students who fail to overcome these hurdles. At the same time, the provision of remedial courses is perceived by the public as indicating a lack of standards, rather than as an important mechanism for setting a basic skill standard for college graduates. Currently, college remediation functions both as a second-chance policy for poorly prepared students and as a form of institutional quality control that prevents students from graduating unless and until they demonstrate basic skills. Critics of remedial education seem to overlook the importance of remedial education for maintaining academic standards.

Access to College as Demotivator of High School Students

The next claim we will consider is that the spread of college expectations among academically weak high school students has created perverse incentives that demotivate students during high school, and lead them to reduce their work effort:

> Although there is nothing wrong with students having optimistic hopes, we would be concerned if they responded to those hopes *by reducing their effort*. (Rosenbaum 2001, 62; emphasis added)

> Since anyone can enter college, no matter how poorly they do in high school (because of open admissions), students believe they can wait until college to exert effort. (Rosenbaum and Person 2003, 12)

> What could be wrong with letting students have "high expectations"? . . . The first opportunity cost of the college-for-all norm is that students' high expectations may inadvertently encourage them to see high school as irrelevant and thus to make poor use of it. . . . As a result the college-for-all norm may lead to a lack of effort. (Rosenbaum 2001, 79–80)

This is a novel thesis. Previous scholars who have studied the relationship between students' college plans and their postsecondary attainment tended to stress the positive association between college plans and educational outcomes (Adelman 1999; Alexander and Cook 1979; Hauser and Anderson 1991; Kerckhoff 1977; Morgan 1998). Rosenbaum and his coauthors, in contrast, seem to be the first to argue that "high expectations" or "optimistic hopes" for college among weak students would lead to a negative outcome, a lack of effort during high school. We will call this the "effort reduction thesis."

The observation that most American high school students don't work very hard at their studies is a long-standing one that far predates the expansion of college going. In their studies of "Middletown" in the 1920s, the Lynds discovered that most high school students spent very little time doing homework or studying, even A students and those enrolled in advanced courses (Lynd and Lynd 1956, 185,195, 215). August de Belmont Hollingshead's classic study (1975), *Elmtown's Youth*, undertaken around 1941, revealed the same pattern: "The high schools' work load is so light that very few students have to study more than *an hour or two a week* outside of school hours" (Hollingshead 1975, 108; emphasis added).

Research carried out in 1957 for James Coleman's (1961, 11) famous book *Adolescent Society*, a study of Elmtown and nearby communities, argued that teachers and parents had lost "direct control over the levers they could apply to motivate children." Adolescent peer culture had taken over that motivational role. Popularity with peers came from involvement in athletics, from good looks, and from being an activities leader much more than from being an academically high-achieving student. Thus, teenage peer culture failed to reward academic effort. More recently, Laurence Steinberg (1996) attributed the causes of student disengagement and low effort in today's high schools to social promotion; to a teen culture that disparages academic success; to students' focus on part-time work; and to disengaged parents. However, none of these studies linked a lack of effort in high school to unrealistic expectations about what it takes to succeed in college.

To our knowledge, the only systematic historical survey of student effort, as measured by time spent on homework outside school, is that undertaken by Brian Gill and Steven Schlossman (2003). After analyzing survey data from the 1940s through the 1990s, they concluded, "The main historical trend over the past half-century is that of continuity. American high school students in the late 1940s and early 1950s studied no more than their counterparts did in the 1970s, 1980s, or 1990s" (332).

The implication of these various community and historical studies is that a lack of academic effort among most high school students has been the norm for many decades, long predating the upswing in attendance at community colleges and other institutions with open admissions policies. What, then, led Rosenbaum to identify low academic effort with unrealistic college expectations among weak students?

Rosenbaum did not attempt a historical examination of student effort. Rather, he analyzed data from a survey of high school seniors in twelve schools in the Chicago area. Those analyses showed, for high school seniors as a whole, irrespective of achievement level, that certain beliefs are associated with lower effort at school. One belief scale included the statements "My courses give me useful preparation I'll need in life"; "School teaches me useful skills"; "Getting a good job depends on how well you do in school"; and "I need more schooling to avoid dead-end jobs." The other scale included the statements "Even if I do not work hard in school, I can still make my future plans come true"; "What I do not learn in school, I can always pick up later"; "Students with bad grades often get good jobs after high school"; and "Without a good education, it is likely that I will end up with the kind of job I want."

In our view, neither of these scales measures Rosenbaum's (2001, 58) assertion that "students who believe they can attain a college degree in spite of low achievement . . . exert little effort in high school." We undertake a more direct test of the effort reduction thesis. The U.S. Department of Education's National Educational Longitudinal Study (NELS), which spans the high school years of the class of 1992, allows us to test whether or not academically weak students who nevertheless believe they can graduate from college reduce their effort in high school. (A student's belief that she or he can "attain a college degree"—not just attend college—was the criterion that Rosenbaum [2001] employed, and we follow his example here.) In our analyses that follow, we select students with weak skills when they enter high school, and we compare the academic progress of weak students who nevertheless expect to graduate from college with otherwise-equivalent academically weak students who don't expect to graduate from college.

Table 7.6 presents conventional ordinary least squares (OLS) regression models predicting outcomes solely for students who had average grades of C or below from sixth through eighth grade. Each regression controls for sociodemographic characteristics of students and schools and for students' course grades when the effect of college plans is assessed. They show that, among academically weak students, those with college graduation plans were significantly less bored, spent more time on homework in the twelfth grade, increased their homework effort more between eighth and twelfth grade, had higher twelfth grade reading/math scores, and made greater progress in test scores between eighth and twelfth grade, compared to students with similarly low grades who did not expect to graduate from college.

Table 7.7 presents logistic regressions for the same low-grades group. Within this group of academically weak students, those who expected to obtain a degree were more likely to take a "new basics"[27] curriculum, to take the ACT or SAT, to earn a high school diploma, to enroll in college, and to earn a degree. In no case was there any evidence that college expectations significantly impaired engagement or effort or performance among weak students.

We also ran regression analyses using a different definition of weak student: those whose reading and math test scores placed them in the bottom quintile of their cohort during eighth grade. These again show that academically weak students with college graduation plans increased

Table 7.6 Effects of Degree Plans on Engagement and Achievement of Weak Students (Unstandardized OLS Regression Coefficients)

	Academic Disengagement Scale (BORED)	Twelfth-Grade Homework Effort	Twelfth-Grade Homework Effort (Controlling for Eighth-Grade Effort)	Twelfth-Grade Achievement Test Score	Twelfth-Grade Achievement Test Score (Controlling for Eighth-Grade Score)
College degree plans	-.091*	3.595***	3.575***	2.242***	1.199***
Hispanic	-.196***	-2.188***	-2.183***	-1.025*	.486
Black	-.282***	-1.529*	-1.513*	-3.021***	-1.764**
Asian	-.416***	1.923*	1.932*	1.940*	1.140
Other	-.381***	-.590	-.598	-4.361***	-1.488*
Male	-.018	.179	.182	1.042**	1.036***
Family SES	.068*	.503	.520	2.423***	1.568***
Middle school grades	-.226***	.852	.787	1.929***	.445
Private school	-.009	-2.146***	-2.193***	2.887***	.660+
High-poverty school	-.041	-.160	-.109	-.336	.190
High-minority-enrollment school	-.096*	1.291*	1.292*	-.648	-1.268**
Eighth-grade homework	—	—	.050	—	—
Eighth-grade test scores	—	—	—	—	.655***
Constant	3.036***	8.532***	8.423***	39.531***	13.022***
Pseudo R^2	.1082	0.0525	0.0529	.1813	.4883
Number of cases	1,508	1,055	1,055	1,508	1,508

Source: Authors' analyses of NELS88 data.

Note: Academically weak students defined here as those having a high school GPA of C or below.

+$p < 0.10$; *$p < .05$; **$p < .01$; ***$p < .001$

Table 7.7 Effects of Degree Plans on Engagement and Achievement Among Academically Weak High School Students (Unstandardized Logistic Regression Coefficients)

	Student Came to Class Unprepared	Student Took "New Basics" Curriculum	Student Took SAT or ACT Test	Student Earned High School Diploma	Student Enrolled in College	Student Earned a College Degree
College plans	-.212+	1.055***	.692***	.517***	1.079***	.332**
Hispanic	.154	-.498	.474**	.571***	.646***	-.595***
Black	-.234	.724*	.757***	.216	-.185	-.616**
Asian	.964***	.329	1.121***	2.460***	.932***	-.870***
Other	.733*	-1.538**	.894***	-.777**	-.691**	-.949**
Male	.440***	-.227	-.220**	.175	-.430***	.080
Family SES	.148*	1.977***	.787***	.623***	1.164***	-.117
Middle-school grades	-.494**	1.964***	1.225***	1.114***	-.056	.588***
Private school	-.667***	-.955**	.026	1.523***	1.091***	.160
High-poverty school	.435**	.285	-.385*	-.371**	.657***	-.098
High minority-enrollment school	-.185	-.308	.394*	.343*	-.098	.165
Constant	.968***	-6.616***	-2.440***	-1.665***	.421+	-1.559***
Pseudo R²	.0325	.2877	.1095	.1221	.1894	.0302
Number of cases	1,508	1,217	1,051	1,505	1,508	1,508

Source: Authors' analyses of NELS88 data.

Note: Academically weak students defined as those with C grades or lower before eighth grade.

+p < 0.10; *p < .05; **p < 0.01; ***p < 0.001

their homework hours more between eighth and twelfth grades, spent significantly more time on homework in twelfth grade, had higher twelfth-grade scores, and made more improvement on skills tests between eighth and twelfth grades than academically and demographically similar students who lacked college plans. This academically low-achieving group with college graduation plans were significantly less likely to come unprepared to class, more likely to take a "new basics" curriculum, more likely to take the ACT or SAT, and were more likely to enroll in college and earn a degree than similar weak students without college plans.

In order to reduce selection biases—background differences between students with college plans and students without such plans—we next used a sample of students matched on their propensity score for having college expectations, using the same outcome measures. Table 7.8 presents the results of the "matched-sample" propensity-score models alongside probabilities obtained from the conventional OLS or logistic regression models with sociodemographic controls, for the subpopulation of grade C and below students.[28] The table shows the average probability of, say, coming to class unprepared for academically weak students who have degree expectations compared to that for similar students who did not have degree plans, controlling for students' race and ethnicity, gender, family SES, middle school grades, and several school characteristics. The overall pattern for the propensity score–matched models strongly confirms the picture previously obtained from conventional OLS and logistic models: Among students with a C average or worse, those with college degree expectations fare better academically. For one dependent variable out of eleven—the probability of earning a degree—a coefficient that was significant for the conventional model wasn't statistically significant in the propensity model. For ten other outcomes, degree plans were associated with better effort and outcomes during high school, both in conventional regression models and in propensity score–matched models that reduce selection bias. In no case were degree expectations associated with worse outcomes or greater disengagement among academically weak students.

Critics of the college-for-all norm suggest that academically weak students who, knowing that some colleges have open admissions policies, aspire to graduate from college, subsequently reduce their effort, and make little progress in high school. These critics offer very weak evidence for this claim: a cross-sectional survey of high school seniors in Chicago that links self-reported student effort in twelfth grade to opinion scales about the importance of college for life.

Previously, scholars have noted that since the 1920s, American high school students have expended little effort in high school. Survey researchers have detected no decrease in homework effort in the decades since access to college has increased. Our longitudinal analyses of the

Table 7.8   Effect of College Graduation Expectations on Educational
            Engagement and Achievement; Comparing Bivariate and
            Propensity Score Analyses, Students with C Grades or Lower

Outcome	Estimated Value from Conventional Regression	Estimated Value from Matched Sample
Probability of coming to class unprepared		
Eighth-grade college degree plans	.5460+	.5497**
No degree plans	.5978	.6383
Number of cases	1,508	720
Estimated score on academic disengagement scale		
Eighth-grade college degree plans	2.401*	2.420*
No degree plans	2.492	2.535
Number of cases	1,508	720
Estimated twelfth-grade homework effort		
Eighth-grade college degree plans	13.032***	12.535***
No degree plans	9.436	9.409
Number of cases	1,055	524
Estimated change in homework effort, eighth to twelfth grades		
Eighth-grade college degree plans	13.032***	12.535***
No degree plans	9.457	9.407
Number of cases	1,055	524
Probability of completing "new basics" curriculum		
Eighth-grade college degree plans	.0345***	.1441***
No degree plans	.0123	.0343
Number of cases	1,217	587
Probability of taking the ACT or SAT test		
Eighth-grade college degree plans	.5334***	.5495***
No degree plans	.3640	.4232
Number of cases	1,051	524
Estimated twelfth-grade achievement test score		
Eighth-grade college degree plans	43.744***	43.541**
No degree plans	41.501	42.207
Number of cases	1,508	720
Estimated improvement in achievement test scores, eighth to twelfth grades		
Eighth-grade college degree plans	14.221***	10.899**
No degree plans	13.022	9.959
Number of cases	1,508	720
Probability of graduating with a high school diploma		
Eighth-grade college degree plans	.6871***	.6943**
No degree plans	.5671	.5876
Number of cases	1,505	720

(Table continues on p. 182.)

Table 7.8   *Continued*

Outcome	Estimated Value from Conventional Regression	Estimated Value from Matched Sample
Probability of enrolling in college		
Eighth-grade college degree plans	.7245***	.7107***
No degree plans	.4721	.5172
Number of cases	1,508	720
Probability of earning a college degree		
Eighth-grade college degree plans	.4104**	.4077
No degree plans	.3305	.3527
Number of cases	1,508	720

Source: NELS88.
+p < 0.10; *p < .05; **p < 0.01; ***p < 0.001

NELS follow academically weak students from the beginning of high school who nevertheless expect to complete a college degree, and compare them to similar weak students who don't expect to earn a degree. We measured low achievement in two different ways: low GPA and low math and English test scores. We found that, by either definition, academically weak students who enter high school with "high expectations" of graduating from college increase their effort and improve their performance during high school.

In conclusion, blaming open access to college for low student effort in high school is unwarranted. One may speculate that weak students might work harder if it were made more difficult to enter college, but there is no evidence of this in historical studies or elsewhere. What we can actually measure suggests that academically weak high school students with degree plans exert significantly more effort than their peers, the opposite of what the demotivation or effort reduction thesis predicts.

Conclusion

This chapter has examined several criticisms of expanded access to college. None of the critics' hard claims are convincing when compared to the empirical record. Degrees have not become devalued. College pays off quite well for most graduates, even for college goers who don't complete their degrees. College pays off economically for students with weak high school backgrounds as well as for better-prepared students.

Graduation rates are not as dire as the "86 percent failure rate" suggests. That striking number was an artifact of the way failure was defined.

If one includes only students who enter college and allows that women and economically disadvantaged students take a longer time to graduate, then graduation rates look much healthier, and seem to be getting better in recent years. There is still much room for improvement, but there is no "dropout boom."

Community colleges are not the academic dead ends that commentators once feared. More students than in earlier years are in the transfer pipeline to get B.A.s, and after they transfer they are on average as successful as matriculants to four-year colleges. The earnings data show that getting an A.A. degree pays off more than entering the labor market directly after one has graduated from high school. A few vocational majors in community college pay especially well, better than certain B.A. majors. However, community college students do drop out and "stop out" in very high numbers. This seems to be a reflection of their family background and academic preparation. We should indeed be looking into ways of reducing dropout rates. Still, students who fail to complete a degree nevertheless do better economically than high school classmates who did not enter higher education at all.

Remedial education represents the failure of middle and high schools to impart basic skills to all students, and thus is nothing to be proud of. In fact, however, the proportion of students in four-year colleges that are "bogged down" taking remedial courses has been quite small. The political firestorm that broke out around remediation in public universities was out of proportion to the number of students affected. We believe that remediation served as a convenient scapegoat for politicians seeking to reduce state funding for higher education, push for tuition hikes, or limit enrollments.

Students in community colleges are not gravely disadvantaged by taking remedial courses, and those who get through such courses have improved chances of graduation. Most strikingly, critics of mass education fail to acknowledge that remedial course work represents an important form of quality control. Colleges that are open to all high school students do not let students advance to the degree until they show proficiency in basic skills, and they require students lacking those skills to pass remedial courses. As we showed, very large proportions of minority college graduates have taken and passed remedial courses and obtained degrees in recent years. If, as some commentators propose, remediation had no place in college, then half of African American B.A. recipients would have been denied the opportunity to earn a degree.

Finally, the claim that open college access has undermined the work ethic of high school students has little basis in fact. On the contrary, we found that college graduation plans motivate weak students to work harder in high school, and we documented the payoff of having college plans in terms of higher grades, better test scores, and increased effort during high school—one more reason for encouraging academically weak students to aspire to college.

Claims about booms in the number of dropouts, worthless diplomas, and bogged-down and demotivated students help persuade legislators and opinion leaders that college access has gone too far. Such arguments sway the public and embolden those who want to push institutions of higher education to be more selective and restrictive in their admissions. Unfortunately, to those who are advancing a policy agenda, it rarely matters whether their complaints are factually grounded, as long as the assertions are plausible and well publicized.

Our research suggests that the critics' main claims are factually flimsy. That does not mean that we are uncritical fans of mass higher education. There are many reasons to be worried. We share with others a deep concern that too many students are failing in high school. In addition, the current rates of "stopout" and dropout from college are undesirable, even if they are not nearly as high as critics suggest. We believe that these rates have more to do with financial and family pressures and less about student's academic abilities than critics allow, but that is another story. We share with other scholars a commitment to keeping intellectual standards high in college, and we acknowledge that this is more difficult when students enter college with skills deficits. But the goal of improving mass higher education is not served by propagating fictions and exaggerations about its current functioning.

= Chapter 8 =

The Bottom Line:
The Difference That Open
Access Makes

Enrollment in higher education expanded over sixfold since the middle of the twentieth century, and the number of degree-granting institutions more than doubled.[1] Some observers saw this as a tide of mediocrity washing away standards and eroding academic excellence. In retrospect, we can see that the swelling ranks of prospective students intensified competition for entry into the most sought-after colleges. From the Ivy League to the flagship campuses of state universities, most top-ranked colleges were able to admit an ever smaller proportion of applicants, and their freshmen's SAT scores kept rising (table 8.1). Thus, for the top-ranked institutions—which enroll only a small percentage of the nation's students—the expansion of higher education coincided with increased academic selectivity and stronger students.

On the other hand, the number of academically weak students who aspired to college increased dramatically during this period, also impacting numerous nonselective colleges. By 1992, almost 60 percent of high school graduates with C minus or lower averages were proceeding to college, compared to less than a quarter of such students in 1972 (table 8.2). Eight out of ten high school graduates are heading to college today, compared to about half in the early 1970s. Entry rates have increased across the board for every category of ethnicity, gender, socioeconomic status, and high school academic record.

As this influx indicates, the majority of U.S. colleges and universities have evolved toward nonselective admissions. Two-year colleges have absorbed a disproportionate and increasing share of the poorest and least well-prepared high school students (see table 8.2). Nevertheless, substantial proportions of graduates with C grades in high school (30 percent) and others with grade point averages of C minus or lower (15 percent) are being admitted into four-year colleges. Unlike the situation at CUNY, this nationwide acceptance of less-prepared students by four-year colleges does not seem to have been a deliberate

Table 8.1   The Changing Academic Selectivity of Some Leading Universities

	Percentage of Applicants Accepted			Verbal SAT Score Range	
	1980	1998	2005	1998	2005
Harvard	16	13	11	700–790	700–800
Princeton	20	12	11	670–770	680–770
Stanford	19	15	12	670–770	670–770
Yale	20	18	11	670–770	690–790
Dartmouth	23	22	19	660–760	670–770
Chicago	66	58	40	640–740	670–770
Duke	37	30	23	640–730	660–750
Northwestern	55	29	30	620–720	650–740
Vanderbilt	67	58	38	590–680	620–710
Ann Arbor, MI	72	69	62	590–660	580–680
Austin, TX	74	61	51	540–650	540–660
Berkeley, CA	70	36	25	570–700	580–710
Chapel Hill, NC	46	37	36	560–670	590–690
Madison, WI	83	77	66	520–650	560–670

Sources: Peterson's Annual Guide to Undergraduate Study (1982) and *Kaplan's College Catalogue* (1999, 2006).
Note: The admissions percentages refer to undergraduate applicants, whereas the SAT verbal scores refer to the 25th and 75th percentiles of the incoming freshman class.

policy shift, but rather an evolution or adaptation to changing application patterns.

Does Open Access Make a Difference?

Just how much of a difference has this expansion made? In previous chapters we documented the individual payoffs to college attendance for students in general and for academically weak students in particular. We also documented the impact on the second generation. But here we want to assess something different: the aggregate importance of the shift towards broad access—the social consequences of educational inclusion. One way of approaching this is to consider a hypothetical world in which educational expansion and open access never occurred. Suppose we rolled back the clock to an era of more stringent college admissions. How much of a difference would it have made if a more selective system of access to higher education had remained in place?

Answering this question is more complicated than it seems. Critics who refer to "unqualified" students rarely say exactly what they mean, so it is left to us to define a more selective model for college admissions. If we were to roll back the clock, one plausible requirement would be that all students entering a four-year institution should have earned a high school average of B minus or higher. Students who did not meet

Table 8.2   Trends in College Attendance Among High School Graduates, by Cohort (Percentages)

	1972[a]	1982[b]	1992[c]	1982 Two-Year	1982 Four-Year	1992 Two-Year	1992 Four-Year
Percentage of all high school graduates	53.2%	66.0%	81.4%	27.1%	38.9%	35.0%	46.4%
Race							
White	53.9	68.6	82.9	26.9	41.7	34.2	48.7
Black	51.4	57.2	69.7	26.4	30.8	29.2	40.5
Hispanic	38.7	54.3	79.5	30.2	24.1	48.4	31.1
Gender							
Male	52.8	62.7	79.6	23.8	38.9	35.6	44.0
Female	53.5	69.1	83.1	30.2	38.9	34.4	48.7
SES							
Top quintile	78.8	88.3	98.3	21.6	66.7	22.3	76.0
Second quintile	61.8	78.0	90.5	28.8	49.2	38.1	52.4
Third quintile	49.9	61.0	81.1	29.7	31.3	42.7	38.4
Fourth quintile	40.6	50.3	65.0	27.5	22.8	37.1	27.9
Bottom quintile	33.2	36.8	57.6	22.8	14.0	38.0	19.6
Grades[d]							
A	82.5	94.5	97.4	11.7	82.8	14.2	83.2
B	64.0	82.4	88.7	26.8	55.6	33.8	54.9
C	41.2	66.1	77.0	33.1	33.0	46.6	30.4
C– or below	23.4	45.1	58.9	28.7	16.4	43.4	15.5

Sources:
[a]National Longitudinal Survey 1972 Cohort (1972 to 1986), weighted by FU5WT. Data on educational attainment are self-reported.
[b]High School and Beyond weighted by FU4WT. Data on educational attainment come from transcript data.
[c]National Educational Longitudinal Survey 1988 Sophomores, followed to 2000, weighted by F4PNHWT. Data on educational attainment come from transcripts.
[d]From transcript surveys.

this standard would not be able to enroll in such a college but could instead attend a two-year community college.

Some commentators (Rosenbaum 2001) argue that students with very low high school averages have little chance of graduation even from a two-year institution, so we need to create a bottom cutoff for community colleges as well. Following this reasoning, we decided that students with high school averages of C or C plus would qualify for entry into a community college, under our more restrictive admissions policy, but those students with high school averages of C minus or worse would be deemed unsuitable for any higher education.

If the pathway to college were narrowed along these lines, what would be the impact? We apply this more selective admissions model to the college students whose records we assessed in the previous chapters: our point of departure is the actual collegiate level at which entering freshmen were placed for the CUNY and national NLSY samples (table 8.3).[2]

Among entrants to four-year schools across four samples, between 47 percent and 60 percent had at least a B minus average, the minimum for admission to a four-year institution, according to the more selective model we are applying.[3] The remainder fell below this threshold and would not be admitted to a four-year school under our more stringent admissions model. Thus, somewhere near half of students who actually attended four-year colleges in recent decades would not have been able to do so under the more stringent admissions policy. Among these students with averages below B minus, a substantial share had averages of C minus or less: between 15 percent and 30 percent of students who actually attended a four-year college in recent decades would not have been able to attend any kind of college at all under the more stringent policy.

Sharp differences between whites and minorities are visible. Black and Hispanic students were far more likely than whites to have entered four-year institutions with weaker high school averages. Consequently, if entering a four-year college had required a B minus or better average, only 18 percent of the African American men and only 26 percent of the African American women who actually attended CUNY's four-year colleges could have enrolled. The national figures are similar: under the more restrictive standard, only 28 percent of African American men and 42 percent of African American women who actually attended four-year colleges would have been admitted. Hispanic students would have fared better under higher admissions standards than African Americans, though not as well as whites. Even among whites, the tougher admissions standard would have culled over a quarter of them from four-year colleges (table 8.3). In sum, there would be much less race and class diversity in four-year colleges, had open admissions not occurred.

Students with very weak high school records are, of course, more prevalent in community colleges than in four-year institutions. James Rosenbaum (2001) argued forcefully that students with C minus or worse high school averages are very unlikely to make it through community college and are wasting their time there. If admissions policies had reflected that viewpoint, nearly half of the men and a third of the women who actually attended community colleges in the national sample would not have been able to do so.

These figures of low-GPA students who would not have been admitted under more stringent policies drive home another important point about open access. CUNY is widely known as having instituted a policy of open admissions in 1970. The NLSY data show that by the beginning

Table 8.3   Changes in Level of College Placement Under Selective Admissions (Percentages)

	CUNY Women				
Original Placement Under Open Access		Placement Under Selective Admissions			
		White	Black	Hispanic	All
Four-year	Four-year	72.6	25.9	53.5	51.9
	Two-year	21.0	32.1	32.9	28.4
	No college	6.4	42.0	13.6	19.7
Two-year	Two-year	58.6	30.8	52.7	47.4
	No college	41.4	69.2	47.3	52.6

	CUNY Men				
Original Placement Under Open Access		Placement Under Selective Admissions			
		White	Black	Hispanic	All
Four-year	Four-year	63.2	17.9	38.6	59.0
	Two-year	24.7	28.0	33.5	25.5
	No college	12.1	54.1	28.0	15.4
Two-year	Two-year	27.9	16.2	26.5	25.8
	No college	72.1	83.8	73.5	74.2

	National Women				
Original Placement Under Open Access		Placement Under Selective Admissions			
		White	Black	Hispanic	All
Four-year	Four-year	73.2	42.1	51.3	60.1
	Two-year	15.8	23.7	21.9	19.2
	No college	11.0	34.2	26.8	20.7
Two-year	Two-year	75.3	54.8	62.2	65.9
	No college	24.7	45.2	37.8	34.1

	National Men				
Original Placement Under Open Access		Placement Under Selective Admissions			
		White	Black	Hispanic	All
Four-year	Four-year	58.9	27.6	37.7	46.7
	Two-year	20.5	22.6	26.7	22.0
	No college	20.6	49.8	35.5	31.3
Two-year	Two-year	60.4	37.9	53.6	52.5
	No college	39.6	62.1	46.4	47.5

Sources: CUNY Women File, CUNY File, and NLSY79–Adult File.

of the next decade, large proportions of students with low GPAs were attending four-year institutions nationwide. Thus, by the 1980s, open access had become the de facto college admissions model for the nation.[4]

How would a more stringent admissions policy have affected people's lives? To answer this question we will examine several outcomes under both an open-access and a selective model. We will first consider educational attainment, in particular, the rate of B.A. attainment. Next, we compare a variety of economic outcomes under the open access and selective admissions models. Finally, we look at the second generation and consider this question: Would changes in mothers' level of college placement be associated with changes in educational outcomes such as their children's college entry?[5]

The Influence of College Selectivity on Degree Attainment

Figure 8.1 shows that about 41 percent of African American women at CUNY actually earned B.A. degrees. Under the more selective access policy, only 19 percent would have done so. In other words, a policy of open access more than doubled the proportion of black women who earned a B.A. It also increased the number of B.A.s Hispanic women earned, from 25 percent to 39 percent.[6] Whites also benefited, but the dividend was not as great as for minority women, most likely because their level of college entry was less dependent on open access. Nationally there is a similar pattern, albeit with smaller effects. Open access increased the proportion of all students—minority as well as white, men as well as women—who completed B.A.s.[7]

The main finding of these analyses, then, is that the broad access to college that has characterized American higher education over the last few decades has—by augmenting opportunity and by fueling perceptions that college is truly accessible—had a large effect in boosting B.A. attainment among all groups, and especially among minority students.

Economic Outcomes

How much difference does open access make for economic outcomes over the long term? To answer this question, we first estimated the earnings consequences of open admissions as compared to selective admissions policies for both the CUNY and national surveys.[8] We know each person's actual annual earnings under the relatively open admissions policies of recent decades, and we contrasted this with what each person would have earned if he or she had been subject to the more selective entry policy described above. Only people who would have been redirected to a community college or to no college at all under a more selective admissions

Figure 8.1   Influence of Open Access and Selective Admissions Models on Baccalaureate Attainment,[a] by Ethnicity (Percentages)

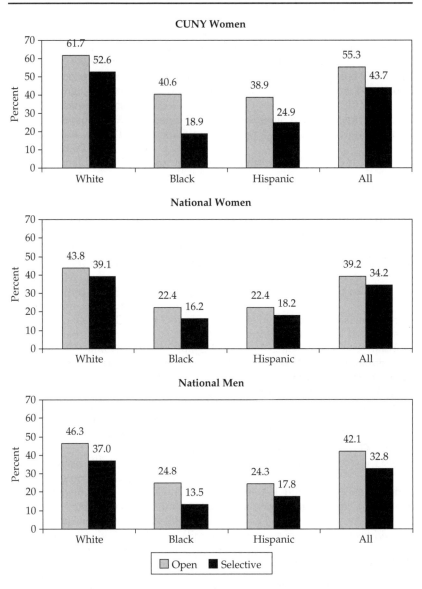

Sources: CUNY Women File and NLSY79–Adult File.
[a]Includes advanced degrees.

policy would have earned a different amount. To determine what those people's earnings would have been, we used a regression model derived from the whole sample that predicted a person's earnings from level of college entry (or no college), family class background and race, high school preparation, IQ score, and so on.

As table 8.4 shows, open access boosted earnings. For example, under open access CUNY women were earning an average of $44,112 per year. Had these women been subject to a selective admission system, their earnings would, on average, have been $36,380, a difference of more than $7,700 annually.[9] Every ethnic group exhibited substantial benefits, although open access appears to have been relatively more valuable for the earnings of white women than for minorities. On average, white women were earning about $9,700 more than they otherwise would have. The comparable benefit for black women is $5,000, and among Hispanic women it is over $7,800. In different terms, open access added 12 percent to the earnings of black women, 19 percent to those of Hispanics, and 21 percent to those of whites.

The picture for women nationally is similar to the one at CUNY: on average, white women's earnings under open access were 29 percent greater than they would have been under selective admissions. The earnings bonuses were 11 percent for black women and 16 percent for Hispanic women. The national picture for men is similar to this. Although whites benefited more than minority men, ethnic differences were narrower than in the case of women. All in all, then, open access provided clear earnings benefits by boosting the level of college that students could enter.

These gains are apparent in other economic indicators, including home ownership. Open admissions generates an 11 percent boost to black home ownership and an 8 percent boost to Hispanics. The national NLSY survey also documented the value of the home: for home-owning women and men, the value of their homes was greater under open access (table 8.4).

Ownership of resources such as a retirement plan, health insurance, equities, and savings are important for well-being. Under open access at CUNY, women possessed these resources more often than they would have otherwise. Overall, 56 percent owned all of them. Without open access the proportion would fall to 49 percent. Among black women, 57 percent owned such assets, compared with 46 percent who would have had access to them under a selective college admissions model. Another way to look at these kinds of economic resources is to consider their value. In the national data, for both women and men the value of economic resources was greater under an open access policy than it would have been otherwise. The boost was greater among minorities than among whites. For example, under open admissions white women

Table 8.4 Influence of Open Access and Selective Admissions Models on Economic Well-Being, by Ethnicity[a]

	Open Access				Selective Admissions			
	White	Black	Hispanic	Total	White	Black	Hispanic	Total
CUNY women								
Mean annual full-time personal earnings	$45,501	$43,113	$42,058	$44,112	$35,796	$38,111	$34,190	$36,380
Percentage home ownership	75.3	52.9	56.8	65.6	73.8	47.2	52.5	62.3
Percentage has all economic resources[b]	57.5	56.8	49.3	56.1	53.7	45.8	40.7	49.4
National women								
Mean full-time personal earnings	$36,584	$26,273	$29,550	$32,559	$25,957	$23,400	$24,969	$25,021
Value of home[c]	$176,267	$107,552	$111,832	$159,800	$155,981	$93,998	$125,435	$143,043
Value of other economic resources[d]	$167,325	$31,689	$40,924	$127,075	$108,240	$9,070	$21,116	$79,260
National men								
Mean full-time personal earnings	$58,231	$39,147	$44,320	$53,580	$50,621	$33,133	$39,183	$46,479
Value of home	$178,710	$118,657	$144,625	$167,011	$150,452	$96,166	$134,806	$140,907
Value of other economic resources	$199,777	$58,897	$71,274	$167,120	$121,764	$29,739	$52,261	$101,470

Sources: CUNY Women File and NLSY79–Adult File.

[a] Filtered for college entrants whose level of entry changed from open access to more selective admissions model.

[b] Economic resources consist of a retirement plan or stocks, savings, health insurance, and vacations.

[c] Calculated only for those who own homes.

[d] Value of economic resources consists of value of savings, CDs, stocks, investments, retirement plan, and trust or estate.

Table 8.5   Influence of Open Access and Selective Admissions Models on Children's College Going, by Ethnicity[a] (Percentages)

	Open Access			
	White	Black	Hispanic	Total
Children of CUNY women				
Went to college[b]	89.5	80.8	81.2	82.7
Children of national women				
Went to college	69.6	58.0	67.6	61.4
	Selective Admissions			
	White	Black	Hispanic	Total
Children of CUNY women				
Went to college[b]	84.9	73.9	77.2	77.2
Children of national women				
Went to college	52.2	45.8	60.8	48.5

Sources: CUNY Children's File and NLSY79–Children File.
[a]Includes only children of women college entrants who changed level of college entry from open access to selective admissions models.
[b]Calculated for children who graduated from high school in both samples.

were 35 percent better off, on average, than they would have been under a selective admissions model; blacks were 71 percent better off; as were 48 percent of Hispanics.[10]

In summary, open access increased former students' personal earnings, their chances of owning a home, and, if they owned one, its value. It increased the chances of having other resources such as equities and health insurance. In some but not all cases, the benefits of open access are more substantial for minorities than whites.

The Second Generation

What about the children of this earlier generation of college goers? One of the most significant educational events in our data sets on children is whether they entered college. Children's college attendance obviously raises the chances that they will get more highly rewarded jobs, in a sense validating their parents' mobility out of lower-income or impoverished status. From our analyses in earlier chapters, we know that the educational attainment of mothers is positively associated with the odds that their children will enter college. How much—if at all—did collegiate open access for the mothers augment their children's chances for college entry? As table 8.5 indicates, because of open access, college entry rates for the second generation are about 5 percent higher in the CUNY sample, and

13 percent greater in the national sample. In both samples, these second-generation benefits are apparent for all ethnic groups.

A Bottom-Line Perspective

We have seen that in both the CUNY and the national samples, a policy shift that allowed students with lower high school GPAs to attend college resulted in important long-term benefits for students and their children. Were there also public benefits? When the open admissions policy was initiated at the City University of New York, policymakers who argued in its favor supposed that broadening educational opportunity for low-income and impoverished students would eventually convert "tax eaters" into taxpayers. In effect, it would convert net consumers of public funds into net producers. This was a variant of a position expressed around twenty years later and in a different context by the Republican leader Newt Gingrich, who asserted that too many people in the society were riding in the cart when they should be helping to pull the cart. These comments refer to a concept of "the public good." Is broad access to college a public good? If it is, one way it can be expressed is by aggregating individual benefits. In the aggregate they might constitute a wider societal benefit.

To examine this we focus on one economic outcome, annual earnings. If one aggregates all of the individual earnings benefits accruing from open access, how much are economic resources augmented, and what are some of the possible consequences? To explore this question, we started with estimates of annual individual earnings.[11] We then projected the individual earnings benefits to the whole population of beneficiaries. In the case of CUNY we estimated the number in each ethnic group whose entry to CUNY was made possible by its open admissions program. Overall, the total number of entering freshmen from 1970 to 1972 was about 100,000 people, and the proportion of each ethnic group was projected to this base. We included only those who worked full-time in the year 2000. The numbers of individuals in the respective ethnic subgroups of the population are shown in the first column of table 8.6 (additional details of our procedure are given in note b of the table).

When our individual estimates of dollar benefit for the year 2000 are projected to the totals in each ethnic group, aggregate payoffs seem very substantial. For CUNY as a whole, the additional payoff to women was over $102 million for those whose entry to a four-year college or to a community college was made possible by broader access. That is to say, in total they earned $102 million more in the year 2000 than they would have if the open admissions policy had not been in effect.

For the national sample (NLSY) we aggregated individual benefits by projecting the proportion of individuals in each ethnic and gender

Table 8.6   Aggregate Annual Dollar Benefits of Open Access, by Gender and Ethnicity

	Number Working Full-Time	Average Annual Dollar Benefit[a]	Aggregate Dollar Benefit (in Millions)[b]
CUNY women			
Whites	6,413	$9,705	$62.2
Blacks	4,887	5,002	24.4
Hispanics	2,038	7,868	16.0
Total benefit to all open access students			$102.6
National men and women			(In billions)[b]
White men	2,838,593	$ 7,610	$21.6
White women	1,246,866	10,627	13.3
Black women	489,500	2,873	1.4
Black men	507,699	6,014	3.1
Hispanic women	158,267	4,581	0.8
Hispanic men	256,075	5,137	1.3
Total benefit to all open access students			$41.5

Sources: CUNY Women File and NLSY79–Adult File.

[a]Calculated from figures shown in table 8.3.

[b]Aggregate dollar benefits were calculated as follows: For the CUNY sample, we began with the aggregated population in the 1970 to 1972 cohorts, 99,000, of which 51,127 were women. From our "mother sample" data, 66.4 percent were white women, 18.9 percent were black, and 11.4 percent were Hispanic. Of these, the percentage working full-time was 62.9 percent of whites, 79.8 percent of blacks, and 79.5 percent of Hispanics. We then calculated the percentage whose level of entry to college was changed according to our procedures for producing a "selective" admissions system. Thus, the number working full-time whose admissions level was changed is displayed in the first column of the table. We then multiplied the average dollar benefit for each group by the number of people in that group. The product, "aggregate dollar benefit," is presented in the third column.

For the NLSY79 sample, we began with the number of people in each ethnic and gender group between the ages of thirty-five and forty-four in the March 2000 Current Population Survey (U.S. Census Bureau). We then applied the percentage of full-time workers from the NLSY. We also applied the percentage of the NLSY who entered college. We multiplied this figure by the percentage whose level of college entry would have been affected under our model of selective admissions. These numbers are displayed in the first column of the table. Each number was multiplied by the average dollar benefit for each group, displayed in column two of the table. The products are shown in column three.

category who benefited from open access (the procedural details are provided in note b of table 8.6) to the national population (between the ages of thirty-five and forty-four). When benefits are projected from individuals in the sample to the population, aggregate dollar benefits are in the billions for every ethnic group except Hispanic women, who fall just short of this threshold, with an aggregate increment of $800 million. Across all groups the aggregate payoff was over $41 billion more in a single year than it would have been if there had been no broad opportunity for college.

Impressive as they seem, these estimates of benefit, which were calculated for a single point in time, the year 2000, convey only a partial sense of the economic benefits of open access. Obviously, these figures would increase dramatically if all the years of the affected persons' work careers were taken into account.

Undoubtedly, very substantial economic benefits have resulted from the college opportunity created by open access policies. The aggregated group payoffs indicate that under inclusive admissions, the billions of dollars in additional earnings add substantially to the tax base at federal, state, and local levels. Of course, a portion of the bonus goes to finance higher education, both institutionally and in the form of student financial aid. With regard to the latter, we note that the $41 billion national open access benefit amassed in one year alone is more than three times the approximately $12 billion spent by the federal government on Pell grants (student grants) in 2003 (Heller 2005).

The Difference It Made: A Summing Up

The results we have reviewed highlight what opening the gates of academe did in contrast to what might have been lost if students designated as "unqualified" or "not college material" had been excluded from four-year schools or turned away from college entirely. Why a society would want to roll back the clock and forgo these benefits is a puzzle. Nationwide, opening the gates has also provided a great boost to equity, helping to fuel the growth of the black and Hispanic middle classes and improving the prospects for students from low-income family backgrounds.

Of course, these findings are not an excuse to give up on educational reform. More still needs to be done to improve the quality of high school preparation for disadvantaged students. For example, more effort could be made to provide an equitable distribution of opportunities to take a college preparatory curriculum and to provide wider access to advanced placement tests for college credits. And policy needs to be developed to help increase college completion rates as well as to shorten the time it takes many students—especially minority and low-income ones—to graduate.

But critics who would like to see a return to earlier days would have us believe that the open admissions era in American higher education has been an all-around failure and has hurt those it aimed to help. Our research suggests that the opposite is true: open access to college has provided important benefits for many disadvantaged students who otherwise would not have completed college degrees. Much would have been lost if these students had not been able to attend.

Our research shows that, on average, the credentials these students earned are worth about as much as those of other degree holders. Certainly premonitions that degrees would have little worth in the labor market are not borne out by earnings data. And of the highest importance is the fact that a poor mother entering college raises the odds that life chances in the next generation will be improved.

Notwithstanding the great benefits stemming from it, open access is not a panacea. Although it has diminished the effects of cumulative disadvantage—the roots of which lie early in the life course—it has not erased them. The weaker a student's high school preparation, the lower are his or her chances of completing a degree in college. Even under open access, students who are disadvantaged by weak preparation in high school are far more likely to start college in two-year institutions. This placement in turn diminishes the chances that these entrants will eventually complete B.A. or higher degrees. Lower educational attainment leads to diminished earnings prospects. And for students who complete a B.A. because open access gave them that opportunity, years may be added to the time it takes them to cross the academic finish line because of initial academic weaknesses, starting in a two-year institution, fragile economic circumstances, and being a parent while in college. Additional time to degree diminishes the odds of going on to graduate school and cuts down on the edge provided by work experience after degree completion. Minority students are the ones most likely to experience these continuing disadvantages. Adding to these greater difficulties in women's educational careers are subsequent ones in which the potential benefits of college, including their children's chances of going to college, are partly undercut when educated women have to make it through life or go through long periods without spouses or partners.

These effects of cumulative disadvantage are clearly ameliorated by open educational opportunity; conversely, under selective college admissions their impact would be far harsher. Students with weak high school records would much more likely be turned away from college, or at best, restricted to the two-year college tier. For those turned away, subsequent chances of unemployment would be much greater or work opportunities would typically be restricted to the lowest rungs of the occupational ladder. Community colleges would account for a larger share of college credentials, so that more graduates would find themselves in the least-rewarded jobs available to those with postsecondary credentials. Long-term economic prospects would be far dimmer and college chances in the second generation would be slimmer. In short, life chances under open access have greater promise, relative to the bleaker outlook for disadvantaged individuals under selective admissions.

Even though race and ethnicity cast a long shadow that college attendance cannot totally erase, open access higher education is a critically important policy that has helped many disadvantaged students whom some would write off as unqualified. Because of open access, inequalities in educational attainment and economic well-being are substantially narrower than they otherwise would have been.

Epilogue: The Retreat from Open Access

Even though open access provides important benefits to individuals and contributes to the public good, recent trends in public policy have been moving in the opposite direction, threatening to erode the influence of higher education in advancing social and economic equity. Among the most important changes are those that have been occurring in fiscal policies. Since the mid-1970s, the share of state appropriations for higher education as a proportion of all state spending has spiraled downward, so that by 2005 the investment effort of the states was 65 percent of where it stood in 1976 (Heller 2005; Mortenson 2005a).[12] Since state funds are the largest single source of support for public colleges (Bowen, Kurzweil, and Tobin 2005), these cutbacks have great significance for their finances.

Partly to offset loss of revenue, tuition at public colleges has skyrocketed.[13] Since public institutions enroll the overwhelming proportion (over 80 percent) of the nation's undergraduates, a large proportion of college costs has in effect been shifted to students themselves.

Although rising tuition would be expected to impose the greatest difficulties of college affordability for low-income students, over the last three decades they have been helped, at least partly, by need-based financial aid, for example through the federal Pell grant program, which began in the early 1970s (Heller 2005). Pell grants have played an important role in enabling low-income students to attend college, but their contribution in defraying college expenses has not kept up with increasing tuition: in 1976 Pell awards covered about 72 percent of costs at the average public four-year school. By 2003, a maximum award contributed only 38 percent, or about half this much (Heller 2005).

This shrinking contribution of need-based grants is partly the result of a shift toward merit-based ones. For example, in the state of Georgia, all who graduate high school with a B average are entitled to a full tuition scholarship at any public college in the state, or, if they attend an in-state private college, they receive a grant of $500 (Bowen, Kurzweil, and Tobin 2005; Heller 2005).[14] Since there is an association between academic grades and family income, this merit-based aid ends up being allocated disproportionately to students from middle- and upper-income families.

At the federal level, loan programs have outpaced grants as a source of support. Loans do not defray college costs as grants help to do, but they do delay payments—presumably to a time when former students, having presumably attained degrees, are benefiting from the higher earnings they receive. Among low-income students, loans provide less of an incentive for college going than grants (Bowen, Kurzweil, and Tobin 2005, 201–3).

Tax policy has become another financial aid vehicle, as most new federal financial aid has been provided through the tax code (Burman et al. 2005). For example, tax credits allow taxpayers to deduct a share of tuition costs from federal taxes (Heller 2005). Such credits mostly benefit middle and upper middle-income families.

The growing role of loans, merit-based grants, and tax credits reflects increasing political support for financial assistance to middle- and even upper-income families. Indeed, Thomas G. Mortenson (2005b) points out that given the current financial aid structure, the poorest families have the largest need that is not covered by financial aid. So even though the amount of financial aid of all kinds has increased, in its newer forms it has been less helpful to the students most in need.

As a consequence of these financial aid trends, proportionally fewer students from low-income and minority families are likely to enter college. But inadequate funding to meet college costs has more complex results than just preventing enrollment. Students with unmet financial need may, in an effort to control costs, delay matriculation immediately after high school, or may choose less expensive shorter-term programs such as two-year community college studies or technical programs in proprietary schools. They may attend college part-time, or interrupt their attendance by temporarily dropping out to save money. Such choices undoubtedly extend the time needed to graduate, and likely diminish the level of credential eventually attained—a certificate or A.A. degree rather than a B.A. or postgraduate degree. Indeed, these choices can ultimately reduce the chances of crossing the educational finish line at all. One of the ironies of inadequate financial aid can be that it creates a vicious circle: by forcing some students to extend the time needed to complete a degree, the aid they do receive may run out as a result of time limitations—further diminishing academic chances.

In the mid-1960s, federal policy aimed to equalize higher education opportunity by expanding programs to enroll students of low and moderate income. The aim, as summarized by Leonard E. Burman et al. (2005, v) was "not only [to] improve college attendance rates

. . . but also [to] provide such students with broader institutional choices and better chances of completing college. These intentions remain unfulfilled. While the college participation rates of low-income students have improved over time, the gap in attendance between them and students from the highest income quartile is still nearly 30 percentage points. Even after controlling for ability . . . , the gap remains at 22 percent (Dynarski 1999). Moreover, low- and moderate-income students are disproportionately enrolled in two-year institutions and even more heavily in short-term programs in for-profit and technical schools.

In addition to issues of financial aid, continuing controversy about who is and who is not college material threatens to undercut access for students whose educational backgrounds have not prepared them so well. The issue is often framed in terms of the legitimacy of remediation in higher education. The sources of opposition to remedial courses or programs run the gamut from those who think that students classified as underprepared should not be in college at all to those who feel that the burden of such programs should be shouldered entirely by community colleges. Some places have policies specifying that students should not be allowed to register for regular courses until they have completed remedial courses and demonstrated skills proficiency. Under still other policies, remedial students and/or their high schools can be charged by colleges when they offer work that—it is claimed—should have been completed in high school (Long 2005).

If policies on remediation prevent some students from entering B.A. programs or delay them from taking regular college courses, then the proportion of students who ultimately earn at least a bachelor's degree will be diminished, and the odds of earning any degree will be lower.

These various trends create challenges for supporters of open access. On the one hand it is critical to demonstrate successes, as we hope the research presented in this volume (and as Bowen and Bok [1998] and Greenberg [2002] have shown for affirmative action in elite colleges). It is important as well to advance the unfinished business of improving academic preparation in the secondary schools and to do more to improve college graduation rates. In part these two aims are linked. Better academic preparation should increase both the speed with which students complete college and the odds of their doing so. Financial aid targeted to the needs of low-income students should also diminish the likelihood of delayed completion and college dropout.

In view of recent developments in financial and academic policy, there can be no complacency about the future of broad access to college. Many public officials, while not consciously opposed to access for low-income and minority students, have advanced policies that mostly are helpful to more affluent segments of the college student population, thus shrinking the resources available for the least advantaged. In the debate over academic policy, the voices opposed to broad access are far from quiet. The battle for college opportunity continues.

= Appendix A =

Data Sources and Methods

Most of the analyses presented in this book draw their data from two large surveys, one of which we call the CUNY survey, and the other the NLSY (National Longitudinal Survey of Youth). Both studies are longitudinal, following representative samples of women for decades from roughly their late teens until they had reached middle age by the year 2000. This substantial time span (CUNY's was longer than the NLSY because it was started earlier, in 1972) proved especially important because many of these women dropped out of college, but some later returned and completed their degrees after a hiatus of a decade or more (when the degree is eventually completed, these sorts of interruptions are called "stopouts"). Those dynamics would have been lost if our data had ended earlier, in the years shortly after college.

Both surveys collected multiple indicators of women's current well-being (earnings, household income, home ownership, and occupational, educational, and family situation). As we report in chapter 3, different indicators may paint incongruent pictures; in particular, women's earnings and household incomes often diverge, depending on marital history.

These two surveys contain rich data about the families in which the women grew up—their parents' income and education and occupation, and the women's high school background—allowing us to distinguish between the effects on women's lives of college attendance versus other advantages or disadvantages such as the woman's class background or having a good high school education, or race or marriage.

Finally, both studies were unusual in containing data about three generations: the parents of the women, the women themselves, and the children of these women. The surveys collected information about the children's educational progress and academic skills. Other variables captured how parents raised their children: the kinds of cognitive stimulation and cultural enrichment they provided. Together these data allow us to examine how maternal education influenced the life chances of the offspring in these families (see chapters 4 and 5).

In this methodological appendix we discuss the main features of these two surveys, and also explain a statistical technique that we employed, known as the counterfactual model of causal inference, or, more informally, as "propensity score matching."

The CUNY Longitudinal Survey Data Set

Our survey, undertaken in 2000, was carried out especially for this book. It was based on a cohort of undergraduate women who first entered the various campuses of the City University of New York (CUNY) between 1970 and 1972. CUNY is the nation's largest urban public university and enrolled about 250,000 undergraduates in that period.

Prior to the early 1970s, CUNY had developed into an academically quite selective institution, and few students of color attended. In 1970, bowing to political pressures, the university undertook a radical shift in policy and opened its doors to all graduates of New York City's high schools. On the basis of their high school records, some entering students were only admitted into CUNY's community colleges, which offered two-year associate's of arts, or A.A., degrees, whereas better-prepared students were allowed to enter the four-year colleges to work toward bachelor's of arts, or B.A., degrees.

Open admissions, as the new admissions policy became known, quickly made a huge difference to the demography of the CUNY student body: far more black and Hispanic students were admitted than in years past, and the representation of students from poor and working-class backgrounds soared. Because this policy represented such a big shift, CUNY undertook a large research effort at that time to study the new students. With support from the Exxon and Ford foundations, researchers systematically sampled entering cohorts of students in the early 1970s, collecting information on their high school records, race and ethnicity, and family background (including parental education, occupation, and income), the students' educational and career aspirations, and so on. That baseline study also tracked college grades and graduation through the year 1975 (Lavin, Alba, and Silberstein 1981).

The CUNY baseline data set provided an unusual window into the effects of increased access to higher education. It is especially well suited to studying a population of working-class and poorer college students, many of whom had relatively weak high school preparation. The baseline sample included over 18,000 women, and their social security numbers were recorded. By 1975, some of the women had graduated, others had left CUNY without completing a college degree, and yet others had transferred to other universities.

In the late 1990s, we decided to trace these ex-students and administer a new follow-up survey to determine their final educational attainment, discover their work histories after college, and document their family and financial situation. We also sought information from mothers about the educational outcomes of their children.

We first carried out a pilot study to test our questionnaire and to discover whether we could successfully trace these CUNY women decades later. The pilot study revealed that although the majority of the women still lived near New York City—in New York, New Jersey, and Connecticut—many had scattered around the country. We decided to use a telephone survey to contact them wherever they lived. We developed a questionnaire to collect information from each woman about her life since entering college, and also data on her children's education and accomplishments, from elementary school through college. For women who had more than two children, we asked about the eldest child and about the youngest child over five. A computer-aided telephone interviewing (CATI) program enabled interviewers to follow a "skip pattern" so that only appropriate questions were posed to, say, married women, or to those with children of a certain age.

Relatively few Asian and Native American women attended CUNY in the 1970s, so the follow-up survey limited itself to white, African American, and Hispanic women, of whom there were 18,067 in the baseline database.

We divided the baseline women along three dimensions: race or ethnicity (black, white, or Hispanic), level of college entry (two-year community college versus four-year college), and number of college credits taken by 1975 (fewer than fifteen credits versus more than fifteen). This created a sampling frame containing twelve cells, and we then randomly selected women from each cell to create a sample for the follow-up study.

The number of women selected from each cell reflected certain analytical needs. We deliberately oversampled minority women because examining ethnic contrasts in long-term outcomes was to be an important goal for this study. We also oversampled students who did not get very far in CUNY ("low-credit students," who completed fifteen or fewer credits by 1975) because these low-credit students function as a comparison group when we assess the long-term effects of earning a degree or of exposure to college. In total, we created a stratified random sample of 2,857 women.

Between 1999 and 2001, a commercial survey research firm—Schulman, Ronka, & Bucuvalas, Inc. (SRBI)—located 2,491, or 87 percent, of our 2,857 subjects. SRBI undertook a demanding search protocol that traced members of the CUNY sample through their social security numbers; they consulted three large consumer credit databases that are constantly updated with reports from merchants and utility companies; a separate commercial database that lists address changes (for example, when a magazine subscription or mail is forwarded); and a national registry of deceased persons. Using all these resources, SRBI was able to locate addresses for all but 366 of the follow-up sample nearly thirty years after they had entered college. Eighty-four of the 2,857 women had died in the intervening years.

Under our supervision, SRBI carried out a CATI survey with each woman. Letters were sent to all located respondents, explaining our study and inviting them to participate. We included a stamped postcard so that respondents could indicate the phone number where they preferred to be contacted, and set up a toll-free phone number so subjects could phone into the study center to schedule an interview. We also contacted our subjects by telephone: the credit databases often contained phone numbers or addresses, and when necessary, interviewers used reverse directories to obtain phone numbers for a given address, and phoned respondents directly. Using these approaches, we were able to contact the overwhelming majority of our sample—153 were lost to the study because they had no listed telephone. An additional 199 people were lost to the survey because they refused to be part of our sample, a number that we kept low by paying respondents for being interviewed.

Phone interviews were mainly carried out during the year 2000. In cases where the phone was not answered, or the respondent was unavailable, the protocol required up to ten callbacks over a period of several months. A typical interview lasted about thirty minutes. At the end of this process, we obtained 1,971 completed interviews.

Our survey's response rate was 71 percent: the original 2,857-person sample, minus the 84 deceased, or 2,773; 1,971 complete interviews divided by 2,773 = .71, or 71 percent.

Data from this follow-up survey in 2000 were merged with information that had been collected on these women when they attended college during the early 1970s (the baseline survey). We then compared the baseline survey information for the women whom we successfully re-interviewed in the year 2000 with the same baseline variables for women whom we tried but failed to interview during the follow-up. There were no significant differences between these two groups, suggesting that nonrespondents were not systematically different than respondents, at least on baseline variables. We also compared the characteristics of "easy-to-interview" respondents with "difficult-to-interview" respondents whom we had to call back multiple times or offer a larger payment before we successfully interviewed them. Again, we found no significant differences, suggesting that nonresponse bias was not a major problem in the CUNY follow-up.

We had selected our follow-up sample from the 18,000 baseline women by drawing a certain number of people from each of twelve cells, each cell representing a particular combination of ethnicity, level of entry, and credits earned. To adjust for this stratified sampling, and to ensure that the follow-up sample correctly represented the proportions of each ethnic group, level of entry, and credit level that were present in the early 1970s baseline, we developed sampling weights for each respondent. The value of this weight was the reciprocal of the probability of being selected from the baseline list into the follow-up sample, given the person's cell. After adding these weights, we checked whether the follow-up sample was equivalent to the baseline sample on other baseline variables. The weighted follow-up sample closely mirrored the baseline sample, as shown by table A.1. This makes us confident that the women interviewed in 2000 accurately represent the population of women who attended CUNY in the early 1970s.

Missing Data

In survey research, respondents occasionally refuse or fail to answer one or more questions, resulting in missing data for those particular questions. In general, the frequency of missing data in our CUNY survey was low; the most frequently missing data—for around 19 percent of respondents—was for family income, measured in the baseline survey in the early 1970s. (This is a much lower frequency of missing data than is found for household income in other well-regarded surveys such as the General Social Survey of the National Opinion Research Center at the University of Chicago [NORC].) We adopted a widely used technique known as multiple imputation to "fill" these missing data points. This approach uses the statistical relationships found among variables in a data set to predict or impute several possible values for cases where a data value is missing. We accomplished this with a computer program called Amelia (the program and statistical documentation for this technique are available on the web at http://gking.harvard.edu/stats.shtml). Using Amelia produces five data sets that are identical except for the imputed values for missing variables. The Amelia software associated with the STATA software package allows one to run regression models for each of the five imputed data sets separately, and then average those regression coefficients and related statistics across the five analyses (King et al. 2001). The regression results presented throughout this volume were arrived at by means of this technique for "filling" missing data.

The NLSY Data Set

Although the CUNY data set is a good vehicle for studying the long-term effects of college attendance on a population that includes many minority and working-class students, it represents the experiences of only one (very large) multicampus university, albeit the one that pioneered open admissions. To expand our analyses to the nation as a whole, we sought a data set that included women who attended many different colleges nationwide, and their children. A government-funded survey, the National Longitudinal Survey of Youth, or NLSY79, met

Table A.1 Comparison of Original Sample and Follow-Up Sample, in Percentages, Except as Noted

Variables	Original Sample	Follow-up Sample, Stratified	Follow-up Sample, Weighted
Race			
Black	20.2	32.2	19.9
White	67.8	35.6	68.1
Hispanic	12.0	32.2	12.0
Age at college entry			
Under seventeen	13.3	9.3	13.5
Eighteen	64.6	61.3	65.1
Nineteen	10.2	14.6	10.3
Over twenty	10.7	13.9	10.4
Missing	1.2	0.9	0.8
Family income at entry			
Under $4,000	7.7	11.2	7.3
$4,000 to 9,999	36.7	46.6	36.4
$10,000 to 14,999	23.6	18.2	23.5
$15,000 to 19,999	8.0	5.6	8.5
Over $20,000	4.9	3.2	5.4
Missing	19.1	15.2	18.9
Father's education			
Grammar school	14.5	19.4	13.6
Some high school	23.8	25.9	23.6
High school graduate	30.3	24.6	30.6
Some college	13.0	12.0	13.2
College degree	7.2	4.9	8.3
Postgraduate degree	3.2	2.2	3.0
Missing	7.9	11.0	7.7
Mother's education			
Grammar school	13.2	19.8	12.8
Some high school	23.7	27.1	23.3
High school graduate	41.7	32.4	41.0
Some college	10.6	9.9	11.4
College degree	4.6	3.9	5.2
Postgraduate degree	1.3	1.0	1.4
Missing	5.0	5.9	4.9
Mean total units of high school academic courses	12.37	11.94	12.39
High school GPA			
Under 70	13.9	14.4	13.8
70 to 74.5	18.2	19.2	18.3
75 to 79.9	23.1	26.5	23.8
80 to 84.9	19.4	19.3	18.3
Over 85	20.4	15.3	21.3
Missing	5.0	5.3	4.5

(Table continues on p. 208.)

Table A.1 *Continued*

Variables	Original Sample	Follow-up Sample, Stratified	Follow-up Sample, Weighted
Level of entry to CUNY			
Four-year college	43.4	50.5	43.7
Community college	55.0	49.5	56.3
Missing	1.7	0	0
CUNY status as of June 1975			
Dropout	45.1	46.5	45.3
Persister	21.4	24.8	21.0
Graduate	33.5	28.7	33.8
Mean cumulative CUNY GPA as of June 1975	2.42	2.27	2.41
Standard deviation	(.858)	(.821)	(.859)
Mean cumulative CUNY credits as of June 1975	62.15	58.36	62.01
Standard deviation	(41.11)	(38.75)	(41.11)
Number of remedial courses taken at CUNY			
None	58.1	46.6	57.6
One to two	29.3	31.4	29.8
Three to four	8.8	13.6	8.9
More than four	3.9	8.4	3.7

Source: CUNY Files.

these requirements. The Bureau of Labor Statistics, a branch of the U.S. Department of Labor, administers and funds this ongoing longitudinal survey and several related surveys. The tasks of survey design, development of instruments, and data distribution are subcontracted to the Center for Human Resource Research (CHRR) at Ohio State University. Data collection for the NLSY79 has been carried out partly by the U.S. Census Bureau and partly by the National Opinion Research Center at the University of Chicago.

Many scholars use the NLSY79, and it is viewed as an authoritative source of longitudinal data. The Bureau of Labor Statistics provides an extensive web site about this survey, containing technical details of the sample, the questionnaire and variables, and response rates at http://www.bls.gov/nls/nlsy79.htm. The Center for Human Resource Research (2004) also provides a printed user's guide.

For our purposes, the NLSY79 has two important advantages compared to the CUNY survey. It follows women who attended high school

but never entered college, which is a more powerful contro
assessing the consequences of attending college. It also prov
ments of maternal IQ and of children's academic skills, obtain
the administration of pencil and paper tests at various po
childhood, and assessments of parenting based on home
data are very expensive to collect, and we did not attempt to do so ror
our CUNY survey. One disadvantage of using the NLSY was that it
started later, in 1979; another was that its first wave of data collection
included many women who were still in high school in the years from
1970 to 1972 rather than entering college. As a result, the NLSY survey
has not followed its sample for as many years after college as the CUNY
survey did, and the NLSY children are somewhat younger, on average.
In the year 2000, when we did our follow-up study, the NLSY women
were aged thirty-five to forty-two (the latest data we obtained); the
average age of the CUNY women in 2000 was about forty-seven.

Beyond this, in our NLSY analyses we were limited to whatever
questions the designers of the survey had chosen, while for our CUNY
study we had control over the design of variables. For example, our
CUNY study had better information on women's academic preparation
in high school than our NLSY analyses.

The NLSY79 sample included approximately 6,000 young women
who were representative of their whole age cohort nationwide at that
time. The NLSY79 deliberately oversampled African American, Hispanic,
and economically disadvantaged women. A baseline survey about these
young women and their families was conducted in 1979, and the subjects
were re-interviewed in intervals of about two years until the year 2000.
These surveys were mainly carried out in person, but telephone interviewing was used for some years. When women in this sample had
children, their children were added to the study, and those children
periodically undertook standardized educational assessments and tests
in the years thereafter. Particular analyses focused either on the women
or on the children.

The NLSY collected information on each woman's family of origin,
her IQ, her educational attainment, her marital and work history, and
her economic status. Descriptive statistics on the main variables we used
are discussed in chapter 2. The children's data are presented and discussed
in chapter 4.

Data Analysis: The Counterfactual Model
of Causal Inference

The most common method of statistical modeling encountered in sociology and economics employs the technique known as ordinary least
squares (OLS) regression. Most estimates of the impacts of higher

education on individuals use regression techniques. However, scholars have become increasingly concerned about one potential problem in regression models as conventionally used. Typically, one's goal in modeling is to estimate the causal effect of one particular variable (termed a treatment variable) on an outcome, while controlling for other potentially confounding variables (Lieberson 1985). In this book, for example, we repeatedly estimate the effect of college attendance on some aspect of an adult's later life, and we would like this quantitative estimate to reflect the "pure" effect of college, separate from a person's class background, IQ, or other confounding influences. In the past, researchers believed they had accomplished this by building regression models containing covariates or controls representing those potentially confounding influences. So long as important background variables were controlled for, scholars believed their estimates of the treatment variable (such as education) were reasonably accurate. Over the last two decades, however, statisticians have questioned this belief, and have argued for new techniques that better estimate the effect of a treatment variable.

The perceived problem with conventional regression is that this technique is susceptible to "selection bias." Individuals who have the "treatment" (for example, attend college) differ on average from those who do not receive the treatment (don't go to college), in terms of their values on many covariates. The effects of these background differences can become incorporated into the estimated coefficient for the treatment variable, creating an upward or downward bias and undermining causal inference (Winship and Morgan 1999). Statisticians have developed a theoretical and mathematical framework, known as the "counterfactual model of causal inference," to address this problem (Heckman and Hotz 1989; Heckman et al. 1998; Rosenbaum and Rubin 1983, 1985). An informative website dedicated to this concern and the resulting new technique may be found at http://www.wjh.harvard.edu/~winship/cfa.html.

The counterfactual approach may be understood by analogy to an experimental design with random assignment of subjects into treatment and control groups. In such an experiment, the random assignment of subjects into the two groups assures that both groups are identical on all background characteristics, so that any difference subsequently observed between the control and treatment groups on an outcome is attributable to the treatment alone.

Something analogous is achieved in a counterfactual model by first building a model that predicts the dichotomous treatment variable. This yields a propensity score (explained later). A sample is then constructed using this propensity score, such that the treatment and control group are "matched"—close to identical on background characteristics, which removes or drastically reduces any selection bias.

In many of the analyses reported in this book, the "treatment" is attending college. In such a case, a logistic regression is first carried out that predicts who attends college. That model includes all available variables that might distinguish students who receive the treatment—attend college—from those who do not. Nonlinear as well as linear versions of predictors are included in this model, and interaction terms between predictors are added. The resulting logistic regression equation predicts for each person in the sample the probability of that student's going to college. This probability statistic is known as a propensity score, and it takes values between 0 and 1.

A second step, known as caliper matching, then matches or pairs each person possessing a certain propensity score who did receive the treatment (entered college) with a different person who has a nearly identical propensity score (likelihood of going to college), but who actually did not receive the treatment (did not enter college). A computer algorithm in the STATA statistical package generates these matched pairs of respondents, selecting at random from treated and untreated individuals whose propensity scores are within .01 of each other. The second person in each pair functions like a member of a control group, providing a "counterfactual" estimate of what the outcome for the treated individual would have been if that person had not received the treatment.

Statisticians argue that for propensity matching to approximate an experiment with random assignment, it is not necessary that the treatment group be identical to the control group on every predictor, so long as the two groups are correctly matched on the single propensity for treatment (Rosenbaum and Rubin 1983). Nevertheless, as a precaution, practitioners examine the balance between the treatment and control group on many predictors (see Harding 2003). Following this practice, for each predictor we calculated a standard bias that equals the difference between the mean value of a given predictor for the treatment group and the mean value of that predictor for the controls, divided by the standard deviation of the predictor (Rosenbaum and Rubin 1985). In all the analyses reported in this book the matching "worked" in the sense that matching greatly reduced the standard biases on each predictor variable, and hence minimized the risk of selection bias.

Although the propensity score is calculated using measured variables ("observables"), some researchers have demonstrated through simulations that selection bias due to unobserved variables may also be reduced by propensity score matching (DiPrete and Engelhardt 2000). If that were the case, propensity score matching would further reduce risks of selection bias in regression analyses.

The last step in a counterfactual analysis employs the sample matched on the propensity score to compare the treatment group with the control group on a dependent or outcome variable. OLS or logistic regression may be used to estimate the effect of the treatment on the outcome for the matched sample. The resulting coefficient for the treatment dummy indicates the estimated average effect of treatment for those who receive the treatment. In our case, it might be the average effect on the likelihood of becoming married of entering college rather than ending one's education as a high school graduate; or the average effect of completing a B.A. on one's child's math and reading score at age seven, after minimizing selection bias and controlling for the effects of various background variables.

In preparing the research for this book we routinely performed both conventional regression analyses and propensity score–matched models. In most tables, where we anticipated that selection effects might be greater, we present the results of both techniques. In other places, to simplify presentation, we only report one of the approaches, but we assure the reader that where this is the case, it is because the results of both techniques are almost identical.

One other aspect of propensity score–matched models may puzzle the reader: the sample size, or N, is typically smaller in a propensity analysis than for the corresponding regression model. This can occur for two reasons. The first case is apparent when less than half of the sample received the treatment. If, say, one-third of the sample went to college, and each of these college individuals is matched with one person who did not go to college, then the resulting matched sample will only have two-thirds of the number of cases in it as the original unmatched sample (the one-third who were treated plus one untreated match for each).

A second reason why propensity matching can lower the N is that some individuals have such very high or very low propensity scores that a match cannot be found for them. Imagine a student from a very affluent family who has a high IQ and a perfect 4.0 GPA in high school, and takes many rigorous classes in high school. That person will have an extremely high propensity to attend college. The propensity technique attempts to match this person with someone having an equally high propensity of going to college, who did not in fact go to college. Perhaps there is no one in the sample with such a high propensity who did not go to college, in which case a match is impossible. A similar logic would apply at the other extreme: it may be hard to match a person with a very low propensity to go to college because there is no one with that score who actually went to college. The result is that propensity models exclude some cases because it cannot match them.

A conservative bias is created by the reduction of sample size following propensity score matching. The smaller N may cause some coefficients that were statistically significant in a conventional regression to become nonsignificant in the propensity model, even though the size of the coefficient may not have changed. We draw the reader's attention to this in the text, when it occurs.

A potentially more serious issue occurs if the lower sample size means the matched sample looks substantially different from the unmatched regression sample, on various variables, because of the cases that have been dropped. Since we routinely used both techniques for each analysis and compared the results, we did check to be sure that matched samples were appropriately constructed.

In sum, the reader should view our use of the counterfactual model of causal inference as a precaution against selection bias. In most cases the substantive findings were not changed by the use of this new technique, but its use alongside conventional regression modeling should provide additional confidence in our findings.

═ Appendix B ═

Additional Tables

**Table B.1 Determinants of Entry to a Four-Year College,
(Logistic Coefficients)**

Determining Factor	CUNY Women		National Women	
	Model 1	Model 2	Model 1	Model 2
Constant	.539***	−11.264***	.238***	−1.422***
Ethnicity[a]				
Black	−1.112***	.704***	−.191**	.320***
Hispanic	−.920***	.184	−.481***	.073
Parents' highest grade completed		.173**		.225***
Low-income family of origin[b]		.043		.009
Grades in high school academic courses		.104***		.528***
Units of academic courses in high school[c]		.291***		.564***
Rank in high school		.015**		
Age at entry to college		−.107**		−.039**
Had a child before entering college		−.597		−.402**
Pseudo R-square	.040	.313	.005	.104

Sources: CUNY Women File and NLSY79–Adults.
[a]Reference category is white women; women whose ethnicity is "other" are not included in either sample.
[b]Defined as less than $10,000 in 1970 dollars.
[c]Measured in the NLSY as a dummy variable: followed a college preparatory curriculum in high school.
*p < .05; **p < .01; ***p < .001

Table B.2 Determinants of B.A. Attainment (Logistic Coefficients)

	CUNY Women			National Women		
Determinant	Model 1	Model 2	Model 3	Model 1	Model 2	Model 3
Constant	.477***	-7.491***	-3.093*	-.443***	-4.98***	-.787
Ethnicity[a]						
Black	-.860***	.270	.423*	-.864***	-.038	-.239
Hispanic	-.931***	-.126	.014	-.928***	-.105	-.282
Parent's highest grade completed		.113	.029		.357***	.159***
Low-income family of origin[b]		-.192	-.067		-.378*	-.318*
Average in high school academic courses		.060***	.013		1.028***	.726***
Academic courses in high school[c]		.197***	.089**		.918***	.499***
Rank in high school		.003	-.002			
Degree aspirations[d]						
Associate's degree			-1.232***			-1.299***
Bachelor's degree			-.510**			-.427***

(Table continues on p. 216.)

Table B.2 *Continued*

Determinant	CUNY Women			National Women		
	Model 1	Model 2	Model 3	Model 1	Model 2	Model 3
Started at a community college			-.973***			-.987***
Liberal curriculum in college			.446**			
Took remedial courses in college[e]			-.195			
GPA in first year of college			.752***			
Worked full-time as an undergraduate						-1.564***
Age at entry to college			.000			-.051*
Had child within five years of entering college			-.255			-1.362***
Pseudo R-square	.029	.148	.263	.031	.232	.363

Sources: CUNY Women File and NLSY79–Adults.

[a]Reference category is white women; women whose ethnicity is "other" are not included in the CUNY sample.

[b]Defined as less than $10,000 in 1970 dollars.

[c]Measured for NLSY women as a dummy for followed a college preparatory curriculum in high school.

[d]Reference category consists of those who aspire to a postgraduate degree.

[e]A variable for number of remedial courses taken in college was not significant either; the issue of "degree" of remediation is explored further in chapter 7.

*p < .05; **p < .01; ***p < .001

Table B.3 Percentage of Women Completing Highest Degree Within Different Time Spans

	CUNY Women				National Women			
	White	Black	Hispanic	All	White	Black	Hispanic	All
Associate's degree								
Within two years	42.4	18.8	24.4	34.2	40.1	28.3	39.1	38.3
Three to four years	33.6	31.9	40.0	34.2	23.8	22.6	26.1	23.8
Five to six years	5.5	13.0	6.7	7.4	7.8	9.4	8.7	8.1
Seven or more years	18.6	36.2	38.9	24.2	28.3	39.6	26.0	29.9
Unweighted N of cases	127	120	121	368	176	127	76	379
Bachelor's degree								
Within four years	47.2	15.1	22.4	40.2	60.0	38.7	32.0	57.0
Five to six years	27.1	29.1	24.5	27.2	16.9	25.8	20.0	17.8
Seven to fourteen years	12.8	33.7	22.4	16.7	16.2	22.5	32.0	17.4
Fifteen or more years	13.0	22.1	30.6	15.9	6.9	12.9	16.0	7.8
Unweighted N of cases	203	173	163	539	400	139	71	610
Postgraduate degree								
Within six years	32.1	7.3	14.3	28.2	16.7	0.0	9.1	15.4
Seven to ten years	26.6	20.0	25.7	25.8	37.4	33.3	54.5	37.9
Eleven to fourteen years	11.4	18.2	20.0	12.7	22.1	20.0	18.2	21.8
Fifteen or more years	30.0	54.5	40.0	33.3	23.8	46.7	18.2	24.9
Unweighted N of cases	167	118	121	406	149	33	33	215

Sources: CUNY Women File and NLSY79–Adult File.

Table B.4 Determinants of Time to B.A. (OLS Coefficients)

Determinant	CUNY Women			National Women		
	Model 1	Model 2	Model 3	Model 1	Model 2	Model 3
Constant	6.320**	19.945***	11.862**	5.488	9.6907***	11.441***
Ethnicity[a]						
Black	2.706***	.752	-.537	1.095***	.680	.645
Hispanic	2.920***	1.418	.569	2.154***	1.839***	1.667***
Parent's highest grade completed		-.249	-.123		-.125	-.010
Low-income family of origin[b]		.312	.329		-.589	-.609
Average in high school academic courses		-.095	-.007		-1.023***	-.695***
Academic courses in high school[c]		-.280**	-.134		-.604*	-.302
Rank in high school		-.014	-.002			
Degree aspirations[d]						
Associate's degree			.323			.899
Bachelor's degree			-.164			.416
Started at a community college			2.685***			2.953***
Liberal curriculum in college			-.238			
Took remedial courses in college			.475			
GPA in first year of college			-1.23**			
Worked full-time as an undergraduate						3.402***
Age at entry to college			.013			-.239***
Had child within five years of entering college			3.0629**			.951**
Adjusted R-square	.035	.086	.155	.032	.071	.192

Sources: CUNY Women File and NLSY79–Adults.

[a] Reference category is "white women"; women whose ethnicity is "other" are not included in the CUNY sample.
[b] Defined as less than $10,000 in 1970 dollars.
[c] Measured for NLSY women as a dummy variable: followed a college preparatory curriculum in high school.
[d] Reference category is aspires to a postgraduate degree.
*p < .05; **p < .01; ***p < .001

Table B.5 Labor-Market and Family-Context Variables, CUNY and NLSY

	CUNY				National[a]			
Variable	White	Black	Hispanic	All	White	Black	Hispanic	All
Cumulative college GPA	2.64	1.94	2.12	2.46		b		
Employment status								
Not working	14.2	12.5	12.3	13.7	15.0	10.6	11.7	14.1
Working part-time	22.5	6.8	7.8	18.0	29.2	15.0	22.1	26.6
Working full-time	63.3	80.7	79.9	68.3	55.9	74.4	66.2	59.3
Worked all or nearly all of the past 15 years[c]	61.0	84.6	80.0	67.4	64.2	62.2	61.4	63.7
Employment sector								
For-profit or private	47.2	33.8	43.6	44.3	59.4	57.5	56.3	58.9
Nonprofit	23.1	27.9	23.9	24.0	12.6	9.8	9.5	12.0
Government or public	19.9	34.1	27.1	23.3	17.4	28.6	27.2	19.7
Self-employed	9.9	4.2	5.5	8.4	10.6	4.1	6.9	9.5
Marital status								
Married or partnered	74.6	43.3	59.1	67.2	73.5	39.1	63.3	67.9
Divorced or separated	11.8	30.6	26.8	16.9	16.9	30.5	20.9	19.1
Widowed	1.8	5.4	3.2	2.6	.5	2.2	1.3	.8
Never married	11.8	20.7	10.9	13.3	9.1	28.3	14.6	12.3
Ever had a marital disruption		b			37.2	55.7	48.5	40.1
Number of children	1.65	1.66	1.64	1.65	1.71	1.81	1.89	1.74
Age of mother when she had first child	28.9	25.4	26.8	28.0	26.1	22.3	23.9	25.4

(Table continues on p. 220.)

Table B.5 Continued

Variable	CUNY				National			
	White	Black	Hispanic	All	White	Black	Hispanic	All
Timing of first child								
Before entering college	.8	16.0	6.4	4.2	12.3	25.1	22.0	14.8
Within five years of entering college	7.0	23.4	20.6	11.5	16.8	28.9	24.8	19.1
Five to ten years after entering college	27.8	21.7	28.0	26.7	23.9	13.3	18.4	22.0
More than ten years after								
entering college	40.1	16.8	24.8	34.2	23.2	11.0	14.9	20.9
No children	24.3	22.2	20.2	23.4	23.7	21.7	19.9	23.2
Ever was a single mother[d]	23.2	62.0	50.0	33.5	37.6	64.9	54.3	42.8
Spouse is currently employed	95.1	79.6	87.7	92.6	97.7	94.4	98.8	97.5
Spouse's mean personal earnings[e]	$65,530	$41,396	$42,397	$60,561	$60,883	$42,293	$52,581	$58,904
Spouse's occupational prestige	52.9	45.4	47.6	51.7	48.8	37.9	45.4	47.6
Spouse's educational attainment[f]								
High school diploma or less		b			34.0	41.2	41.1	35.1
Some college					10.8	18.2	14.0	11.6
Associate's degree					11.7	18.2	15.0	12.5
Bachelor's degree					23.8	15.8	15.9	22.6
Postgraduate degree					19.7	6.7	14.0	18.2
Lives in New York metropolitan area	69.5	66.4	57.5	67.6		b		

Sources: CUNY Women File and NLSY79–Adults.

[a]National data include only white, black, and Hispanic women who entered college from the 1996, 1998, and 2000 waves of the NLSY79–Adults file.

[b]Data not available.

[c]For the CUNY women, this item measures women who worked "all or nearly all of the time" over the past fifteen years, and for NLSY women, it measures women who worked more than 75 percent of the time over the past ten years.

[d]Calculated only for mothers.

[e]Estimated for CUNY women by subtracting personal earnings from household income for married women. Data are not estimated for national women.

[f]Spouse's educational attainment is taken from spouse's highest grade completed; we have no independent verification that these represent actual degrees attained.

Table B.6 Home Ownership (Unstandardized Logistic Coefficients)

	Model 1	Model 2	Model 3	Model 4	Model 5
CUNY Women					
Constant	.55691***	1.5759***	-2.6221*	-4.8026***	-2.3571
Some college[a]	.04381		-.21458	-.21683	-.57455
Associate's degree	.35394		.18247	.29726	-.26025
Bachelor's degree	.85023***		.35864	.37172	-.03501
Advanced degree	1.2134***		.56344*	.52743	.20607
Black[b]		-1.3703***	-.81412***	-.40837*	-1.516***
Hispanic		-1.0827***	-.65432***	-.53556**	-1.1165**
Age			.00701	.01573	.00746
Low-income family of origin[c]			-.34997*	-.27605	-.35197*
Parents' highest grade completed			.06669	.05005	.07039
Grades in high school academic courses			.04566***	.03992**	.04667***
Units of high school academic courses			-.00825	.00756	-.01073
Married or partnered				1.0294***	
Any children				1.1352***	
Ever a single mother				-.83296***	
Spouse's prestige				.0188	
Black—some college					.80205
Black—associate's degree					.88655
Black—bachelor's degree					.8199
Black—advanced degree					.73744
Hispanic—some college					.40796
Hispanic—associate's degree					.71116
Hispanic—bachelor's degree					.52935
Hispanic—advanced degree					.50706
Pseudo R-square	.0354	.0609	.1008	.2347	.1034

(Table continues on p. 222.)

Table B.6 *Continued*

	Model 1	Model 2	Model 3	Model 4	Model 5
National Women					
Constant	.29601***	1.2763***	-.59461	-1.6855*	-.46958
Some college	.02489		-.00941	.01932	-.1149
Associate's degree	.50249***		.32747*	.20795	-.08051
Bachelor's degree	.96392***		.39008**	.26514	.36978*
Advanced degree	1.286***		.5518***	.43376	.15546
Black		-1.48***	-.99318***	-.62302***	-1.0637***
Hispanic		-.96264***	-.68886***	-.65313***	-.99513***
Age			.03167	.02877	.03091
Low-income family of origin			-.18833*	-.1425	-.19787*
Parents' highest grade completed			-.05365***	-.0578***	-.05358***
Grades in high school academic courses			.26793***	.1869**	.26538***
AFQT			.01144***	.01245***	.01173***
Married or partnered				1.3649***	
Any children				.64166***	
Ever a single mother				-.44842***	
Spouse's prestige				.00573*	
Black—some college					.05489
Black—associate's degree					.54301*
Black—bachelor's degree					-.21559
Black—advanced degree					.96796*
Hispanic—some college					.37602
Hispanic—associate's degree					.83694*
Hispanic—bachelor's degree					.47222
Hispanic—advanced degree					.73339
Pseudo R-square	.0287	.0743	.1152	.2157	.1183

Source: CUNY women file and NLSY79–Adults.

[a]Reference category is an early dropout in the CUNY sample, defined as having less than sixteen college credits, and a high school graduate in the NLSY.

[b]White is the reference category. Women of "other" ethnic groups are not included in the CUNY or NLSY samples.

[c]Defined as less than $10,000 in 1970 dollars.

*p< .05; **p< .01; ***p< .001.

Table B.7 Logged Value of Home, National Women (Unstandardized OLS Coefficients)

	Model 1	Model 2	Model 3	Model 4	Model 5
Constant	11.263***	11.715***	11.107***	10.713***	11.19***
Some college[a]	.18789***		.13189**	.12742**	.08094
Associate's degree	.28417***		.19042**	.15625*	.07519
Bachelor's degree	.69183***		.41981***	.32717***	.33983***
Advanced degree	.74296***		.42416***	.33641***	.37802***
Black[b]		-.6014***	-.31806***	-.21953***	-.47618***
Hispanic		-.1493***	.12958*	.12534*	.05672
Age			-.00361	-.00348	-.0047
Low-income family of origin[c]			-.18985***	-.16973***	-.18973***
Parents' highest grade completed			.02699***	.02252***	.0275***
Grades in high school academic courses			-.00227	-.01582	-.00421
AFQT80			.00441***	.00414***	.00453***
Married or partnered				.3056***	
Any children				.05153	
Ever a single mother				-.07347	
Spouse's prestige				.00583***	
Black—some college					.20243
Black—associate's degree					.32271*
Black—bachelor's degree					.26114*
Black—advanced degree					-.03924
Hispanic—some college					.03117
Hispanic—associate's degree					.18749
Hispanic—bachelor's degree					.16497
Hispanic—advanced degree					.23988
Adjusted R-square	.0824	.0664	.1704	.2177	.1715

Source: NLSY79–Adults
[a]Reference category is a high school graduate.
[b]White is the reference category. Women of "other" ethnic groups are not included.
[c]Defined as less than $10,000 in 1970 dollars.
*p < .05; **p < .01; ***p < .001

Table B.8 Logged Value of Other Financial Assets[a] of National Women (Unstandardized OLS Coefficients)

	Model 1	Model 2	Model 3	Model 4	Model 5
Constant	8.4943***	9.7935***	7.3346***	6.8777***	7.3748***
Some college[b]	.37174***		.25308*	.2261*	.25453
Associate's degree	.77534***		.47454***	.32572*	.31706
Bachelor's degree	1.9839***		1.1121***	.77728***	1.0622***
Advanced degree	2.1202***		1.0512***	.65852***	1.0868***
Black[c]		−1.4829***	−.64819***	−.33868**	−.53913**
Hispanic		−.92102***	−.11473	−.09642	−.36661
Age			.00535	.00957	.00509
Low-income family of origin[d]			−.34016***	−.27083**	−.34665***
Parents' highest grade completed			.04047*	.02754	.04025*
Grades in high school academic courses			.16527*	.09832	.16397*
AFQT80			.01604***	.01432***	.0161***
Married or partnered				.86162***	
Any children				−.43556***	
Ever a single mother				−.32118***	
Spouse's prestige				.01493***	
Black—some college					−.16898
Black—associate's degree					−.12465
Black—bachelor's degree					−.07836
Black—advanced degree					−.10294
Hispanic—some college					.22839
Hispanic—associate's degree					.8684**
Hispanic—bachelor's degree					.41379
Hispanic—advanced degree					−.14
Adjusted R-square	.1067	.0732	.2025	.2671	.2030

Source: NLSY79–Adults

[a] Assets consist of the total dollar value of savings, CDs, stocks, other investments, retirement plans, and estates, and are top-coded at $350,000.

[b] Reference category is a high school graduate.

[c] White is the reference category. Women of "other" ethnic groups are not included.

[d] Defined as less than $10,000 in 1970 dollars.

*p < .05; **p < .01; ***p < .001

═ Notes ═

Chapter 1

1. That progress has slowed since the 1980s, and the United States now lags behind several other industrialized nations in the proportion of young people entering higher education. See Claudia Goldin and Lawrence Katz (2001).

2. See William G. Bowen and Derek Bok (1998). See also Bowen, Martin Kurzweil, and Eugene Tobin (2005) for analyses of equity issues in access to college.

3. In their book, *The Shape of the River*, Bowen and Bok (1998) estimated that about 20 percent of U.S. universities are selective, in the sense of having many applicants competing for each opening. The bulk of universities and colleges admit all applicants who meet basic entrance requirements.

4. Douglas Massey et al.'s study (1993) of minority freshmen at Ivy League and other selective colleges, *The Source of the River*, found that many black freshmen in those colleges are relatively well off in terms of socioeconomic origins. The large majority of minority college students in the United States attends less selective institutions and comes from considerably less advantaged family backgrounds.

5. More details on each of the data sets and our analytical methods are provided in each of the following chapters and in the appendix A of this book.

6. William J. Bennett (1990), *The De-Valuing of America*.

7. Susan P. Choy (2002) defines the "traditional undergraduate" as "one who earns a high school diploma, enrolls full time immediately after finishing high school, depends on parents for financial support, and either does not work during the school year or works part time." Only 27 percent of today's undergraduates are traditional by this definition, and those who take a classical liberal arts curriculum at a residential college constitute an even smaller subset.

Chapter 2

1. During the 1950s and 1960s going to college became more and more popular in New York City, but the number of places at CUNY remained constant in the face of a great increase in the number of applications for admission. This produced heightened competition for places even in the system's community colleges.

2. Variants of CUNY's use of high school rank to determine admission have spread in the last few years to other state university systems such as Texas and California. In the wake of court cases and legislative actions against race-based affirmative action, university systems have instead adopted a policy of admitting those in the top ranks of every high school class. A class ranking cut-off applies equally to all applicants, but it disproportionately benefits minority applicants wherever schools are highly segregated.

3. In addition, CUNY stipulated that transfer to a B.A. program with full credit was to be guaranteed for all community college graduates.

4. For a more-detailed description of the processes leading up to the open-admissions policy, see David E. Lavin, Richard D. Alba, and Richard A. Silberstein (1981) and Lavin and David Hyllegard (1996).

5. Part of the reason CUNY's program was perceived as unique is that it came on the heels of a decade or so in which admissions to four-year colleges in the system were very competitive, requiring in some years high school averages of near 90 for entry to some schools.

6. Details of the survey samples and statistical methods are provided in appendix A.

7. See the variable "Mean College Preparatory Credits" in table 2.1. Students were expected to accumulate four college-preparatory credits per year from the freshman through senior years of high school. Therefore, a difference of four credits would be the equivalent of one year, and two credits would represent a half year.

8. In the last year before open admissions, 1969, 75 percent of all minority entrants (combining blacks and Hispanics into one "minority" category) were placed in community colleges, compared with 40 percent of all whites. So ethnic inequality in initial positioning, while substantial, was narrower after open admissions than before. Also, while minority enrollments in the CUNY system grew dramatically under open access, their presence in senior colleges leapt upward even more startlingly, almost sevenfold between 1969 and the early 1970s. The proportional increase of minority enrollments in community colleges was smaller: around a fourfold increase in these schools. For whites the comparable figures are much less dramatic: their post-open-admissions enrollment increase less than doubled in both four-year and community colleges. In short, even in the face of consider-able inequality across the two tiers of CUNY, minority enrollment in B.A. programs increased proportionally far more than it did in community col-leges and far more than whites' enrollment. Consequently, minority repre-sentation in the four-year-college tier was more equal to whites' than it had been before.

9. A couple of other variables had modest effects. One is social origin: having parents with more education added to the chances of enrolling in a four-year institution. Student age made some difference: older students were more likely to choose community colleges. Probably these students entered after a hiatus during which many undoubtedly had encountered frustration

in the labor market. Being older perhaps made them feel that they had less time to pursue a more lengthy college education, as some undoubtedly had spouses, children, and other obligations.

10. Inspection of z score coefficients which are not presented here shows high school variables to be the most important determinants

11. Unlike the CUNY data findings, in the national data, having a child makes community college entry more likely.

12. That is, 68 percent of women in the Current Population Survey who ever entered college had completed a degree by the year 2000.

13. For this analysis the sample consisted of all respondents who earned a B.A. That includes women who earned M.A.s and advanced degrees, such as Ph.D.s or professional degrees, since the B.A. is a prerequisite for admission to postgraduate study.

14. We have no direct measure of full-time work while in college for the CUNY women. However, we do know from an earlier study (Lavin and Hyllegard 1996) that black and Hispanic students, both for men and women, were more likely to hold full-time jobs than whites. In the earlier study, which examined respondents who had been out of college for twelve to fourteen years, this variable lowered the chances of B.A. attainment.

15. Federal statistics and other research (for example, Astin and Oseguera 2002) sometimes use multiple time periods for tracking graduation. Even so, these time spans are shorter than the ones available in our data.

16. The fact that these time-to-complete figures tend to be longer for CUNY than for the national NLSY data does not mean that CUNY students are taking longer to complete degrees. It partly reflects the fact that the CUNY survey spans more years than the NLSY data. In the CUNY survey, a woman who graduated thirty years after entering college in 1970 counts toward the mean time to graduation. Cases where women took a long time to graduate strongly influence the mean graduation time. In the NLSY, the longest period tracked was twenty-one years; graduates who took over twenty-one years do not get included in calculating the mean time to degree. Beyond this, many NLSY women were still in high school when that survey began. For those women, NLSY has only tracked them for about seventeen years beyond the time of their likely college entry.

17. These results differ from those reported by Clifford Adelman (2004, 22, table 2.3). On average, B.A. recipients took between four and five years to graduate, and ethnic differences never even reach one year. However, since Adelman's studies do not look at cohorts for longer than twelve years, those who took extended time to complete degrees cannot be included in the averages. In addition, Adelman refers to students who earned less than ten credits as "incidental students," and does not count them either in graduation rates or in calculations of time to degree.

18. In examining how long it took to earn one's highest degree, we note that many women who completed postgraduate degrees also completed B.A.s, but they are not counted as B.A. recipients. If we counted them among the

pool of those who earned B.A.s, time to degree would be shorter. Thus, for whites the overall time to B.A. for all who earned this degree is 6.3 years, a year less than for the group who did not go further. All of the black women who earned a B.A. averaged 9.0 years, and all of the Hispanics averaged 9.2 years. Corresponding figures in table 2.4 for the women who didn't go beyond the B.A. are 10 and 11 years.

19. In the national sample, advanced degrees appear to take *less* time than M.A.s. This seeming anomaly is probably a function of their shorter follow-up period: for many advanced degree recipients, especially from low-income backgrounds and with family responsibilities, the path to completion is interrupted. Many eventual completers at this level were probably still in graduate school in 2000 or had not returned for graduate study (waiting perhaps to complete child-care responsibilities).

20. Although taking remedial courses appeared to extend time to degree by around a half year, this finding is not statistically significant. Perhaps this is because most students took only one or two remedial courses, and some of these did carry credit, or at least partial credit. For these reasons, students who took remediation were not significantly slowed down, despite widespread belief to the contrary.

21. In the CUNY sample our measure of work did not clearly identify those who worked full-time. However, in the NLSY79 there is such a measure and we have used the estimate in that sample and applied it to our analysis for the CUNY women. We feel confident in doing this, because in an earlier study (Lavin and Hyllegard 1996), full-time work emerged as the single most important influence on time to B.A.

22. In the national case, high school record (grades) continued to affect time to degree. Undoubtedly, this is because unlike the CUNY regression, no measure of freshman grades is available.

Chapter 3

1. Relative to other measures such as job prestige, earnings are a particularly significant outcome for women, since they typically receive less pay than men who hold jobs of similar social standing (England 1979).

2. In these regression analyses, payoffs from higher education in the national sample (the NLSY) appear greater than for the CUNY sample (table 3.2). This is because the comparison group in the NLSY regression consists of high school graduates who never entered college, whereas in the CUNY sample the comparison is with college entrants who dropped out before completing one semester. Thus, rather than compare sizes of coefficients across the two samples, we draw the reader's attention to the similar patterns revealed by the regressions in the CUNY and NLSY surveys.

3. Largely this is because the earnings of minority women (especially blacks) who dropped out early were far lower than those of whites (see table 3.1). Thus degree completion provides a very substantial boost for minority

women, relative to the rather weak earnings base of those who left higher education early. This does not mean that minority women were necessarily earning more than whites, but it does mean that payoffs to minority women were proportionately greater.

4. The CUNY data set, on the other hand, uses early dropouts as the reference point and as a consequence, most likely underestimates payoffs from both credits and credentials.

5. Of course, one cannot assume that individuals are always employed in occupations directly related to their fields of concentration, but it is likely that there is an association between the two.

6. The only qualification to this picture of linear association concerns the economic status of the A.A. degree. Among whites and Hispanics, the household income of women who had "some college" appears equal to or slightly better than it is for those who completed an associate degree. Among blacks, however, there appears to be a substantial household income payoff from the A.A., relative to those who did not graduate.

7. Apparently, child support, maintenance payments, and so forth do not come close to replacing the contributions of spouses or partners resident in the household.

8. See table B.5.

9. There is one exception to the finding that whites' property resources are greater than minorities (even with controls): home value among Hispanic women nationally. After parental education, income, and respondent college attainments are controlled, these women own homes that are more valuable than those of whites. This means that if Hispanic women had parents whose educational attainments and income were the equivalent of whites', and if they had gone as far in terms of acquisition of college credentials, they would own more valuable homes than the whites.

10. Spouse prestige is significant only in the national sample.

11. Aside from the boost Hispanic women received from holding an A.A. degree (model 5), there are no significant interactions of ethnicity with degree attainment. In effect, education pays off about the same for every group.

12. The value of assets was lower among women with children. However, since there is little to choose among white and minority women in the likelihood of having children, this does not help to explain ethnic differences.

Chapter 4

1. The average household income was expressed as a ratio of the poverty-level income for a family of that size. Using this ratio also corrects for inflation over time.

2. For a discussion of the effects of poverty on child outcomes see Greg J. Duncan and Jeanne Brooks-Gunn (1999) and Lee Rainwater and Timothy Smeeding (2003).

3.   As we pointed out in the previous chapter, the large racial differences in household income reflect the fact that black women are much less likely than white women to live in a two-adult household. But in their personal earnings and occupational prestige, black women are much closer to their white and Hispanic counterparts.

4.   See, for example, Sara McLanahan and Gary Sandefuhr (1994), Robert Haveman and Barbara Wolf (1994), Timothy Biblarz and Adrian Raftery (1999), and Kevin Lang and Jay Zagorsky (2001). The issue of marital status and children's outcomes is discussed in more detail in chapter six.

5.   See George Farkas (1996), Farkas and Kurt Beron (2001), and Betty Hart and Todd R. Risley (1995, 1999).

6.   See Jay Heubert and Robert Hauser (1998) for a review of prior studies, and a discussion of the negative impact of being held back or retained in grade. A study by Karl Alexander, Doris R. Entwisle, and Susan L. Dauber (1994) is one of the very few reporting that being retained in grade improves students' subsequent academic performance.

7.   Paul Attewell et al. (2004) and U.S. Census Bureau (2004).

8.   We translated the logistic coefficient for a given background variable into a probability, setting each of the control variables to its mean value.

9.   The contributions of fathers will be explored in chapter 6.

10. The two outcomes that did not meet statistical significance were being held back a grade, and entering college. The observed effect was substantial for child attending college, but the sample size for the matched propensity-score technique was small ($N = 359$), for this outcome, reducing the power of the test.

11. We did this using regression models on child educational outcomes where the predictors were maternal B.A. plus all the grandparent background variables plus race, maternal IQ, and two psychological scales.

12. The sample sizes for children going to college were too small to undertake separate models for each racial-ethnic group in the NLSY.

Chapter 5

1.   To be sure, there are thinkers who dispute this viewpoint: some give more weight to genetics in the formation of a child's personality, and others have emphasized the importance of peers for a child's development. See, for example, Judith Rich Harris (1998).

2.   In the U.S. context, E. Donald Hirsch Jr. (1987) offers a broader concept, called by him cultural literacy, which is a person's knowledge of historical events, important people, social institutions, literary allusions, and popular phrases and sayings. He links this to children's success in reading at school. Other scholars cast an even wider conceptual net, including in the concept of cultural literacy vocabulary, diction, and style of speech, which are also

associated with class and racial background (Bernstein 1975; Farkas and Beron 2001; Hart and Risley 1995, 1999; Heath 1983, 1999).

3. A different term, "human capital," is used by other social scientists to refer to knowledge and education that has a utilitarian purpose. Human capital is a person's knowledge and skills that increase the bearer's economic productivity in the workplace and therefore his or her earnings capacity (Becker 1963, 1981; Becker and Lewis 1973; Becker and Tomes 1986). The human capital framework acknowledges formal education as a central source of human capital, along with on-the-job experience and family social-ization (Mulligan 1997). Pierre Bourdieu doesn't use the human capital concept, preferring cultural capital. He strongly underplays any utilitarian or skill aspect of cultural capital in favor of its cultural dimension, and emphasizes its origins in family socialization within a particular social class rather than in education.

4. For example, when Bourdieu (1986, 265) writes about "objectified social capital"—the physical stock of writings, art objects, instruments, and architecture—he notes that, in today's society, where "embodied cultural capital is constantly increasing, it can be seen that, in each generation the edu-cational system can take more for granted." Once again, the educational sys-tem is denied agency in expanding cultural capital itself; it can only transmit the more socially widespread cultural capital with which it is provided.

5. The notion of achieved cultural capital is inimical to Bourdieu's purpose; it may even be an oxymoron for him. He notes, "Cultural capital can be acquired . . . in the absence of any deliberate inculcation, and therefore quite unconsciously. . . . Because . . . it is subject to a hereditary transmission which is always heavily disguised or even invisible, it defies the old, deep-rooted distinction the Greek jurists made between inherited properties . . . and acquired properties, . . . i.e. those which an individual adds to his heritage. It thus manages to combine the prestige of innate property with the mer-its of acquisition" (Bourdieu 1986, 245). For Bourdieu, cultural capital is inherited but masquerades as an acquisition or achievement.

6. Such courses are required in Columbia University's core undergraduate curriculum.

7. There is no objective or scientific criterion for deciding what constitutes a large, medium, or small effect size, but social scientists tend to view effects of less than .3 standard deviations as small, those from about .3 to .5 standard deviations as medium, and anything over .5 standard deviation as large. See Robert Rosenthal and Ralph Rosnow (1991). These are only rules of thumb, however, and scholars will differ in their interpretations of what constitutes an important effect. For one thing, error in measurement tends to lower effect sizes below what researchers would observe if they could measure variables more exactly.

8. The *Digest of Educational Statistics* for 2001 (National Center for Education Statistics 2001) reports that in the United States as a whole, about 13 percent of children attend private schools, pre-K through grade twelve.

9.   See U.S. Census Bureau (2001), table 26, "Mobility Status of the Population by Selected Characteristics."

10. A scheduled school move would be when a child graduates elementary school and enters middle school, or leaves middle school and enters a high school. These kinds of expected moves are not included in our measure of mobility.

11. The creators' rationale for combining these superficially unrelated items into one scale would probably be that all the items in the scale load together in a factor analysis and have good reliability.

12. In technical terms, they fail to load onto one factor; they do not form a statistically reliable scale.

13. See Rosenthal and Rosnow (1991).

Chapter 6

1.   In this second case, the causation runs in both directions: single mothers are less likely to go to college in the first place, and going to college also reduces the likelihood of a woman's subsequently bearing a child out of wedlock.

2.   The use of propensity scores is discussed in more detail in the methodological appendix to this volume.

3.   A related rhetorical strategy downplays the effect of family structure by suggesting that if only a hypothetical intervention were made to change a person's value on intervening variables, then the disadvantageous effect of the treatment would not matter. For example, Biblarz and Raftery (1999, 354) suggest that "single mothers who are able to secure adequate positions in the social structure—indicated by their employment and occupation—can offset the negative effect of the loss of the father, and their children will do approximately as well (in education) as those from two-biological-parent families." This gives the impression that it is SES and not single parenting that is the genuine problem. Although it is true that a disadvantage resulting from a family type can be offset by some other positive factor (more wealth, a better job, more maternal education, or living in a neighborhood with excellent schools), this does not change the causal situation in the real world: that children in single-parent families are poorer on average and have worse outcomes than children in two-parent families.

4.   These issues are detailed in three recent and fairly comprehensive reviews of the neighborhood literature (see Newman and Small 2001; Pebley and Sastry 2004; Sampson, Morenoff, and Gannon-Rowley 2002).

5.   We were unable to carry our propensity matching for African Americans separately because of sample size limitations.

6.   In her book *What Money Can't Buy*, the sociologist Susan Mayer (1997, 143) argued that "the effect of parental income [on children's outcomes] is nowhere near as large as many . . . imagine." She finds that children's test scores "are likely to improve by one or two points when their parents' income doubles." At the same time, she finds that the "cumulative impact [of family income] across all outcomes may be substantial." Our analyses are consistent

with her view; insofar as we find that family structure, parental education, job complexity, and several other noneconomic variables have important impacts on children's educational outcomes, over and above family income. Nevertheless, after removing these other influences, the effects of income on children's chances are not trivial.

Chapter 7

1. See U.S. Census Bureau (1993).

2. See U.S. Census Bureau (2005). A public controversy is under way regarding the proportion of students who graduate from public high schools in the United States. Critics of public education have excoriated the Census Bureau for overstating graduation rates and understating dropout rates. They claim that there is a crisis in public schooling, evidenced by very high dropout rates and academically underprepared graduates. In response, supporters of public education have argued that graduation rates have been increasing over time, and there is little evidence that students are less prepared than in previous decades. They note that larger numbers of high school students are taking more-advanced course work than a decade or two ago, and accuse the critics of provoking a public panic in order to further their political agenda of school vouchers and privatization of K-through-twelve education. Lawrence Mishel and Joydeep Roy (2006) present one side of this debate, and Jay Greene and Marcus Winters (2005) provide another. Derrick Jackson provided an account of the controversy in his column in the *Boston Globe* on June 28, 2006.

3. Two government agencies provide conflicting estimates of undergraduate enrollment nationwide: the National Center for Education Statistics (2004, table 7.1) provides the estimate cited in the text. This is a projected estimate of 14.845 million undergraduates in 2005 that is based on actual measurements through 2002. NCES's equivalent figure for 2003 was 14.46 million. These NCES numbers are derived from a survey of postsecondary educational institutions, each of which reports its enrollment in the fall.

    Using a different data set, a survey of a large representative sample of American households known as the Current Population Survey, the U.S. Census Bureau (2005, table E) reported total undergraduate enrollment of 13.4 million in October 2003, 1 million fewer students than the NCES estimates. The census reports that two-thirds of these undergraduates are enrolled in four-year institutions. Most (81 percent) students at four-year colleges attend full-time, and most are young. However, 13 percent of full-time undergraduates at four-year schools are so-called mature students aged twenty-five or older. By contrast, in two-year colleges fewer undergraduates are full-time students (58 percent) and more (27 percent) are twenty-five or older. The 2003 survey reports that among full-time college students, nearly 15 percent work full-time and another 35 percent work part-time.

    Points of contrast are that NCES reports considerably higher nationwide undergraduate enrollment (14.5 million compared to the CPS's 13.4 million). NCES also reports that 55 percent of undergraduate enrollment is in four-year colleges, whereas the CPS reports 66 percent. There is no simple way of reconciling these discrepancies.

4. See National Center for Education Statistics (2004, indicator 20).

5. This figure describes the percentage of high school graduates from three cohorts—the classes of 1972, 1982, and 1992—who entered college in the years following high school graduation. It shows that the proportion of graduates proceeding directly to college has increased each decade, to its present high of 81.4 percent. It also provides separate analyses of the proportion of high school graduates with high school GPAs of C minus or worse who went on to college. Evidently, in more recent cohorts, too, weak high school students are much more likely to enter college. These data are drawn from three separate government studies: the National Longitudinal Study of the High School Class of 1972 (NLS72), the High School and Beyond Longitudinal Study of 1980 Sophomores (HS&B), and the National Educational Longitudinal Study of 1988 (NELS88). Our analyses in figure 7.1 are for college entrants only. Adelman (2004, 24) provides similar analyses, showing the same trend, but he reports college attendance percentages slightly lower than ours. We suspect the difference may occur because we limited our sample to high school graduates.

6. At the national level only an indirect measure of the number of students who have been held back a grade is available: government reports that indicate the percentage of children whose age is above the modal age of children in their grade (U.S. Census Bureau 2005). This measure combines students who have been held back a grade with students who began elementary school at an older age than the norm, possibly by parental choice (known as "red-shirting"). Examining those statistics, one finds that rate of being above modal age among blacks is 37.4 percent, compared to 29.4 percent for non-Hispanic whites.

7. Between eighteen and twenty-four, only 7 percent of whites are high school dropouts, compared to 14 percent of blacks and 28 percent of Hispanics (U.S. Census Bureau 2005). Here, a dropout is defined as someone aged eighteen to twenty-four who has not completed high school and is no longer enrolled in high school.

8. The percentage of white graduates immediately transitioning to college is reported for 2004, whereas the rates for blacks and Hispanics are three-year averages for the years 2001 to 2003. There are fewer black and Hispanic students in the survey, so that the year-to-year rates for these racial-ethnic groups fluctuate more dramatically than for whites. For this reason, I have reported the NCES's three-year averages for these two minorities. Data on this indicator are available on the web at: http://www.nces.ed.gov/programs/coe/2006/section3/table.asp?tableID=487.

9. Longitudinal data that follow cohorts of high school graduates beyond high school graduation paint a rosier picture regarding race gaps in college attendance. For the 1992 high school cohort, Adelman (2004, 23) finds no significant differences in college access rates between whites and African Americans.

10. A poor family is defined here as one in the lowest quartile of family income and an affluent family is one in the top income quartile. The figures above are derived from October CPS data for 2003, as reported by Thomas G. Mortenson (2005b). Also see the NCES figures cited in note 8.

11. One exception to this view is an essay by Pedro Carneiro and James Heckman (2003, 77), in which they say, "After a half century of progress, cohorts born after 1950 did not improve much, or at all, on the educational attainment of their predecessors." They base this conclusion on cross-sectional survey data (one CPS survey for the year 2000) comparing the percentage of persons born in each year who are high school dropouts, high school graduates, or college graduates. Graphing these data gives the impression that younger cohorts have fewer years of education than older birth cohorts do. This is an error of interpretation, and not a real finding. The reason that more fifty-year-olds in the year 2000 survey seem to have earned college degrees than twenty- or thirty-somethings is that many of those younger people are still completing degrees during their thirties and forties. Those late degrees appear in the statistics for fifty-year-olds, but have not yet happened for the younger cohorts in Carneiro and Heckman's graph, and so go uncounted. Education is no longer complete by early adulthood. By the time younger birth cohorts reach their fifties they will have outperformed their predecessors. If one looks at longitudinal data instead of a cross-sectional survey, it is clear that more high school students are continuing to college today than in any earlier period. In addition, a larger percentage of each successive birth cohort finishes college. There has been no drop or stagnation in educational attainment over time and the growth trend continues. See Jennifer Cheeseman Day and Kurt Bauman (2000).

12. Before the 1990s, economists tended to explain increasing inequality in wages as results of institutional factors such as intensified international competition and decreased unionization, the growth and expansion of various industry sectors, a shifting occupational composition within industries, and so on (for example, Bluestone and Harrison 1988). This view was superseded by an argument that linked the spread of technology (especially computers) to wage changes. Several scholars found that people who worked with computers earned more than employees with similar education who did not use computers (Krueger 1993), and this became generalized to a thesis that technological change was skill-biased, that is, that it required more-educated workers, whose higher salaries reflected their greater skills. This idea in turn was used to explain the increased polarization of incomes that was occurring within industries and occupations (Bound and Johnson 1992; Katz and Murphy 1992; Levy and Murnane 1992). The notion of skill-biased technological change has its critics, however. David Card and John E. DiNardo (2002) suggest that the timing of the increase in wage inequality does not fit that of the spread of computer use.

13. A brief history of the GI Bill of 1944 and its consequences is provided at http://www.75anniversary.va.gov/history/gi_bill.htm.

14. African American ex-servicemen had a much harder time than white ex-servicemen in taking advantage of the educational benefits for the GI

Bill of 1944, but the bill nevertheless represented an important advance. See Hilary Herbold (1995) and Ronald Roach (1997).

15. After considering various potential indicators of the quality of undergraduate education, William G. Bowen, Martin Kurzweil, and Eugene Tobin (2005, 64) conclude, "We see no reliable way of answering definitively either of two questions of interest: Is American undergraduate education better today than in the past? And is it better than undergraduate education outside the United States?"

16. Notwithstanding the long-term increase in the value of a degree, there are fluctuations in the value of a college credential that are linked to recessions and expansions. In a recent newspaper article, the economist Paul Krugman ("Left Behind Economics," *New York Times,* July 14, 2006) discusses evidence that except for the very richest strata, almost all Americans, including college graduates, have experienced income loss in the last year or two.

17. Neither the NELS88, which followed students for about eight and a half years after high school graduation in 1992, nor the High School and Beyond data, which followed students for ten years after high school graduation in 1982, are suitable for assessing the economic payoffs to different levels of higher education. Employees whose labor-market experience is only three or four years past completing their degree are usually far from the earning power they will have from age thirty-five on.

18. Table 7.2 reports personal earnings data in the year 2000 for full-time workers for the NLSY data set. Regression models include the following controls: race and gender dummies, age, mother's and father's highest grade completed, family income when respondent was fourteen, mother's and father's occupational prestige when respondent was fourteen, dummies indicating whether or not respondent or parent was foreign-born, dummies indicating whether or not respondent's mother and father were employed when respondent was fourteen, respondent's high school academic GPA, the total number of academic courses respondent took in high school, respondents' self-esteem and self-mastery scale scores, respondents' Armed Forces Qualification Test score, dummies indicating whether or not respondent was married or had a child before his or her eighteenth birthday. The propensity score–matched models include these controls, as well as several interaction terms, quadratics, and dummy variables to capture nonlinear effects of these predictors. In addition, the matched cases are only paired with same-race and same-gender respondents: one who went to college, the other who did not.

19. See David Leonhardt ("The College Dropout Boom," *New York Times,* May 24, 2005) and Karen Arenson ("Bonus Planned for Colleges Whose Students Finish on Time," *New York Times,* January 26, 2005, late edition, 1B).

20. Rosenbaum (2001, 68, 80, 82). This figure was subsequently publicized in *The American Teacher* (Rosenbaum 2004), the nation's largest-circulation journal for teachers, and also in a publication aimed at high school counselors (Rosenbaum 2003).

21. According to the National Center for Education Statistics (2003a, 23), approximately 33 percent of B.A. recipients take more than six years after high school graduation to obtain their degrees, and 19 percent take more than ten years. We used this to estimate longer-term graduation rates.

22. In part, this shift in perception of the community colleges as a route for mobility depends on what yardstick is used for comparing student success. The research literature in the 1960s and 1970s tended to contrast earnings and other outcomes of community college students compared to students who graduated from four-year colleges. By that comparison, community college graduates clearly earn less. On that basis, critics viewed community college students as second-class citizens.

    By contrast, current research (including our own) is more likely to compare community college students with persons of similar background who went no further than high school graduation. By that criterion, community college students clearly earn more than they would have done if they had not gone to college.

    Thus, attending community college seems to be a positive step.

23. The 7.5 percent figure comes from our analyses of the NLSY (see Levey 2005).

24. See W. Norton Grubb (1993, 1995a, 1995b, 1997, 2002); Thomas Bailey, Gregory Kienzl, and David Marcotte (2004), Dougherty (1994), Thomas Kane and Celia Rouse (1995a, 1995b); U.S. Census Bureau (2004a); and Card (1999).

25. This phenomenon is known popularly as remedial education, although many educators avoid that label, preferring terms such as "developmental education," "skills courses," or "college preparation" courses.

26. Paul Attewell et al. (2006).

27. In 1983, the National Commission on Excellence in Education published its well-known report, "A Nation At Risk: The Imperative for Educational Reform," which called for a major overhaul of American schools. (The report is available online at: http://www.ed.gov/pubs/NatAtRisk/index.html.) One of the report's main recommendations was to institute a "New Basics" curriculum, a set of more rigorous courses required for high school graduation. The New Basics included four years of high school English, three years of mathematics, and three years of both social studies and science. A half year of computer science was also mandated. This coursework is known as "The New Basics Curriculum." Many college-bound students go beyond this minimum, for example by taking one or more foreign languages in high school, but taking the New Basics is viewed as the mark of a well-prepared student.

28. The sample sizes for the propensity models are considerably smaller than the N's for the equivalent conventional models in this table. This shrinkage in sample size is typical in matched propensity score models, for two reasons: first, cases are lost because the technique pairs just one control case with each treated case. If fewer than half of the cases in the sample received the treatment, as is the case in this analysis, the maximum number of cases included in the analysis will be twice the number of cases in the treatment group. For example, approximately one-third of the NELS respondents with C grades

or lower had college expectations. Therefore, even if every C student with college expectations was matched with a C student without college aspirations, the number of cases in the propensity analysis would shrink from approximately 1,500 to approximately 1,000. Second, sample-size shrinkage occurs in propensity models because not all students can be matched to within .01 on their propensity to have college graduation plans. In our analysis of the effects of college expectations for students with C grades or lower, we found suitable matches for 360 of the 519 treatment cases. The treated cases that were not matched (and therefore excluded from the matched analysis) were cases that fit the college aspirant profile so well that it was impossible to find a respondent with similar characteristics in the no-college-plans control group. Shrinkage reduces statistical power in the matched models, creating a conservative bias in significance testing, but this is worthwhile given the reduction in selection bias that propensity matching provides.

Chapter 8

1.   The total enrollment in higher education was 2,281,000 in the fall of 1950 (National Center for Education Statistics 1993, 76, table 24). Estimated total enrollment in 2005 was 14,628,000 (National Center for Education Statistics 2005, indicator 7). The number of degree-granting institutions increased from 1,851 in the academic year 1949–1950 to 4,197 in 2001–2002 (National Center for Education Statistics 2003b).

2.   To gauge the effects of imposing these selective admissions standards, to estimate what level of college entry would be under a more selective admissions model, we divided college admissions averages (GPA in academic courses) into the following categories: C minus or below; C to C plus; and B minus or higher. College entrants in the C minus or below category were moved to the non-college-entrant (high school graduate only) category. College entrants in the C to C plus category were moved to two-year colleges. Students in the B minus or higher category remained as four-year-college entrants. Students were only moved down, so students in the B minus or higher category who in reality entered a two-year college remained classified as two-year college entrants.

3.   For example, in the top panel of table 8.3, we see that 51.9 percent of CUNY women who in actuality enrolled in four-year colleges would have been able to enroll in those colleges because they had a B minus or better high school average. In the next panel, 59 percent of CUNY men could have entered a four-year college because they had a B minus or better average. Likewise, 60 percent of women and 46.7 percent of men in the NLSY could still have entered four-year institutions under the more restrictive policy. Returning to the top panel of table 8.3, 28.4 percent of those actually admitted into four-year colleges would have had to enter a two-year college because their grades were between C and C plus, and 19.7 percent of students who actually entered a four-year college would have been unable to attend any college at all under the more restrictive admissions criterion of a C or better high school average.

4.   Estimates about the effects of changed admissions criteria upon level of college placement are based on assumptions that might not hold true in practice. Different admissions models can themselves alter perceptions and behavior in ways that affect the estimates. For example, Jerome Karabel (1998), in assessing the effects of the termination of affirmative action at Berkeley, shows that the announcement of the program's end actually diminished the number of minority applications, even before it was actually terminated. At the other end, the announcement of the initiation of open admissions at CUNY produced applications from minority students whose records would have been strong enough for admissions even without the new program but who otherwise would not have applied. These students' perception was that the new policy made it possible for them to attend (Lavin, Alba, and Silberstein 1981).

5.   Here is how we projected effects of a selective admissions model on various outcomes: We used logistic regression to predict B.A. attainment (or higher) under the more selective model. In the CUNY sample we controlled for ethnicity, parents' income and education, college admissions average, total units of academic courses in high school, rank in high school graduating class, academic self-rating, degree aspirations, age at college entry, had a child before entering college, and level of college entry. The controls in the NLSY were ethnicity, parents' income and education, college admissions average, total units of high school academic courses, results of the 1980 Armed Forces Qualification Test, self-esteem and mastery scales, age, had a child before entering college, level of college entry (two- or four-year college), and worked full-time in college (regressions were run separately for men and women).

     If the level of entry did not change under the more selective model, respondents who had earned a B.A. kept this level of attainment. If a respondent was moved to the high school category, she or he received a value of 0 for B.A. attainment. If a respondent was moved from a four-year college to a two-year college, B.A. attainment rate was predicted using logistic regression with coefficients from the original logistic regression predicting B.A. attainment, but the coefficient for level of college entry was replaced with the coefficient for the new, two-year, level of college entry. Because this was a logistic regression, the values for B.A. attainment were converted to probabilities using the equation $1/(1+\exp(-x))$, where x is the log odds produced by the logistic regression.

     The same technique was used to predict the other outcomes: full-time earnings, home ownership, value of home (in the NLSY), other economic resources, value of other economic resources (NLSY), and children's outcomes. If a respondent was moved to the "no college" category, she or he received the coefficient for the educational attainment category "early college dropout" in the CUNY data (which do not include any non–college entrants, so the results are conservative estimates of the true effect of not attending college), and the coefficient for a high school graduate in the NLSY data set. If the outcome was continuous, as with earnings, OLS regression was used and it was not necessary to convert the estimated value. Findings are presented only for respondents whose level of college entry changed under the more selective admissions model.

Data sets used in this chapter are the following: women from the CUNY women's data set; children from the CUNY women's data set; CUNY men from the CUNY "1970 to 1972 entrants" file; national women and men from the NLSY79-adult file, and children from the NLSY79-children file. Appropriate weights were used for the NLSY and CUNY samples. Only whites, blacks, and Hispanics are included.

6. Because our thirty-year follow-up of former CUNY students includes only women, we have no data for men on actual B.A. attainment over this time period.

7. Actual graduation rates in the NLSY are consistently lower than in the CUNY sample. We believe this is largely due to the fact that women in the former are, on average, about ten years younger and typically entered college for the first time in the early 1980s, as compared with the early 1970s in the CUNY case. Also, the CUNY sample is organized as a cohort, whereas the NLSY is composed of women who were between fourteen and twenty-four years old in the base year. Across the two samples our main focus is on the comparative influence of the two admissions models rather than on the magnitude of graduation rates.

8. In assessing what economic outcomes would have looked like in the absence of open access, the reader should be aware that we have focused only upon the former students whose level of entry was changed under the selective model. Individuals whose level of entry was not affected by the selective model are not included in our assessments. This provides an incisive way of gauging the impact of each model on economic outcomes.

9. The benefits we speak of are net benefits, calculated after controlling for other determinants of earnings. In the selective admissions model, we substituted the new level of college placement for the original value. For the details of this procedure, see the earlier description in note 4.

10. These proportional changes are computed as follows, say, for the case of black women: the difference between $31,689 (value under open access) and $9,070 (value under selective admissions) is $22,619, or 71 percent of the open access value of $31,689.

11. See table 8.4.

12. The contraction in these expenditures has occurred in all fifty states, according to Mortenson (2005a).

13. It has been increasing in the private sector as well, which is more expensive to begin with. Still, increases have been proportionately greater in public institutions.

14. As William G. Bowen, Martin Kurzweil, and Eugene Tobin (2005) have pointed out, the distinction between merit- and need-based aid is sometimes misleading, since some students who qualify for merit aid are also financially needy.

References

Adelman, Clifford. 1998. "The Kiss of Death? An Alternative View of College Remediation." *National CrossTalk* 8(3): 11.

———. 1999. *Answers in the Toolbox: Academic Intensity, Attendance Patterns, and Bachelor's Degree Attainment.* Washington: U.S. Department of Education; available at: http://www.ed.gov/pubs/Toolbox/toolbox.html (accessed October 23, 2006).

———. 2004. *Principal Indicators of Student Academic Histories in Post-Secondary Education, 1972–2000.* Washington: U.S. Department of Education, Institute of Education Sciences, Available at: http://www.ed.gov/rschstat/research/pubs/prinindicat/prinindicat.pdf.

Ainsley, John, John Foreman, and Michael Sheret. 1991. "High School Factors That Influence Students to Remain in School." *Journal of Educational Research* 85(2): 69–80.

Alba, Richard, and David Lavin. 1981. "Community Colleges and Tracking in Higher Education." *Sociology of Education* 54(4): 223–37.

Alexander, Karl, and Martha A. Cook. 1979. "The Motivational Relevance of Educational Plans: Questioning the Conventional Wisdom." *Social Psychological Quarterly* 42(3): 202–13.

Alexander, Karl, Doris R. Entwisle, and Susan L. Dauber. 1994. *On the Success of Failure.* Cambridge: Cambridge University Press.

———. 1996. "Children in Motion: School Transfers and Elementary School Performance." *Journal of Educational Research* 90(1): 3–12.

Alexander, Karl, and Aaron Pallas. 1983. "Private Schools and Public Policy: New Evidence on Cognitive Achievement in Public and Private Schools." *Sociology of Education* 56(4): 170–82.

Amott, Teresa, and Julie Matthaei. 1991. *Race, Gender, and Work: A Multicultural Economic History of Women in the United States.* Boston: South End Press.

Anderson, Karl. 1984. "Institutional Differences in College Effects." *ERIC Digest* (ED 256204). Washington: U.S. Department of Education, Educational Research Information Center.

Arendell, Terry. 1986. *Mothers and Divorce.* Berkeley: University of California Press.

Astin, Alexander W., Kenneth C. Green, and William S. Korn. 1987. *The American Freshman: Twenty Year Trends, 1966–1985.* Los Angeles: University of California, Graduate School of Education, Higher Education Research Institute.

Astin, Alexander W., and Leticia Oseguera. 2002. *Degree Attainment Rates at American Colleges and Universities.* Los Angeles: University of California, Los Angeles, Higher Education Research Institute.

Attewell, Paul. 1987. "The Deskilling Controversy." *Work and Occupations* 13(3): 323–46.

Attewell, Paul, David Lavin, Thurston Domina, and Tania Levey. 2004. "The Black Middle Class: Progress, Prospects, and Puzzles." *Journal of African American Studies* 8(1–2): 6–19.

———. 2006. "New Evidence on College Remediation." *Journal of Higher Education* 77(5): 886–924.

Bailey, Thomas, Gregory Kienzl, and David Marcotte. 2004. "Who Benefits from Postsecondary Occupational Education? Findings from the 1980s and 1990s." CCRC Brief 23. New York: Columbia University, Teachers College, Community College Research Center.

Barnett, Rosalind, and Caryl Rivers. 1998. *She Works/He Works: How Two-Income Families Are Happy, Healthy, and Thriving.* Cambridge, Mass.: Harvard University Press.

Bauman, Kurt, and Camille Ryan. 2001. "What's It Worth? Field of Training and Economic Status, 1996." *Current Population Reports.* Washington: U.S. Government Printing Office, for U.S. Census Bureau.

Becker, Gary. 1963. *Human Capital with a Special Reference to Education.* Chicago: University of Chicago Press.

———. 1981. *A Treatise on the Family.* Cambridge, Mass.: Harvard University Press.

Becker, Gary S., and H. Gregg Lewis. 1973. "On the Interaction Between the Quantity and Quality of Children." *Journal of Political Economy* 81(2): S279–88.

Becker, Gary S., and Nigel Tomes. 1986. "Human Capital and the Rise and Fall of Families." *Journal of Labor Economics* 84(4): S142–62.

Bennett, William. 1994. *The De-Valuing of America.* New York: Touchstone.

Berg, Ivar. 1970. *Education and Jobs: The Great Training Robbery.* New York: Praeger.

Berman, Eli, John Bound, and Stephen Machin. 1998. "Implications of Skill-Biased Technological Change: International Evidence." *Quarterly Journal of Economics* 113(4): 1245–79.

Bernstein, Basil. 1975. *Class, Codes, and Control.* New York: Routledge.

Bettinger, Eric, and Bridget Terry Long. 2004. "Shape Up or Ship Out: The Effects of Remediation on Students at Four-Year Colleges." NBER working paper 10369. Cambridge, Mass.: National Bureau of Economic Research. Available at: www.nber.org/papers/w10369.

Bianchi, Suzanne M., and John Robinson. 1997. "What Did You Do Today? Children's Use of Time, Family Composition, and the Acquisition of Social Capital." *Journal of Marriage and the Family* 59(2): 332–44.

Biblarz, Timothy, and Adrian Raftery. 1999. "Family Structure, Educational Attainment, and Socioeconomic Success: Rethinking the 'Pathology of Matriarchy.' " *American Journal of Sociology* 105(2): 321–65.

Biblarz, Timothy, Adrian Raftery and Alexander Bucur. 1997. "Family Structure and Mobility." *Social Forces* 75(4): 1319–41.

Blau, Peter M., and Otis Dudley Duncan. 1967. *The American Occupational Structure.* New York: John Wiley.

Bloom, Allan. 1988. *The Closing of the American Mind.* New York: Simon & Schuster.

Bluestone, Barry, and Bennett Harrison. 1988. *The Great U Turn: Corporate Restructuring and the Polarization of America*. New York: Basic Books.

Boesel, David, and Eric Fredland. 1999. *College for All? Is There Too Much Emphasis on Getting a Four-Year Degree?* Washington: U.S. Department of Education, Office of Educational Research and Improvement, National Library of Education. Available at: www.ed.gov/pubs/CollegeForAll/title.html.

Bound, John, and George Johnson. 1992. "Changes in the Structure of Wages in the 1980s: An Evaluation of Alternative Explanations." *American Economic Review* 83(June): 371–92.

Bourdieu, Pierre. 1986. "The Forms of Capital." In *Handbook of Theory and Research for the Sociology of Education*, edited by John Richardson. New York: Greenwood Press.

Bourdieu, Pierre, and Jean Passeron. 1977. *Reproduction in Education, Culture and Society*. Los Angeles: Sage Press.

Bowen, William G., and Derek Bok. 1998. *The Shape of the River: Long-Term Consequences of Considering Race in College and University Admissions*. Princeton: Princeton University Press.

Bowen, William G., Martin Kurzweil, and Eugene Tobin. 2005. *Equity and Excellence in American Higher Education*. Charlottesville: University of Virginia Press.

Bowles, Samuel, and Herbert Gintis. 1976. *Schooling in Capitalist America: Educational Reform and the Contradictions of Economic Life*. New York: Basic Books.

Bowles, Samuel, Herbert Gintis, and Melissa Osborne. 2001. "The Determinants of Earnings: A Behavioral Approach." *Journal of Economic Literature* 39(4): 1137–76.

Brenahan, Timothy. 1999. "Computerization and Wage Dispersion: An Analytical Reinterpretation." *Economic Journal* 109(June): 390–415.

Breneman, David W., and William N. Haarlow. 1998. *Remediation in Higher Education*. Washington, D.C.: Thomas B. Fordham Foundation.

Breneman, David W., and Susan C. Nelson. 1981. *Financing the Community College: An Economic Perspective*. Washington, D.C.: Brookings Institution.

Brint, Steven, and Jerome Karabel. 1989. *The Diverted Dream: Community Colleges and the Promise of Educational Opportunity in America, 1900–1985*. New York: Oxford University Press.

Bronfenbrenner, Urie. 1958. "Socialization and Social Class Through Time and Space." In *Readings in Social Psychology*, edited by Eleanor Maccoby. New York: Holt, Rinehart & Winston.

Brooks-Gunn, Jeanne, Greg J. Duncan, and J. Lawrence Aber, eds. 1997. *Neighborhood Poverty*. Volume 1: *Context and Consequences for Children*. New York: Russell Sage Foundation.

———. 1997. *Neighborhood Poverty*. Volume 2: *Policy Implications in Studying Neighborhoods*. New York: Russell Sage Foundation.

Bryk, Anthony, Valerie Lee, and Peter Holland. 1993. *Catholic Schools and the Common Good*. Cambridge, Mass.: Harvard University Press.

Bulcroft, Richard A., and Kris A. Bulcroft. 1993. "Race Differences in Attitudinal and Motivational Factors in the Decision to Marry." *Journal of Marriage and the Family* 55(2): 338–55.

Burman, Leonard E., Elaine Maag, Peter Orzag, Jeffrey Rohaly, and John O'Hare. 2005. "The Distributional Consequences of Federal Assistance for Higher Education: The Intersection of Tax and Spending Programs." Discussion paper 26. Washington, D.C.: Urban Institute.

Caldwell, Bettye M., and Robert H. Bradley. 1984. *Home Observation for Measurement of the Environment.* Little Rock: University of Arkansas Press.

Card, David. 1999. "The Causal Effect of Education on Earnings." In *Handbook of Labor Economics,* edited by Orley Ashenfelter and David Card. Volume 3A. Amsterdam, Netherlands: North Holland.

Card, David, and John E. DiNardo. 2002. "Skill-Biased Technological Change and Rising Wage Inequality: Some Problems and Puzzles." NBER working paper 8769. Cambridge, Mass.: National Bureau of Economic Research. Available at: www.nber.org/papers/w8769.

Carneiro, Pedro, and James Heckman. 2003. "Human Capital Policy." In *Inequality in America: What Role for Human Capital Policies?,* edited by James Heckman and Alan Krueger. Cambridge, Mass.: MIT Press.

Center for Human Resource Research. 2004. *NLSY79 User's Guide 1970–2002.* Prepared for the U.S. Department of Labor. Columbus: Ohio State University, Center for Human Resource Research.

Cherlin, Andrew J., Frank F. Furstenberg, Jr., P. Lindsay Chase-Lansdale, Kathleen E. Kiernan, Philip K. Robins, Donna Ruane Morrison, and Julien O. Teitler. 1991. "Longitudinal Studies of Effects of Divorce on Children in Great Britain and the United States." *Science* 252(June 7): 1386–89.

Choy, Susan P. 2002. "Special Analyses: Nontraditional Undergraduates." In *The Condition of Education 2002.* NCES 2002–025. Washington: U.S. Department of Education, National Center for Educational Statistics.

Clark, Burton. 1960. "The 'Cooling Out' Function in Higher Education." *American Journal of Sociology* 65(6): 569–76.

Clinton, Hillary Rodham. 1996. *It Takes a Village.* New York: Simon & Schuster.

Cloud, John. 2002. "Who's Ready for College?" *Time,* October 14, 2002, 62–3.

Coleman, James S. 1961. *The Adolescent Society: The Social Life of the Teenager and Its Impact on Education.* New York: Free Press.

———. 1988. "Social Capital in the Creation of Human Capital." *American Journal of Sociology* 94(supplement): S95–S120.

———. 1990. *Foundations of Social Theory.* Cambridge, Mass.: Harvard University Press.

Coleman, James, and Thomas Hoffer. 1987. *Public and Private Schools: The Impact on Communities.* New York: Basic Books.

Coleman, James, Thomas Hoffer, and Sally Kilgore. 1982. "Cognitive Outcomes in Public and Private Schools." *Sociology of Education* 55(2 and 3): 65–76.

Collins, Randall. 1979. *The Credential Society: An Historical Sociology of Education and Stratification.* New York: Academic Press.

Conklin, Mary E., and Ann Ricks Dailey. 1981. "Does Consistency of Parental Encouragement Matter for Secondary School Students?" *Sociology of Education* 54(4): 254–62.

Conley, Dalton. 1999. *Being Black, Living in the Red: Race, Wealth, and Social Policy in America.* Berkeley: University of California Press.

Cookson, Peter, and Caroline Hodges Persell. 1985. *Preparing for Power: America's Elite Boarding Schools.* New York: Basic Books.

Corcoran, Mary. 1999. "The Economic Progress of African American Women." In *Latinas and African American Women at Work,* edited by Irene Brown. New York: Russell Sage Foundation.

Corcoran, Mary, Colleen M. Heflin, and Belinda L. Reyes. 1999. "The Economic Progress of Mexican and Puerto Rican Women." In *Latinas and African American Women at Work,* edited by Irene Brown. New York: Russell Sage Foundation.

Crosnoe, Robert. 2001. "Academic Orientation and Parental Involvement in Education During High School." *Sociology of Education* 74(3): 210–30.

Crosnoe, Robert, Rahsmita Mistry, and Glenn Elder. 2002. "Economic Disadvantage, Family Dynamics, and Adolescent Enrollment in Higher Education." *Journal of Marriage and the Family* 64(August): 690–702.

Dauber, Susan L., Karl Alexander, Doris R. Entwisle, and Kerri A. Kerr. 2002. "Framing the Future: The Development of Educational Expectations from Elementary School Through Young Adulthood." Paper presented at the annual meeting of the Southern Sociological Association, Baltimore (April).

Day, Jennifer Cheeseman, and Kurt Bauman. 2000. "Have We Reached the Top? Educational Attainment Projections for the U.S. Population." Working paper 43. Washington: U.S. Census Bureau, Population Division.

Day, Jennifer Cheeseman, and Eric Newberger. 2002. *The Big Payoff: Educational Attainment and Synthetic Estimates of Work-life Earnings.* Special studies, series P23-210. Washington: U.S. Census Bureau. Available at: http://www.census.gov/prod/2002pubs/p23-210.pdf.

DeGraaf, Nan, Paul DeGraaf, and Gerbert Kraaykamp. 1998. "How Does Parental Cultural Capital Affect Educational Outcomes in the Netherlands?" Paper presented at the 1998 meetings of the American Sociological Association, San Francisco (August 21–25).

Deil-Amen, Regina, and James Rosenbaum. 2002. "The Unintended Consequences of Stigma-Free Remediation." *Sociology of Education* 75(July): 249–68.

DiMaggio, Paul. 1982. "Cultural Capital and School Success." *American Sociological Review* 47(2): 189–201.

———. 2001. "Social Stratification, Life-Style, Social Cognition, and Social Participation." In *Social Stratification,* edited by David B. Grusky. 2nd ed. New York: Westview Press.

DiMaggio, Paul, and John Mohr. 1985. "Cultural Capital, Educational Attainment, and Marital Selection." *American Journal of Sociology* 90(6): 1231–61.

DiMaggio, Paul, and Michael Useem. 1982. "The Arts in Class Reproduction." In *Cultural and Economic Reproduction in Education,* edited by Michael Apple. New York: Routledge, Kegan Paul.

DiPrete, Thomas, and Henriette Engelhardt. 2000. "Estimating Causal Effects with Matching Methods in the Presence and Absence of Bias Cancellation." Paper presented to the 2000 Annual Meeting of the American Sociological Association, Washington, D.C. (August 12–16). Available at: http://www.wjh.harvard.edu/~winship/cfa_papers/RESJune12.pdf.

Domina, Thurston. 2005. "Leveling the Home Advantage: Assessing the Effectiveness of Parental Involvement in Elementary School." *Sociology of Education* 78(3): 233–49.

Dougherty, Kevin. 1987. "The Effects of Community Colleges: Aid or Hindrance to Socioeconomic Attainment?" *Sociology of Education* 60(2): 86–103.

246   References

———. 1994. *The Contradictory College: The Conflicting Origins, Impacts and Futures of the Community College.* Albany: State University of New York Press.

———. 2002. "The Evolving Role of the Community College: Policy Issues and Research Questions." In *Higher Education: Handbook of Theory and Research,* edited by John Smart and William Tierney. Volume 17. New York: Kluwer Press.

Downey, Douglas B. 1995. "When Bigger Is Not Better: Number of Siblings, Parental Resources, and Educational Performance." *American Sociological Review* 60(5): 746–61.

———. 2001. "Number of Siblings and Intellectual Development: The Resource Dilution Explanation." *American Psychologist* 56(6–7): 497–504.

Downey, Douglas B., Brian Powell, Lala Carr Steelman, and Shana Pribesh. 1999. "Much Ado About Siblings: Change Models, Sibship Size and Intellectual Development." *American Sociological Review* 64(2): 193–98.

Duncan, Beverly, and Otis Dudley Duncan. 1969. "Family Stability and Occupational Success." *Social Problems* 16(3): 273–85.

Duncan, Greg J., and Jeanne Brooks-Gunn, eds. 1999. *The Consequences of Growing Up Poor.* New York: Russell Sage Foundation.

Dynarski, Susan. 1999. "Does Aid Matter? Measuring the Effect of Student Aid on College Attendance and Completion." Working paper no. 7422. Cambridge, Mass.: National Bureau of Economic Research.

Ellwood, David, and Thomas J. Kane. 2000. "Who Is Getting a College Education? Family Background and the Growing Gaps in Enrollment." In *Securing the Future,* edited by Sheldon Danziger and Jane Waldfogel. New York: Russell Sage Press.

England, Paula. 1979. "Women and Occupational Prestige: A Case of Vacuous Sex Equality." *Signs* 5(Winter): 252–65.

Entwisle, Doris, and Karl Alexander. 1990. "Beginning School Math Competence: Minority and Majority Comparisons." *Child Development* 61(2): 454–71.

Epstein, Joyce. 2001. *School, Family, and Community Partnerships: Preparing Educators and Improving Schools.* Boulder, Colo.: Westview Press.

Epstein, Joyce L., and Mavis G. Sanders. 2000. "Connecting Home, School, and Community: New Directions for Social Research." In *Handbook of the Sociology of Education,* edited by Maureen T. Hallinan. New York: Kluwer Press.

Educational Resources Information Center. 1991. "Highly Mobile Students." *ERIC Digest* (ED338745). Washington: U.S. Department of Education, Educational Research Information Center.

———. 2002 "Student Mobility and Academic Achievement." *ERIC Digest* (ED 466314). Washington: U.S. Department of Education, Educational Research Information Center.

Etzioni, Amitai. 1970. "The High Schoolization of College," *Wall Street Journal,* March 17, 1970.

Farkas, George. 1996. *Human Capital or Cultural Capital? Ethnicity and Poverty Groups in an Urban School District.* New York: Aldine de Gruyter.

———. 2003. "Cognitive Skills and Noncognitive Traits and Behaviors in Stratification Processes." *Annual Review of Sociology* 29(1): 541–62.

Farkas, George, and Kurt Beron. 2001. "Family Linguistic Culture and Social Reproduction: Verbal Skill from Parent to Child in the Preschool and School

Years." Paper presented to the Annual Meeting of the Population Association of America, Washington, D.C. (March 29–31). Available at: http://www.pop.psu.edu/~gfarkas/paa301.pdf.

Fehrmann, Paul G., Timothy Z. Keith, and Thomas Reimers. 1987. "Home Influence on School Learning: Direct and Indirect Effects of Parental Involvement on High School Grades." *Journal of Educational Research* 80(6): 330–37.

Fields, Jason. 2004. "America's Families and Living Arrangements: 2003." *Current Population Reports*, series P20-553. Washington: U.S. Census Bureau.

Fine, Michelle. 1993. "[Ap]parent Involvement: Reflections on Parents, Power, and Urban Public Schools." *Teachers College Record* 94(4): 682–710.

Fish, Stanley. 2005. "Devoid of Content." *New York Times*, May 31, 2005, p. A17.

Flippen, Chenoa. 2001. "Residential Segregation and Minority Home Ownership." *Social Science Research* 30(3): 337–62.

Freeman, Richard B. 1976. *The Overeducated American*. New York: Academic Press.

Fryer, Roland, and Steven Levitt. 2004. "Understanding the Black-White Test Score Gap in the First Two Years of School." *Review of Economics and Statistics* 86(2): 447–64.

Furstenberg, Frank, Thomas Cook, Jacqulynne Eccles, Glen Elder, and Arnold Sameroff. 1999. *Managing to Make It: Urban Families and Adolescent Success*. Chicago: University of Chicago Press.

Gans, Herbert J. 1962. *The Urban Villagers*. New York: Free Press.

General Social Survey. 1972–2000. Data and documentation available at: http://www.norc.org/projects/gensoc.asp.

Gill, Brian, and Steven Schlossman. 2003. "A Nation at Rest: The American Way of Homework." *Educational Evaluation and Policy Analysis* 25(3): 319–37.

Goldberger, Arthur, and Glen Cain. 1982. "The Causal Analysis of the Cognitive Outcomes in the Coleman, Hoffer, and Kilgore Report." *Sociology of Education* 55(2/3): 103–22.

Goldin, Claudia. 1990. *Understanding the Gender Gap: An Economic History of American Women*. New York: Oxford University Press.

Goldin, Claudia, and Lawrence Katz. 2001. "The Legacy of U.S. Educational Leadership: Notes on Distribution and Economic Growth in the 20th Century." *American Economic Review* 91(2): 18–23.

Goldrick-Rab, Sara. 2006. "Following Their Every Move: How Social Class Shapes Postsecondary Pathways." *Sociology of Education* 79(1; January): 61–79.

Gray, Kenneth, and Edwin L. Herr. 1996. "BA Degrees Should Not Be the 'Only Way.' " *Chronicle of Higher Education* 42, May 10, B1.

Greenberg, Jack. 2002. "Affirmative Action in Higher Education: Confronting the Condition and Theory." *Boston College Law Review* 43(May): 521–621.

Greene, Jay, and Marcus Winters. 2005. *Public High School Graduation and College Readiness Rates in the United States*. New York: Manhattan Institute for Policy Research. Available on-line at www.manhattan-institute.org/html/ewp_08.htm.

Grubb, W. Norton. 1993. "The Varied Economic Returns to Postsecondary Education: New Evidence from the Class of 1972." *Journal of Human Resources* 28(2): 365–82.

———. 1995a. "Response to Comment." *Journal of Human Resources* 30(1): 222–28.

———. 1995b. *The Returns to Education and Training in the Sub-Baccalaureate Labor Market: Evidence from the Survey of Income and Program Participation, 1984–1990.* Berkeley: University of California, Berkeley, National Center for Research in Vocational Education.

———. 1997. "The Returns to Education and Training in the Sub-Baccalaureate Labor Market, 1984–1990." *Economics of Education Review* 16(3): 231–45.

———. 2001. "From Black Box to Pandora's Box: Evaluating Remedial/Developmental Education." CCRC Brief 11. New York: Columbia University, Teachers College, Community College Research Center.

———. 2002. "Learning and Earning in the Middle." Part I: "National Studies of Pre-Baccalaureate Education." *Economics of Education Review* 21(4): 299–321.

Guo, Guang. 1998. "The Timing and Influences of Cumulative Poverty on Children's Cognitive Ability and Achievement." *Social Forces* 77(1): 257–87.

Guo, Guang, and Leah K. VanWey. 1999. "Sibship Size and Intellectual Development: Is the Relationship Causal?" *American Sociological Review* 64: 169–87.

Guo, Guang, and Kathleen Mullan Harris. 2000. "The Mechanisms Mediating the Effects of Poverty on Children's Intellectual Development." *Demography* 37(4): 431–47.

Gutman, Herbert G. 1976. *The Black Family in Slavery and Freedom, 1750–1925.* New York: Pantheon.

Hanson, Sandra. 1994. "Lost Talent: Unrealized Educational Aspirations and Expectations Among U.S. Youths." *Sociology of Education* 67(3): 159–83.

Harding, David J. 2003. "Counterfactual Models of Neighborhood Effects: The Effect of Neighborhood Poverty on Dropping Out and Teenage Pregnancy." *American Journal of Sociology* 109(3): 676–719.

Harris, Judith Rich. 1998. *The Nurture Assumption: Why Children Turn Out the Way They Do.* New York: Free Press.

Hart, Betty, and Todd R. Risley. 1995. *Meaningful Differences in the Everyday Experience of Young American Children: The Everyday Experience of One and Two Year Old American Children.* Baltimore: Paul H. Brookes.

———. 1999. *The Social World of Children Learning to Talk.* Baltimore: Paul H. Brookes.

Harwood, Richard. 1997. "Flunking the Grade and Nobody Notices." *Washington Post,* August 25, 1997.

Hauser, Robert M., and Douglas K. Anderson. 1991. "Post High School Plans and Aspirations of Black and White High School Seniors: 1976–1986." *Sociology of Education* 64(4): 22–30.

Hauser, Robert M., and David L. Featherman. 1977. *The Process of Stratification.* New York: Academic Press.

Haveman, Robert, and Barbara Wolfe. 1994. *Succeeding Generations: On the Effects of Investments in Children.* New York: Russell Sage Foundation.

Heath, Shirley Brice. 1983. *Ways with Words.* Cambridge: Cambridge University Press.

———. 1999. "Dimensions of Language Development: Lessons from Older Children." In *Cultural Processes in Child Development,* edited by Anne S. Masten. Mahwah, N.J.: Erlbaum.

Heckert, D. Alex, Thomas C. Nowak, and Kay A. Snyder. 1998. "The Impact of Husbands' and Wives' Relative Earnings on Marital Disruption." *Journal of Marriage and the Family* 60(3): 690–703.

Heckman, James J., and V. Joseph Hotz. 1989. "Choosing Among Alternative Nonexperimental Methods for Estimating the Impact of Social Programs: The Case of Manpower Training." *Journal of the American Statistical Association* 84(408): 862–74.

Heckman, James, Hidehiko Ichimura, Jeffrey Smith, and Petra Todd. 1998. "Characterizing Selection Bias Using Experimental Data." *Econometrica* 66(5): 1017–98.

Heller, Donald E. 2005. "Can Minority Students Afford College in an Era of Skyrocketing Tuition?" In *Higher Education and the Color Line,* edited by Gary Orfield, Patricia Marin, and Catherine L. Horn. Cambridge, Mass.: Harvard Education Press.

Herbold, Hilary. 1995. "Never a Level Playing Field: Blacks and the G.I. Bill." *Journal of Blacks in Higher Education* (Winter): 104–8.

Heubert, Jay, and Robert Hauser, eds. 1998. *High Stakes: Testing for Tracking, Promotion, and Graduation.* Washington, D.C.: National Academy Press.

Heyns, Barbara L. 1997. Review of *Changing the Odds: Open Admissions and the Life Chances of the Disadvantaged,* by David E. Lavin and David Hyllegard. *American Journal of Sociology* (January): 1199–1201.

Hirsch, E. Donald, Jr. 1987. *Cultural Literacy.* New York: Houghton Mifflin.

Ho, Sui-Chu, and J. Douglas Willms. 1996. "Effects of Parental Involvement on Eighth Grade Achievement." *Sociology of Education* 69(April): 126–41.

Hoffer, Thomas, Andrew Greeley, and James Coleman. 1985. "Achievement Growth in Public and Private Schools." *Sociology of Education* 58(2): 74–97.

Hollingshead, August de Belmont. 1975. *Elmtown's Youth and Elmtown Revisited.* New York: John Wiley.

Ignash, Jan. 1997. "Who Should Provide Postsecondary Remedial/Developmental Education?" *New Directions for Community Colleges* 100(winter): 5–20.

Jacobs, Jerry. 1986. "Sex Segregation of Fields of Study." *Journal of Higher Education* 57(2): 135–54.

———. 1995. "Gender and Academic Specialties: Trends Among Recipients of College Degrees During the 1980s." *Sociology of Education* 57(2): 81–98.

———. 1996. "Gender Inequality in Higher Education." *Annual Review of Sociology* 22(1): 153–85.

Jacobson, Jonathan, Cara Olsen, Jennifer King Rice, Stephen Sweetland, and John Ralph. 2001. *Educational Achievement and Black-White Inequality.* NCES 2001–61. Washington: U.S. Government Printing Office, for the U.S. Department of Education, National Center for Education Statistics.

Jencks, Christopher, Susan Bartlett, Mary Corcoran, James Crouse, David Eaglesfield, Gregory Jackson, Kent McClelland, Peter Mueser, Michael Olneck, Joseph Schwartz, Sherry Ward, and Jill Williams. 1979. *Who Gets Ahead?* New York: Basic Books.

Jencks, Christopher, and Meredith Philips, eds. 1998. *The Black-White Test Score Gap.* Washington, D.C.: Brookings Institution.

Jencks, Christopher, Marshall Smith, Henry Acland, Mary Jo Bane, David Cohen, Herbert Gintis, Barbara Heyns, and Stephan Michelson. 1972. *Inequality: A Reassessment of the Effect of Family and Schooling in America.* New York: Basic Books.

Journal of Blacks in Higher Education. 1997. "The Marriage Dilemma of College-Educated Black Women." 17(Autumn): 52–53.

Kane, Thomas, and Cecilia Rouse. 1995a. "Comment on W. Norton Grubb: The Varied Economic Returns to Post-secondary Education: New Evidence from the Class of 1972." *Journal of Human Resources* 30(1): 205–21.

———. 1995b. "Labor-Market Returns to Two- and Four-year Colleges." *American Economic Review* 85(3): 600–14.

Kao, Grace, and Jennifer Thompson. 2003. "Racial and Ethnic Stratification in Educational Achievement and Attainment." *Annual Review of Sociology* 29(1): 417–42.

Kaplan, Diane S., Xiaoru Liu, and Howard B. Kaplan. 2001. "Influence of Parents' Self-Feelings and Expectations on Children's Academic Performance." *Journal of Educational Research* 94(6): 360–70.

Karabel, Jerome. 1972. "Community Colleges and Social Stratification." *Harvard Educational Review* 42(4): 521–62.

———. 1998. "No Alternative: The Effects of Color-Blind Admissions in California." In *Chilling Admissions: The Affirmative Action Crisis and the Search for Alternatives*, edited by Gary Orfield and Edward Miller. Cambridge, Mass.: Harvard Civil Rights Project and the Harvard University Publishing Group.

———. 2005. *The Chosen: The Hidden History of Admission and Exclusion at Harvard, Yale, and Princeton.* New York: Houghton Mifflin.

Karen, David, and Kevin J. Dougherty. 2005. "Necessary but Not Sufficient: Higher Education as a Strategy of Social Mobility." In *Higher Education and the Color Line*, edited by Gary Orfield, Patricia Marin, and Catherine L. Horn. Cambridge, Mass.: Harvard Education Press.

Katz, Lawrence, and Kevin Murphy. 1992. "Changes in Relative Wages 1963–1987: Supply and Demand Factors." *Quarterly Journal of Economics* 107(February): 35–78.

Kerbow, David, and Annette Bernhardt. 1993. "Parental Involvement in School: The Context of Minority Involvement." In *Parents, Their Children, and Schools*, edited by Barbara Schneider and James Coleman. New York: Westview Press.

Kerckhoff, Alan C. 1977. "The Realism of Educational Ambitions in England and the United States." *American Sociological Review* 42: 563–71.

Kerckhoff, Alan C., and Richard T. Campbell. 1977. "Black-White Differences in the Educational Attainment Process." *Sociology of Education* 50(1): 15–27.

King, Gary, James Honaker, Anne Joseph, and Kenneth Scheve. 2001. "Analyzing Incomplete Political Science Data: An Alternative Algorithm for Multiple Imputation." *American Political Science Review* 95(1): 49–69.

Kohn, Melvin. 1969. *Class and Conformity: A Study of Values.* Homewood, Ill.: Dorsey Press.

Kozeracki, Carol. 2002. "ERIC Review: Issues in Developmental Education." *Community College Review* 29(4): 83–100.

Krueger, Alan. 1993. "How Computers Have Changed the Wage Structure: Evidence from Microdata, 1984–1989." *Quarterly Journal of Economics* 108 (February): 33–60.

Kuncel, Nathan R., Marcus Crede, and Lisa L. Thomas. 2005. "The Validity of Self-Reported Grade Point Averages, Class Ranks, and Test Scores: A Meta-Analysis and Review of the Literature." *Review of Educational Research* 75(1): 63–82.

Lamont, Michele, and Annette Lareau. 1988. "Cultural Capital." *Sociological Theory* 6(2): 153–68.

Lang, Kevin, and Jay Zagorsky. 2001. "Does Growing Up with a Parent Absent Really Hurt?" *Journal of Human Resources* 36(2): 253–73.

Lareau, Annette. 1989. *Home Advantage: Social Class and Parental Intervention in Elementary Education.* Philadelphia: Falmer Press.

———. 2003. *Unequal Childhoods: Class, Race, and Family Life.* Berkeley: University of California Press.

Larson, Reed. 2000. "Toward a Psychology of Positive Youth Development." *American Psychologist* 55(1): 170–83.

Lavin, David E., Richard D. Alba, and Richard A. Silberstein. 1981. *Right Versus Privilege: The Open Admissions Experiment at the City University of New York.* New York: Free Press.

Lavin, David E., and David Hyllegard. 1996. *Changing the Odds: Open Admissions and the Life Chances of the Disadvantaged.* New Haven: Yale University Press.

Lavin, David E., and Elliot Weininger. 1998. "Proposed New Admissions Criteria at the City University of New York: Ethnic and Enrollment Consequences." Unpublished paper. New York: City University of New York Graduate Center, Sociology Program.

Lee, David S. 1999. "Wage Inequality During the 1980s: Rising Dispersion or Falling Minimum Wage?" *Quarterly Journal of Economics* 114(3): 977–1023.

Lee, Valerie, and David Burkam. 2002. *Inequality at the Starting Gate.* Washington, D.C.: Economic Policy Institute.

Leigh, Duane E., and Albert M. Gill. 1997. "Labor Market Returns to Community Colleges: Evidence for Returning Adults." *Journal of Human Resources* 32(2): 334–53.

Levey, Tania. 2005. "Reexamining Community College Effects: New Techniques, New Outcomes." Paper presented to the Eastern Sociological Society, Washington, D.C. (March 17).

Levy, Frank, and Richard J. Murnane. 1992. "U.S. Earnings and Earnings Inequality: A Review of Recent Trends and Proposed Explanations." *Journal of Economic Literature* 30(September): 1333–81.

———. 2004. *The New Division of Labor: How Computers Are Creating the Next Job Market.* Princeton: Princeton University Press.

Lieberson, Stanley. 1985. *Making It Count: The Improvement of Social Research and Theory.* Berkeley: University of California Press.

Lin, Nan. 2001. *Social Capital: The Theory of Social Structure and Action.* New York: Cambridge University Press.

Long, Bridget Terry. 2005. "The Remediation Debate." *National CrossTalk* 13(4). Available at: www.highereducation.org/crosstalk/ct0405/voices0405-long.shtml.

Long, Larry H. 1992. "International Perspectives on the Residential Mobility of America's Children." *Journal of Marriage and the Family* 54(4): 861–69.

Lucas, Samuel. 1999. *Tracking Inequality: Stratification and Mobility in American High Schools.* New York: Teacher's College Press.

Lynd, Robert S., and Helen Merrell Lynd. 1956. *Middletown: A Study in Modern American Culture.* New York: Harcourt Brace.

MacDonald, Heather. 1994. "Downward Mobility: The Failure of Open Admissions at City University." *The City Journal* 4(3): 10–20.

———. 1997. "Substandard." *The City Journal* 7(3): 11–12.

————. 1998. "CUNY Could Be Great Again." *The City Journal* 8(1): 65–70.

————. 1999. "Room for Excellence?" *The City Journal* 9(4): 6.

MacLeod, Jay. 1987. *Ain't No Makin' It: Aspirations and Attainment in a Low-Income Neighborhood.* Boulder, Colo.: Westview Press.

Marcus, Jon. 2000. "Revamping Remedial Education." *National CrossTalk* 8(1). Available at: http://www.highereducation.org/crosstalk/ct0100/front.shtml.

Marsden, Peter. 1987. "Core Discussion Networks of Americans." *American Sociological Review* 52(1): 122–31.

Martin, Joyce A., Melissa M. Park, and Paul D. Sutton. 2002. "Births: Preliminary Data for 2001." *National Vital Statistics Report* 50(10). Available at: http://www.cdc.gov/nchs/data/nvsr/nvsr50_10.pdf.

Massey, Douglas, Camille Charles, Garvey Lundy, and Mary Fischer. 2003. *The Source of the River: The Social Origins of Freshmen at America's Selective Colleges and Universities.* Princeton: Princeton University Press.

Massey, Douglas S., and Nancy A. Denton. 1993. *American Apartheid: Segregation and the Making of the Underclass.* Cambridge, Mass.: Harvard University Press.

Mayer, Susan. 1997. *What Money Can't Buy: Family Income and Children's Life Chances.* Cambridge, Mass.: Harvard University Press.

Mazzeo, Christopher. 2002. "Stakes for Students: Agenda-Setting and Remedial Education." *The Review of Higher Education* 26(1): 19–39.

McBride, James A. 1996. *The Color of Water.* New York: Riverhead Books.

McCabe, R. 2000. *No One to Waste: A Report to Public Decision-Makers and Community College Leaders.* Washington, D.C.: Community College Press.

McLanahan, Sara, and Gary Sandefur. 1994. *Growing Up with a Single Parent.* Cambridge, Mass.: Harvard University Press.

McNeal, Ralph B., Jr. 1999. "Parental Involvement as Social Capital: Differential Effectiveness on Science Achievement, Truancy, and Dropping Out." *Social Forces* 78(1): 117–44.

Merisotis, Jamie P., and Ronald A. Phipps. 2000. "Remedial Education in Colleges and Universities: What's Really Going On?" *The Review of Higher Education* 24(1): 67–85.

Merton, Robert K. 1968. "The Matthew Effect in Science." *Science,* January 5, 1968, 56–63.

————. 1988. "The Matthew Effect in Science, II: Cumulative Advantage and the Symbolism of Intellectual Property." *Isis* 79(4): 606–23.

Mickelson, Roslyn Arlin. 1990. "The Attitude-Achievement Paradox Among Black Adolescents." *Sociology of Education* 63(1): 44–61.

Miedel, Wendy T., and Arthur J. Reynolds. 1999. "Parent Involvement in Early Intervention for Disadvantaged Children: Does It Matter?" *Journal of School Psychology* 37(4): 379–402.

Milne, Ann M., David E. Myers, Alvin S. Rosenthal, and Alan Ginsburg. 1986. "Single Parents, Working Mothers, and the Educational Achievement of School Children." *Sociology of Education* 59(3): 125–39.

Mishel, Lawrence, and Joydeep Roy. 2006. *Rethinking High School Graduate Rates and Trends.* Washington, D.C.: Economic Policy Institute.

Mohr, John, and Paul DiMaggio. 1996. "The Intergenerational Transmission of Cultural Capital." In *Research on Social Stratification and Mobility,* edited by Michael Wallace. Volume 14. Greenwich, Conn.: JAI Press.

Monk-Turner, Elizabeth. 1990. "The Occupational Achievements of Community and Four-year College Entrants." *American Sociological Review* 55(5): 719–725.

Morgan, Stephen. 1998. "Adolescent Educational Expectations: Rationalized, Fantasized, or Both?" *Rationality and Society* 10(2): 131–62.

———. 2001. "Counterfactuals, Causal Effect Heterogeneity, and the Catholic School Effect on Learning." *Sociology of Education* 74(October): 341–74.

Morrison, Donna Ruane, and Andrew J. Cherlin. 1995. "The Divorce Process and Young Children's Well-Being: A Prospective Analysis." *Journal of Marriage and the Family* 57(August): 800–12.

Mortenson, Thomas G. 2005a. "State Tax Fund Appropriations for Higher Education FY1961 to FY2005." *Postsecondary Education Opportunity* 151(January): 1–12. Available at: http://www.postsecondary.org.

———. 2005b. "Family Income and Higher Education Opportunity 1970 to 2003." *Postsecondary Education Opportunity* 156(June). Available at: http://www.postsecondary.org.

———. 2005c. "College Affordability Trends by Parental Income Levels and Institutional Type 1990 to 2004." *Postsecondary Education Opportunity* 159 (September). Available at: http://www.postsecondary.org.

Moynihan, Daniel Patrick. 1965. *The Negro Family: The Case for National Action.* Washington: U.S. Department of Labor, Office of Planning and Research.

Muller, Chandra. 1993. "Parental Involvement and Academic Achievement: An Analysis of Family Resources Available to the Child." In *Parents, Their Children, and Schools,* edited by Barbara Schneider and James S. Coleman. Boulder, Colo.: Westview Press.

———. 1998. "Gender Differences in Parental Involvement and Adolescents' Mathematics Achievement." *Sociology of Education* 71(4): 336–56.

Muller, Chandra, and David Kerbow. 1993. "Parent Involvement in the Home, School and Community." In *Parents, Their Children, and Schools,* edited by Barbara Schneider and James S. Coleman. Boulder, Colo.: Westview Press.

Mulligan, Casey. 1997. *Parenting Priorities and Economic Inequality.* Chicago: University of Chicago Press.

National Center for Education Statistics. 1993. *120 Years of American Education: A Statistical Portrait.* Washington: U.S. Government Printing Office, for the U.S. Department of Education.

———. 1995. *High School and Beyond: Fourth Follow-up Methodology Report.* NCES 95-426. Washington: U.S. Government Printing Office, for the U.S. Department of Education. Available at: http://nces.ed.gov/surveys/hsb.

———. 1997. *Nontraditional Undergraduates: Trends in Enrollment from 1986 to 1992 and Persistence and Attainment Among 1989–90 Beginning Postsecondary Students.* NCES 97-578. Washington: U.S. Government Printing Office, for the U.S. Department of Education. Available at: http://nces.ed.gov/pubs/97578.pdf.

———. 2001. *Digest of Educational Statistics 2001.* Washington: U.S. Government Printing Office, for the U.S. Department of Education.

———. 2003a. *A Descriptive Summary of 1999–2000 Bachelor's Degree Recipients One Year Later. With an Analysis of Time to Degree.* NCES 2003-165. Washington: U.S. Government Printing Office, for the U.S. Department of Education. Available at: http://nces.ed.gov/pubs2003/2003165.pdf.

———. 2003b. *Digest of Education Statistics.* "Table 173. Historical Summary of Faculty, Students, Degrees and Finances in Degree-Granting Institutions: Selected Years, 1869–70 to 2001–02." Washington: U.S. Government Printing Office, for the U.S. Department of Education.

———. 2004. *The Condition of Education 2004.* NCES 2004-077. Washington: U.S. Government Printing Office, for the U.S. Department of Education. Available at: http://nces.ed.gov/programs/coe/index.asp.

———. 2005a. *College Persistence on the Rise?* NCES 2005-156. Washington: U.S. Government Printing Office for the U.S. Department of Education. Available at: http://nces.ed.gov/pubsearch/pubsinfo.asp?pubid=2005156.

———. 2005b. *The Condition of Education 2005.* "Immediate Transition to College (Indicator 20)." Washington: U.S. Government Printing Office, for the U.S. Department of Education. Available at: http://nces.ed.gov/programs/coe/2005/section3/indicator20.asp.

National Education Longitudinal Survey of 1988. 2006. Available at: http://nces.ed.gov/surveys/nels88.

National Longitudinal Study of the High-School Class of 1972. 2006. Available at: http://nces.ed.gov/surveys/nels72.

National Longitudinal Study of Youth. 2002. "Child and Young Adult Data Users Guide." Columbus: Ohio State University, Center for Human Resource Research. Available at: http://www.bls.gov/nls/y79cyaguide/2000/nlsy79childg0.pdf.

Nelson, Perry S., Jane M. Simoni, and Howard S. Adelman. 1996. Mobility and School Functioning in the Early Grades. *Journal of Educational Research* 89(6): 365–69.

Newman, Katherine. 1999. *No Shame in My Game: The Working Poor in the Inner City.* New York: Alfred A. Knopf and Russell Sage Foundation.

Newman, Katherine, and Mario Small. 2001. "Urban Poverty After the Truly Disadvantaged: The Rediscovery of Family, the Neighborhood, and Culture." *Annual Review of Sociology* 27(1): 23–45.

Noell, Jay. 1982. "Public and Catholic Schools: A Reanalysis of 'Public and Private Schools.' " *Sociology of Education* 55(2/3): 123–32.

Oakes, Jeannie. 1985. *Keeping Track: How Schools Structure Inequality.* New Haven: Yale University Press.

Ogbu, John. 2003. *Black American Students in an Affluent Suburb.* Mahwah, N.J.: Lawrence Erlbaum.

Oliver, Melvin, and Tom Shapiro. 1995. *Black Wealth/White Wealth.* New York: Routledge.

O'Neill, June, and Solomon Polachek. 1993. "Why the Gender Gap in Wages Narrowed in the 1980s." Part 1. *Journal of Labor Economics* 11(January): 205–28.

Orfield, Gary, and Edward Miller, eds. *Chilling Admissions: The Affirmative Action Crisis and the Search for Alternatives.* Cambridge, Mass.: Harvard Civil Rights Project and the Harvard University Publishing Group.

Painter, Gary, and David Levine. 2000. "Family Structure and Youth's Outcomes: Which Correlations Are Causal?" *Journal of Human Resources* 35(3): 524–94.

Panel Study of Income Dynamics. 2006. Data and documentation available at: http://psidonline.isr.umich.edy/data.

Parcel, Toby, and Elizabeth Menaghan. 1994. *Parents' Jobs and Children's Lives.* New York: Aldine de Gruyter.

Patillo-McCoy, Mary. 1999. *Black Picket Fences: Privilege and Peril Among the Black Middle Class*. Chicago: University of Chicago Press.

Payne, Emily M., and Barbara G. Lyman. 1996. "Issues Affecting the Definition of Developmental Education." In *Defining Development Education: Theory, Research, and Pedagogy,* edited by Jeanne L. Higbee and Patricia L. Dwinell. Carol Stream, Ill.: National Association of Developmental Education. Available at: http://www.nade.net/documents/Mono96/mono96.2.pdf.

Pebley, Anne, and Narayan Sastry. 2004. "Neighborhoods, Poverty and Children's Well-Being." In *Social Inequality,* edited by Kathryn Neckerman. New York: Russell Sage Foundation.

Phillips, Meredith. 1999. "Sibship Size and Academic Achievement: What We Now Know and What We Still Need to Know." *American Sociological Review* 64(2): 188–92.

Phipps, Ronald A. 1998. *College Remediation: What It Is, What It Costs, What's at Stake?* Washington, D.C.: Institute for Higher Education Policy.

Pincus, Fred. 1986. "Vocational Education: More False Promises." *New Directions for Community Colleges* 14(2): 41–52.

Porter, Kathleen. 2002. "The Value of a College Degree." *ERIC Digest* (ED470038). Washington: U.S. Department of Education, Clearinghouse on Higher Education, Educational Research Information Center.

Portes, Alejandro. 2000. "Two Meanings of Social Capital." *Sociological Forum* 15(1): 1–12.

Powell, Arthur G. 1996. *Lessons from Privilege: The American Pre-School Tradition.* Cambridge, Mass.: Harvard University Press.

Pribesh, Shana, and Douglas Downey. 1999. "Why are Residential and School Moves Associated with Poor School Performance?" *Demography* 35(4): 521–34.

Rainwater, Lee, and Timothy Smeeding. 2003. *Poor Kids in a Rich Country: America's Children in Comparative Perspective.* New York: Russell Sage Foundation.

Resnick, Michael, Peter Bearman, Robert Blum, Karl Bauman, Kathleen Harris, Jo Jones, Joyce Tabor, Trish Beuhring, Renee Sieving, Marcia Shew, Marjorie Ireland, Linda Bearinger, and J. Richard Udry. 1997. "Protecting Adolescents from Harm: Findings from the National Longitudinal Study on Adolescent Health." *Journal of the American Medical Association* 278(10): 823–32.

Riley, Richard, C. Kent McGuire, Blane Dessy, and Cynthia Hearn Dorffman. 1999. *College for All? Is There Too Much Emphasis on Getting a 4-Year Degree?* Washington: U.S. Department of Education.

Roach, Ronald. 1997. "From Combat to Campus: G.I. Bill Gave a Generation of African Americans Opportunity to Pursue the American Dream." *Black Issues in Higher Education* 14(3): 26–28.

Rosenbaum, Emily. 1996. "Racial/Ethnic Differences in Home Ownership and Housing Quality." *Social Problems* 43(4): 403–26.

Rosenbaum, James. 2001. *Beyond College for All: Career Paths for the Forgotten Half.* New York: Russell Sage Foundation.

———. 2003. "Beyond College for All: Policies and Practices to Improve Transitions into College and Jobs." *Professional School Counseling* (April).

———. 2004. "It's Time to Tell the Kids: If you Don't Do Well in High School, you Won't Do Well in College (or on the Job)." *American Educator* 28(spring): 8–10.

Rosenbaum, James E., and Anne E. Person. 2003. "Beyond College for All: Policies and Practices to Improve Transitions into College and Jobs." *Professional School Counseling* 6(4): 252–60.

Rosenbaum, Paul R., and Donald Rubin. 1983. "The Central Role of the Propensity Score in Observational Studies for Causal Effects." *Biometrika* 70(1): 41–55.

———. 1985. "Constructing a Control Group Using Multivariate Matched Sampling Methods That Incorporate the Propensity Score." *American Statistician* 39(1): 33–38.

Rosenthal, Robert, and Ralph Rosnow. 1991. *Essentials of Behavioral Research: Methods and Data Analysis.* 2nd ed. New York: McGraw-Hill.

Roueche, John E., and Suanne D. Roueche. 1999. *High Stakes, High Performance: Making Remedial Education Work.* Washington, D.C.: Community College Press.

Rubin, Donald B. 1997. "Estimating Causal Effects from Large Data Sets Using Propensity Scores." *Annals of Internal Medicine* 127(8): 757–63.

Rumberger, Russell W. 2002. "Student Mobility." In *Encyclopedia of Education,* edited by James Guthrie. 2nd ed. New York: Macmillan.

Rumberger, Russell W., and Katherine A. Larson. 1998. "Student Mobility and the Increased Risk of High School Dropout." *American Journal of Education* 107(1): 1–35.

Rumberger, Russell W., Katherine A. Larson, Robert K. Ream, and Gregory J. Palardy. 1999. *The Educational Consequences of Mobility for California Students and Schools.* Berkeley, Calif.: Policy Analysis for California Education.

Ryan, Camille. 2005. "What's It Worth?: Field of Training and Economic Status 2001." *Current Population Reports,* series P70-98. Washington: U.S. Government Printing Office, for U.S. Census Bureau.

Sampson, Robert, Jeffrey Morenoff, and Thomas Gannon-Rowley. 2002. "Assessing 'Neighborhood Effects': Social Processes and New Directions in Research." *Annual Review of Sociology* 28(1): 443–78.

Sanders, Mavis. 1998. "The Effects of School, Family, and Community Support on the Academic Achievement of African American Adolescents." *Urban Education* 33(3): 384–409.

Sandham, Jessica L. 1998. "Mass Plan Would Make Districts Pay for Remediation." *Education Week* 17, February 18, 1998, p. 18.

Schmidt, Peter. 1998. "A Clash of Values at CUNY Over Remedial Education." *The Chronicle of Higher Education* 44, March 20, 1998, A33–34.

Schneider, Barbara, and James S. Coleman, eds. 1993. *Parents, Their Children and Schools.* New York: Westview Press.

Seeley, John R., R. Alexander Sim, and Elizabeth W. Loosley. 1956. *Crestwood Heights: A Study of the Culture of Suburban Life.* Toronto: University of Toronto Press.

Sewell, William H., and Robert M. Hauser. 1975. *Education, Occupation, and Earnings: Achievement in the Early Career.* New York: Academic Press.

Sewell, William H., Robert M. Hauser, and Wendy C. Wolf. 1980. "Sex, Schooling, and Occupational Status." *American Journal of Sociology* 86(3): 551–83.

Shaw, Kathleen M. 1997. "Remedial Education as Ideological Battleground: Emerging Remedial Education Policies in the Community College." *Educational Evaluation and Policy Analysis* 19(3): 284–96.

Singh, Kusum, Patricia G. Bickley, Paul Trivette, Timothy Z. Keith, Patricia B. Keith, and Eileen Anderson. 1995. "The Effects of Four Components of Parental Involvement on Eighth-Grade Student Achievement: Structural Analysis of NELS-88 Data." *School Psychology Review* 24(2): 299–317.

Slater, Robert Bruce. 1994. "The Growing Gender Gap in Black Higher Education." *Journal of Blacks in Higher Education* 3(spring): 52–59.

Smith, Sandra S. 2000. "Mobilizing Social Resources: Race, Ethnic and Gender Differences in Social Capital and Persisting Wage Inequalities." *Sociological Quarterly* 41(4): 509–37.

Sobel, Michael. 1995. "Causal Inference in the Social and Behavioral Sciences." In *Handbook of Statistical Modeling for the Social and Behavioral Sciences*, edited by Gerhard Arminger, Clifford Clogg, and Michael Sobel. New York: Plenum Press.

Soliday, Mary. 2002. *The Politics of Remediation*. Pittsburgh: University of Pittsburgh Press.

South, Scott J. 2001. "Time-Dependent Effects of Wives' Employment on Marital Dissolution." *American Sociological Review* 66(2): 226–45.

South, Scott, Kyle Crowder, and Katherine Trent. 1998. "Children's Residential Mobility and Neighborhood Environment Following Divorce and Remarriage." *Social Forces* 77(2): 667–93.

Speare, Alden, and Frances Kobrin Goldscheider. 1987. "The Effects of Marital Status Change on Residential Mobility." *Journal of Marriage and the Family* 49(2): 455–64.

Spilerman, Seymour. 2000. "Wealth and Stratification Processes." *Annual Review of Sociology* 26(1): 497–524.

Stanfield, Rochelle L. 1997. "Overselling College." *National Journal*, April 15, 1997, 653–56.

Steinberg, Laurence. 1996. *Beyond the Classroom*. New York: Simon & Schuster.

Stevenson, David L., and David P. Baker. 1987. "The Family-School Relation and the Child's School Performance." *Child Development* 58(5): 1348–57.

Swanson, Christopher B., and Barbara Schneider. 1999. "Students on the Move: Residential and Educational Mobility in America's Schools." *Sociology of Education* 72(1): 54–67.

Sweeney, Megan M. 2002. "Two Decades of Family Change: The Shifting Economic Foundations of Marriage." *American Sociological Review* 67(1): 132–47.

Traub, James. 1995. *City on a Hill: Testing the American Dream at City College*. New York: Perseus.

Trimberger, Ellen Kay. 1973. "Open Admissions: A New Form of Tracking?" *Insurgent Sociologist* 4(1): 29–43.

Trombley, William. 1998. "Remedial Education Under Attack." *National CrossTalk* 6(3): 1.

Trusty, Jerry, and Trace Pirtle. 1998. "Parents' Transmission of Educational Goals to Their Children." *Journal of Research and Development in Education* 32(1): 53–65.

U.S. Census Bureau. 1993. *We the Americans: Our Education*. Washington: U.S. Government Printing Office, for U.S. Bureau of the Census. Available at: http://www.census.gov/apsd/wepeople/we-11.pdf.

———. 1998–2002. *Current Population Survey*. March supplement. Data and documentation available at: http://www.bls.census.gov/ferretftp.htm.

———. 2000. *Current Population Survey*. March. Washington: U.S. Government Printing Office, for U.S. Bureau of the Census.

———. 2001. *Statistical Abstract of the United States 2001*. Washington: U.S. Government Printing Office, for U.S. Bureau of the Census.

———. 2004a. "Educational Attainment in the United States 2003." *Current Population Reports*. Series P20, number 550. June. Washington: U.S. Government

Printing Office, for U.S. Bureau of the Census. Available at: http://www.census. gov/prod/2004pubs/p20-550.pdf.

———. 2004b. "Table P-24: Educational Attainment—Full-Time Year-Round, Workers 25 Years Old and Over by Median Earnings and Sex: 1991 to 2004." *Current Population Survey.* Annual Social and Economic Supplements. Washington: U.S. Government Printing Office for U.S. Bureau of the Census. Available at: http://www.census.gov/hhes/www/income/histinc/p24.html.

———. 2005. "School Enrollment: Social and Economic Characteristics of Students: October 2003." *Current Population Reports.* Series P20, number 554. Washington: U.S. Government Printing Office, for U.S. Bureau of the Census. Available at: http://www.census.gov/prod/2005pubs/p20-554.pdf.

Useem, Elizabeth. 1992. "Middle Schools and Math Groups: Parents' Involvement in Children's Placement." *Sociology of Education* 65(4): 263–79.

Velez, William. 1985. "Finishing College: The Effects of College Type." *Sociology of Education* 58(3): 191–200.

Wagener, Linda, James Furrow, Pamela King, Nancy Leffert, Peter Benson. 2003. "Religious Involvement and Developmental Resources in Youth." *Review of Religious Research* 44(3): 271–84.

Waldinger, Roger. 1996. *Still the Promised City?: African-Americans and New Immigrants in Post-Industrial New York.* Cambridge, Mass.: Harvard University Press.

Warren, John Robert, Robert M. Hauser, and Jennifer T. Sheridan. 2002. "Occupational Stratification Across the Life Course: Evidence from the Wisconsin Longitudinal Study." *American Sociological Review* 67(3): 432–55.

Weber, Max. 1922/1968. *Economy and Society.* New York: Bedminister Press.

White, Halbert. 1980. "A Heteroskedasticity-Consistent Covariance Matrix Estimator and a Direct Test of Heteroskedasticity." *Econometrica* 48(4): 817–38.

Willms, J. Douglas. 1985. "Catholic School Effects on Academic Achievement." *Sociology of Education* 58(2): 98–114.

Wilson, William Julius. 1987. *The Truly Disadvantaged: The Inner City, the Underclass, and Public Policy.* Chicago: University of Chicago Press.

Winship, Christopher, and Stephen L. Morgan. 1999. "The Estimation of Causal Effects from Observational Data." *Annual Review of Sociology* 25(1): 659–707.

Wirt, John, Susan Choy, Patrick Rooney, Stephen Provasnik, Anindita Sen, and Richard Tobin. 2004. "Indicator 6: Past and Projected Undergraduate Enrollments." In *The Condition of Education 2004.* NCES 2004-077. Washington: U.S. Department of Education, National Center for Educational Statistics.

Wonacott, Michael E. 2003. "Myths and Realities: Everyone Goes to College." ERIC report 25. Washington: U.S. Department of Education, Educational Research Information Center.

Woodham, F. 1998. "Report Says Remedial Classes Are Cost Effective." *Chronicle of Higher Education,* December 1, A54.

Youniss, James, Jeffrey McLellan, and Miranda Yates. 1999. "Religion, Community Service, and Identity in American Youth." *Journal of Adolescence* 22(2): 243–53.

Zuckerman, Harriet. 1977. "The Nobel Prize and the Accumulation of Advantage in Science." In *Scientific Elite: Nobel Laureates in the United States.* New York: Free Press

Zwerling, Steven L. 1976. *Second Best: The Crisis of the Community College.* New York: McGraw-Hill.

═ Index ═

Boldface numbers refer to figures and tables.